ORDINARY GRACES

ORDINARY

Christian Teachings on the Interior Life

GRACES

EDITED BY LORRAINE KISLY

INTRODUCTION BY PHILIP ZALESKI

BELL TOWER · NEW YORK

Published by Bell Tower, New York.
Member of the Crown Publishing Group.

Random House, Inc. New York, Toronto,
London, Sydney, Auckland
www.randomhouse.com

Bell Tower and colophon are registered trademarks
of Random House, Inc.

Printed in the United States of America

Design by Jennifer Ann Daddio

Library of Congress Cataloging-in-Publication Data

Ordinary graces : Christian teachings on the interior life /edited
by Lorraine Kisly ; introduction by Philip Zaleski — 1st ed.
    p. cm.
Includes bibliographical references and index.
    I. Spiritual life—Christianity.   I. Kisly, Lorraine.
BV4501.2.067   2000
248—dc21

                                00-026708

ISBN 0-609-60674-3

1 3 5 7 9 10 8 6 4 2

First Edition

Dedicated to
Matthew,
namesake of the Evangelist

CONTENTS

Introduction by Philip Zaleski   ix

Foreword   xv

Cycle One: Joy in Your Father's Works   I

Cycle Two: The Law of Bearing   28

Cycle Three: The True Human Person   56

Cycle Four: The Sacrament of Presence   76

Cycle Five: Preparing the Ground   99

Cycle Six: The Stream of Providence   118

Cycle Seven: The Heart of Struggle   137

Cycle Eight: A Recollected Spirit   167

Cycle Nine: Holy Fire   189

Cycle Ten: Having Nothing, Possessing All Things   216

Acknowledgments and Sources   235

INTRODUCTION

Philip Zaleski

Sometime in the 1850s, on the 24th Sunday after Pentecost, in one of the most justly famous moments in Christian spiritual history, a 33-year-old Russian vagabond chanced to hear the following words from St. Paul read out in church: "Pray without ceasing." The phrase struck the man like a heavenly thunderbolt. Immediately he shouldered his knapsack, pocketed his Bible, and set out to find the answer to this great mystery, the secret of unceasing prayer.

The identity of the Pilgrim remains unknown, although various scholars have attributed his tale to one Russian monk or another. His anonymity seems wholly appropriate, for the Pilgrim is Everyman, man or woman, who longs for an answer to life's deepest mysteries. The Pilgrim's search led him to a specific solution, the Jesus Prayer, a method of interior devotion perfected in the cells of Russian monasteries and discussed in "Cycle Nine" of this splendid collection by Lorraine Kisly. But the Pilgrim's question has been, is now, and always will be Everyman's question. For by seeking to unravel the mystery of prayer, the Pilgrim is asking how to live the Christian life: What must I embrace, what must I surrender, to find my true self? How can I learn to love God, and love my neighbor as myself? How may I abide in Christ?

These questions resound up and down the millennia. We hear them in the Gospels, in the urgent request in Luke, "Lord, teach us to pray," and in the plaintive entreaty of the bewildered young man in Mark, "Good Master, what shall I do that I may inherit eternal life?" We hear them, as *Ordinary Graces* attests, voiced down the centuries by saints and madmen, scholars and mystics, poets and prophets. We hear them today, not only in the books of the great Christian writers of our age—Thomas Merton, Simone Weil, Dietrich Bonhoeffer, and their spiritual kin—but in living rooms, campuses, prison cells, wherever men and women pause long enough to hear the whisperings of the Spirit. To these profound questions there can be no simple answers, for what is at stake is supernally complex, involving the very nature of the human being. The Christian project proposes nothing less than a radical reevaluation of what it means to be human; the Christian is asked to awaken to a new reality—"Arise, O sleeper, and arise from the dead, and Christ shall give you light" as the ancient morning hymn has it—and wipe away the disfiguring crust of years of sin and self-love, a *metanoia* that will reveal each of us as we truly are, an icon of God. To accept this challenge is to take oneself and the world and God seriously. It is to harken to the Psalm: "Create in me a clean heart, O God; and renew a right spirit within me" (Ps. 51:10), and to St. Paul: "If any man be in Christ, he is a new creature: old things are passed away; behold, all things are become new" (2 Cor. 5:17).

How do we shoulder such an overwhelming task? According to Christian tradition, the decisive action belongs to God alone, for God alone can instill faith in the human heart. But the soil of the heart must be prepared to receive the seeds of grace. This cultivation, this striving toward awakening, sanctification, perfection—one can phrase it in so many different ways—has been elaborated in minute detail by the Christian saints. Nonetheless, for reasons both historical and cultural, Christian spiritual practice remains largely unknown to the general public. Many people today are inclined to describe Buddhism as a school of practice and Christianity as a system of belief. The truth is more complicated, for Buddhism has its essential beliefs and Christianity its essential methods. The path that Christ brought is indeed a matter of faith ("He that believeth in me, as the scripture hath said, out of his belly shall flow rivers of living water"—John 7:38)—but it is also, decisively, a Way.

This term *Way* has biblical antecedents: "I am the way, the truth, and the life," says Jesus to Thomas the Doubter. Within this central mode of abiding in Christ, it seems fair to say that there are as many "ways" or methods of practice as there are human beings, for each of us, even those in the most orthodox communions, treads his or her own path to God. From the early monastic experiments of John Cassian, St. Benedict, and St. Scholastica, through the exercises in attention of Simeon the New Theologian, Brother Lawrence's Practice of the Presence, and George Fox's turning toward the inner light, seekers incessantly devise new means for discovering divine reality. Within this immense variety, however, a pattern of ascent toward God may be discerned. Jan van Ruusbroec, perhaps the greatest of the Rhineland mystics, condensed the process into three stages, which he called the Active, the Interior, and the Superessential Life: a threefold process that begins with contrition, self-knowledge, and self-overcoming—especially the maturation of the one absolutely indispensable quality for spiritual growth, humility—and that culminates in a mystical marriage with God. The anthology that you hold in your hands expands fruitfully upon this classical scheme, presenting a 10-rung ladder, or better, a 10-level spiral staircase, as the ascent to God is often indirect, circular, entailing new beginnings at every stage. The first step, as *Ordinary Graces* presents it, takes us just as we are, frail creatures inhabiting a mysterious cosmos, and asks us to see the beauty and order of the natural world as signs of God's presence; subsequent steps involve the art of prayer; how to bear (and bear with) one's neighbor; the illuminations of faith; and so on, culminating in divine union.

In the end, all depends upon God's grace, and upon our willingness to accept God's grace. We may be transformed in the twinkling of an eye or struggle for a lifetime with few signs of progress. What changes we do discern may come haltingly, with plentiful setbacks checkering the inch-by-inch advance. Real change may take place on levels deeper than our eye can see. The effort demanded of us may shake us to our roots, for to sacrifice one's self-love, to deny oneself and take up one's cross daily, as Jesus asks, is no easy task. But be of good cheer. We have the assurance that the entire cosmos is struggling with us. The animals seek God, as the first entry in *Ordinary Graces* proposes: "The birds taking flight lift themselves up to heaven, and instead of hands, spread out the cross of their wings" (Tertullian). The cherubim, seraphim, and other angelic orders seek God; the souls of the dead seek God; all creation seeks God, as St. Augustine so majestically proclaims: "Our hearts are restless until they rest in Thee." Along with this guarantee of cosmic solidarity, we are also promised that those who persevere will not fail; for God himself longs for our renewal:

"Ask, and it shall be given you; seek, and ye shall find; knock, and it shall be opened unto you" (Matt. 7:7).

It is impossible to overestimate the importance of a choice passage of writing, such as those found throughout this book, in sparking or sustaining the spiritual quest. For the faith that declares "In the beginning was the Word," words can be chariots that carry us to God. No matter how crude or small, every word possesses a certain inherent beauty because it contains meaning and thus signifies the orderliness and lucidity of God's cosmos. The Pilgrim is one link in a great chain of people who discovered their hearts opened and their minds transformed by the power of words. The words that prefigure the Word and transform a life may come under any circumstances. The call came to the Pilgrim during divine services, to St. Augustine while pacing in a garden, to Simone Weil while reciting the Lord's Prayer. By echoing this call, the selections in *Ordinary Graces* summon the reader to a deeper spiritual life.

FOREWORD

In the pages ahead, you will encounter "cycles" of passages centered on the teachings of Christ. The voices span decades, centuries, millennia. They are the voices of the early fathers of the church, of Protestants, of Roman Catholics, of Eastern Orthodox; voices of men and women, artists and writers, saints and teachers, each carrying the living resonance of Christ's teaching through the last two thousand years.

Each cycle spirals through levels of experience and insight, gathering at each turn what came before and providing a support for what lies ahead. The third cycle, for example, "The True Human Person," opens with a passage evoking our ordinary passive state, moves through reflections on the causes and consequences of this state, and gradually reveals our need for participation in a greater life. Teachings in this cycle are explored in more depth in those that follow and precede it: will, grace, presence, the neighbor, obstacles, prayer.

While each passage stands alone, each gains strength from the intimate relationship that emerges among voices separated by great geographical, cultural, and temporal distances. These voices are fresh and vivid as they speak to each other and to us because they spring from the present moment. It is when we enter this moment with them that we have ears to hear, eyes to see, and when false divisions within and without begin to pass away.

The graces in the title of this volume are "ordinary" in the sense of usual, commonplace, and available to all. That these ordinary graces are offered at every moment is at the heart of the Christian teaching. No great or special gifts, no extraordinary spiritual talents, are needed to have a center, and to live a life guided by spiritual energies. Indeed, Saint Theophan tells us that this is the *normal* state of a human being. Though the ability to receive these gifts depends on our commitment and readiness, we have been assured that they are being offered, and offered again.

These writings speak to all spiritual seekers, but especially to those wishing to reenter and reanimate their connection to the Christian Way.

A way that begins now.

LORRAINE KISLY

Note: The teachings gathered here represent a fraction of what might have been included. No attempt has been made to be comprehensive or even representative. Only a few paths have been followed, and many others equally valid remain to be explored. Readily available everywhere and the source that inspired all that follows, the uniquely powerful and vivifying words of Jesus Christ in the Gospels and the rest of the New Testament have not been excerpted—though readers of this volume may well find a wish to revisit these primary texts.

Let us pray our dear Lord God that he help us
to mount from a life divided
to a life unified. Amen.
—*Meister Eckhart*

All rising . . . is by a winding stair.
—*Sir Francis Bacon*

CYCLE ONE

JOY IN YOUR FATHER'S WORKS

When we open to the majesty of creation and "the Love that moves the sun and the other stars," we are awakened to wonder. And it is wonder, deepening to awe, that leads to what has been translated as the "fear" of God, and the beginning of wisdom.

The following passages reflect on the natural world, and on human nature; on what changes, and on what abides.

The angels too pray, all of them. The whole creation prays. Cattle and wild beasts pray, and bend their knees, and in coming forth from their stalls and lairs look up to heaven, their mouths not idle, making the spirit move in their own fashion. Moreover the birds taking flight lift themselves up to heaven, and instead of hands, spread out the cross of their wings, while saying something which may be supposed to be a prayer. What more then of the obligation of prayer? Even the Lord himself prayed: to him be honor and power for ever and ever.

TERTULLIAN (160–230)
Carthaginian church father and theologian

My little sisters the birds, you are much beholden to God your Creator, and always and in every place you ought to praise Him. He has given you double and triple gifts; He has given you freedom to go into every place, and also preserved you in the ark of Noah, in order that your kind might not perish from the earth. Again, you are beholden to Him for the element of air which He has appointed for you; moreover, you sow not, neither do you reap, and God feeds you and gives you the rivers and the fountains for your drink; He gives you the mountains and the valleys for your refuge, and the tall trees wherein to build your nests, and as you can neither spin nor sew God clothes you, you and your children. Your Creator loves you much, since He has dealt so bounteously with you: and so beware, little sisters of mine, of the sin of ingratitude, but ever strive to praise God.

FRANCIS OF ASSISI (1182–1226)
Italian monk, saint, and founder of the Franciscan order

For I will consider my Cat Jeoffry.
For he is the servant of the Living God, duly and daily serving him.
For at the first glance of the glory of God in the East he worships in his way.
For this is done by wreathing his body seven times round with elegant quickness.
For then he leaps up to catch the musk, which is the blessing of God upon his prayer.
For he rolls upon prank to work it in.
For having done duty and received blessing he begins to consider himself.

For this he performs in ten degrees.

For first he looks upon his fore-paws to see if they are clean.

For secondly he kicks up behind to clear away there.

For thirdly he works it upon stretch with the fore-paws
extended.

For fourthly he sharpens his paws by wood.

For fifthly he washes himself.

For sixthly he rolls upon wash.

For seventhly he fleas himself, that he may not be interrupted
upon the beat.

For eighthly he rubs himself against a post.

For ninthly he looks up for his instructions.

For tenthly he goes in quest of food.

For having consider'd God and himself he will consider his
neighbor.

For if he meets another cat he will kiss her in kindness.

For when he takes his prey he plays with it to give it a chance.

For one mouse in seven escapes by his dallying . . .

For he purrs in thankfulness when God tells him he's a good
Cat.

For there is nothing sweeter than his peace when at rest.

For there is nothing brisker than his life when in motion . . .

For he can catch the cork and toss it again.

For he is hated by the hypocrite and miser.

For the former is afraid of detection.

For the latter refuses the charge.

For he camels his back to bear the first notion of business.

For he is good to think on, if a man would express himself
neatly . . .

For his ears are so acute that they sting again.

For from this proceeds the passing quickness of his attention.

For by stroaking of him I have found out electricity.

For I perceived God's light about him both wax and fire.

For the Electrical fire is the spiritual substance, which God
sends from heaven to sustain the bodies both of man
and beast.

For God has blessed him in the variety of his movements.

For, tho' he cannot fly, he is an excellent clamberer.

For his motions upon the face of the earth are more than any
other quadrupede.

For he can tread to all the measures upon the musick.

For he can swim for life.

For he can creep.

CHRISTOPHER SMART (1722–1771)

English poet

After this [St. Columba] goes out of the granary and, returning to the monastery, sits down half-way at the place where afterwards a cross, fixed in a mill-stone, and standing to this day, is to be seen at the roadside. And while the saint, weary with age as I have said, rested there, sitting for a little while, behold the white horse, a faithful servant, runs up to him, the one which used to carry the milk-pails to and fro between the byre and the monastery.

He, coming up to the saint, wonderful to tell, lays his head against his breast—inspired, as I believe, by God, by whose dispensation every animal has sense to perceive things according as its Creator Himself has ordained—knowing that his master was soon about to leave him, and that he would see him no more, began to whinny and to shed copious tears into the lap of the saint as though he had been a man, and weeping and foaming at the mouth.

And the attendant, seeing this, began to drive away the weeping mourner, but the saint forbade him, saying, "Let him alone, let him alone, for he loves me. Let him pour out the tears of his bitter lamentation into this my bosom. Lo! now, thou, man as thou art, and possessing a rational soul, couldst in no wise know anything about my departure save what I myself have just now told thee: but to this brute beast, devoid of reason, the Creator Himself has clearly in some way revealed that his master is about to go away from him."

And so saying, he blessed his servant the horse as it sadly turned to go away from him.

ADAMNAN (624–704)
Irish saint, abbot of Iona, and missionary

Christ as recapitulation of creation: as new Adam he encompasses everything human, but he also incorporates the animal realm in himself, since he is lamb, scapegoat, sacrificial ox, ram, and lion of Judah. As bread and as vine he incorporates the vegetative. Finally, in the Passion, he became a mere thing and thus reached the very bottom of the world's structure. This reification is most evidenced in the sacraments and especially in Christ's quantification in Communion wafers and in his multilocation: Christ as printing matrix, as generic article. Such reification has its cause, not at all in a subsequent desacralization of the holy by the Church, but in an intensely personal decision of the Redeemer, and in the strongest possible effects of the redemption itself, whereby the

Lord makes himself irrevocably a thing at the disposal of anyone who requests it.

HANS URS VON BALTHASAR (1905–1988)
Swiss Roman Catholic theologian

By this let nurses, and those parents that desire Holy Children learn to make them possessors of Heaven and Earth betimes; to remove silly objects from before them, to magnify nothing but what is great indeed, and to talk of God to them, and of His works and ways before they can either speak or go.

For nothing is so easy as to teach the truth because the nature of the thing confirms the doctrine: As when we say the sun is glorious, a man is a beautiful creature, sovereign over beasts and fowls and fishes, the stars minister unto us, the world was made for you, &c.

But to say this house is yours, and these lands are another man's, and this bauble is a jewel and this gew-gaw a fine thing, this rattle makes music, &c., is deadly barbarous and uncouth to a little child; and makes him suspect all you say, because the nature of the thing contradicts your words. Yet doth that blot out all noble and divine ideas, dissettle his foundation, render him uncertain in all things, and divide him from God. To teach him those objects are little vanities, and that though God made them, by the ministry of man, yet better and more glorious things are more to be esteemed, is natural and easy.

Your enjoyment of the World is never right, till you so esteem it, that everything in it, is more your treasure than a King's exchequer full of Gold and Silver. And that exchequer yours also in its place and service. Can you take too much joy in your Father's works? He is Himself in everything. Some things are little on the outside, and rough and common, but I remember a time when the dust of the streets were as precious as Gold to my infant eyes, and now they are more precious to the eye of reason.

THOMAS TRAHERNE (1637–1674)
English cleric and poet

When the wonder has gone out of a man he is dead. When all comes to all, the most precious element in life is wonder. Love is a great emotion and power is power. But both love and power are based on wonder. Plant consciousness, insect consciousness, fish consciousness, animal consciousness, all are related by one permanent element, which we may call the religious element in all life, even in a flea: the sense of wonder. That is our sixth sense. And it is the *natural* religious sense.

D. H. LAWRENCE (1885–1930)
English novelist and essayist

All around us, to right and left, in front and behind, above and below, we have only to go a little beyond the frontier of sensible appearances in order to see the divine welling up and showing through. But it is not only close to us, in front of us, that the divine presence has revealed itself. It has sprung up universally, and we find ourselves so surrounded and transfixed by it, that there is no room left to fall down and adore it, even within ourselves. By means of all created things, without exception, the divine assails us, penetrates us and moulds us. We imagined it as distant and inaccessible, whereas in fact we live steeped in its burning layers. *In eo vivimus.*

As Jacob said, awakening from his dream, the world, this palpable world, which we were wont to treat with the boredom and disrespect with which we habitually regard places with no sacred association for us, is in truth a holy place, and we did not know it. *Venite, adoremus.*

PIERRE TEILHARD DE CHARDIN (1881–1955)
French paleontologist and Jesuit priest

In youth, before I lost any of my senses, I can remember that I was all alive, and inhabited my body with inexpressible satisfaction; both its weariness and its refreshment were sweet to me. This earth was the most glorious musical instrument, and I was audience to its strains. . . .

The morning and the evening were sweet to me, and I led a life aloof from society of men. I wondered if a mortal had ever known what I knew. I looked in books for some recognition of a kindred experience, but, strange to say, I found none. Indeed, I was slow to discover that other men had had this experience, for it had been possible to read books and to associate with men on other grounds. The maker of me was improving me. When I detected this interference I was profoundly moved. For years I marched as to a music in comparison with which the military music of the streets is noise and discord. I was daily intoxicated, and yet no man could call me intemperate. With all your science can you tell how it is, and whence it is, that light comes into the soul? . . .

It does seem as if mine were a peculiarly wild nature which so yearns toward all wildness. I know of no redeeming qualities in me but a sincere love for some things, and when I am reproved I have to fall back on to this ground. This is my argument in reserve for all cases. My love is invulnerable. Meet me on that ground, and you will find me strong. When I am condemned, and condemn myself utterly, I think straightway, "But I rely on my love for some things." Therein I am whole and entire. Therein I am God-propped.

What more glorious condition of being can we imagine than from impure to be becoming pure? It is almost desirable to be impure that we may be the subject of this improvement. That I am innocent to myself! That I love and reverence my life! That I am better fitted for a lofty society to-day than I was yesterday! To make my life a sacrament!

What is nature without this lofty tumbling? May I treat myself with more and more respect and tenderness. May I not forget that I am impure and vicious. May I not cease to love purity. May I go to my slumbers as expecting to arise to a new and more perfect day. May I so live and refine my life as fitting myself for a society ever higher than I actually enjoy. May I treat myself tenderly as I would treat the most innocent child whom I love; may I treat children and my friends as my newly discovered self. Let me forever go in search of myself; never for a moment think that I have found myself; be as a stranger to myself, never a familiar, seeking acquaintance still. May I be to myself as one is to me whom I love, a dear and cherished object. What temple, what fane, what sacred place can there be but the innermost part of my own being?

HENRY DAVID THOREAU (1817–1862)

American poet, essayist, and naturalist

I had been sitting in the garden working and had just finished. . . . It was still and peaceful—around me and within me. Too good, in fact, to allow one to think much about anything. I just sat there. Then it began to come, that infinite tenderness, which is purer and deeper than that of lovers, or of a father toward his child. It was in me, but it also came to me, as the air came to my lungs. As usual, the breathing became sober and reverent, became, as it were, incorporeal; I inhaled the tenderness. . . .

This deep tenderness which I felt, first within myself and then even stronger around and above me, extended further and further— it became all-present. I saw it, and it developed into knowing, into knowing all, at the same time it became power, omnipotence, and drew me into the eternal Now.

That was my first actual meeting with Reality; because such is the real life: a Now which *is* and a Now which *happens.* There is no beginning and no end. I cannot say any more about this Now. I sat in my garden, but there was no place in the world where I was not.

During the whole time my consciousness was clear and sober. I sat in the garden and acknowledged it with a smile. There was something to smile over, for time and space, characteristics of the Now which happens were so to speak "outside." But what is the Now which happens? It is the continuously active creation with all its birth throes. I saw time and space as instruments or functions of this creation. They come into existence with it and in the course of it, and with it they come to an end. The Newly Created stands in the Now and discards these tools. The freedom, the real *Being* begins.

JOHANNES ANKER-LARSEN (1874–1957)
Danish novelist

In the Divine Office, the whole world is present. The whole of
mankind is there, as well as the angels and the saints. The whole
world is there, and each of us is a microcosm who contains the
whole. At the end of Lauds every day, we sing Psalms 148–150,
which include everything on heaven and earth—the birds, the fish,
everything. It is very beautiful and it has a transfiguring effect, so
that when you go out and see the hills after the Office, you think
"Ah, yes." And you take the Office out to the hills. It couldn't be
otherwise. If the liturgy weren't cosmic, it wouldn't be worth doing.

> HUGH GILBERT, OSB (contemporary)
> Benedictine abbot of Pluscarden Abbey, Scotland

Mysteries are not dark shadows, before which we must shut our eyes
and be silent. On the contrary, they are dazzling splendours, with
which we ought to sate our gaze, whilst recognizing, however, that
they extend far beyond its capacity, and that our eyes cannot bear
their full radiance. It is in contemplating them, in speaking of them,
that we dispose ourselves to be given even here below as much of
them as God sees fit to impart to us, and to receive one day that
fullness of light which will be the essence of our beatitude.

> ANONYMOUS CARTHUSIAN MONK (contemporary)

Let man, then, examine nature in its lofty and full majesty; let him
banish from his sight the objects that surround him. Let him contemplate this dazzling luminary set as an eternal lamp to illumine
the universe; let the earth appear to him as a dot in comparison to
the immense circumference that this luminary describes, and let

him marvel at the fact that this same vast circumference is but a very small dot compared to that described by the stars which revolve in the firmament.

But if our sight stops there, let our imagination go further. It will grow weary with imagining sooner than nature with providing. All this visible world is but a minute point in nature's ample bosom. No notion comes close to it. In vain do we swell our imaginings, beyond imaginable spaces, we produce but atoms in comparison to the reality of things. It is a sphere whose center is everywhere, whose circumference nowhere. Finally, the fact that our imagination gets lost in this thought is the greatest sign of God's omnipotence.

Once he recovers his senses, let man consider what he is in comparison to what is; let him look upon himself as lost in this remote patch of nature, and from this little prison cell where he is lodged, I mean the universe, let him learn to value the earth, kingdoms, cities, and himself at their true worth. What is a man in the infinite?

But to introduce him to another wonder just as startling, let him investigate the daintiest things he knows. In the littleness of its body, let a mite present him parts that are incomparably smaller, legs with their joints, veins in its legs, blood in its veins, humors in this blood, drops in its humors, vapors in these drops; and dividing still further these latter, let him exhaust himself in these imaginings and let the last object to which he can arrive be now that of our discourse; he will think perhaps that here is the extreme minuteness in nature.

I want to show him therein a further abyss. I want to picture for him not only the visible universe but also the vastness that can be imagined in nature, within the enclosure of this epitome of an atom. Let him see therein an infinity of universes each with its own firmament, its planets, its earth, in the same proportion as in the visible world; in this earth are animals and finally mites in which he will meet again with what the first have proffered; and discovering again in these first the same things endlessly and perpetually, let him lose himself in these wonders as marvelous in their littleness as the others are in their immensity. For who will not be amazed that our body, a little while ago imperceptible in the universe which in turn is imperceptible in the bosom of the all, should be now a colossus, a world, or rather an all, compared to the nothingness to which we cannot reach?

Who examines himself in this fashion will grow frightened of himself, and, feeling himself suspended between the two abysses of nothingness and the infinite in this mass given to him by nature, he will tremble at the sight of these wonders; and I think that as his curiosity changes to admiration he will become more and more disposed to contemplate them in silence rather than to inquire into them with presumption.

For, in the end, what is man in nature? A nothing compared to the infinite, an all compared to nothing, a mean between nothing and everything. Infinitely removed from understanding the extremes, as far as he is concerned the end of things and their beginnings are invincibly hidden in an impenetrable secret, identically incapable as he is of seeing the nothingness from which he is drawn as the infinite wherein he is engulfed.

BLAISE PASCAL (1623–1662)
French scientist, polemicist, and Christian apologist

We live in a world of unreality and dreams. To give up our imaginary position as the center, to renounce it, not only intellectually but in the imaginative part of our soul, that means to awaken to what is real and eternal, to see the true light and hear the true silence. A transformation then takes place at the very roots of our sensibility, in our immediate reception of sense impressions and psychological impressions. It is a transformation analogous to that which takes place in the dusk of evening on a road, where we suddenly discern as a tree what we had at first seen as a stooping man. We see the same colors; we hear the same sounds, but not in the same way.

To empty ourselves of our false divinity, to deny ourselves, to give up being the center of the world in imagination, to discern that all points in the world are equally centers and that the true center is outside the world, this is to consent to the rule of mechanical necessity in matter and of free choice at the center of each soul. Such consent is love. The face of this love, which is turned toward thinking persons, is the love of our neighbor; the face turned toward matter is love of the order of the world, or love of the beauty of the world which is the same thing.

SIMONE WEIL (1909–1943)
French scholar, mystic, and philosopher

One day, the Gospel tells us, the tension gradually accumulating between humanity and God will touch the limits prescribed by the possibilities of the world. And then will come the end. Then the presence of Christ which has been silently accruing in things, will suddenly be revealed—like a flash of light from pole to pole. Breaking through all the barriers within which the veil of matter and the water-tightness of souls have seemingly kept it confined, it will invade the face of the earth. And under the finally liberated action of the true affinities of being, the spiritual atoms of the world will be borne along by a force generated by the powers of cohesion proper to the universe itself, and will occupy, whether within Christ or without Christ (but always under the influence of Christ,) the place of happiness or pain designated for them by the living structure of the Pleroma. "As the lightning comes from the east and shines as far as the west . . . as the floods came and swept them all away . . . so will be the coming of the Son of Man" (Matt. 24:27, 39). Like lightning, like a conflagration, like a flood, the attraction exerted by the Son of Man will lay hold of all the whirling elements in the universe so as to reunite them or subject them to his Body.

PIERRE TEILHARD DE CHARDIN (1881–1955)
French paleontologist and Jesuit priest

From the Incarnation springs the whole doctrine of sacraments—the indwelling of the mortal by the immortal, of the material by the spiritual, the phenomenal by the real. After an analogous manner, we all bear about with us not only the immortal soul but also the glorified body in which we shall be known at the Resurrection, though now it is known only to God, or to those to whom love may reveal it.

It is this that lies at the bottom of Dante's Beatrician Vision: because he loved the mortal Florentine girl, it was given to him to behold her, as it were, walking the earth in her body of glory. And this is why, in the *Commedia*, a stress so disconcerting to the minds of those who like their religion to be very "spiritual" is laid continually upon her bodily beauty. A sure mark of Catholic Christianity is the honoring of the "holy and glorious flesh," and indeed of all material things, because they are sacraments and symbols of the Divine glory.

DOROTHY L. SAYERS (1893–1957)
English novelist, playwright, and Christian apologist

Suppose a curious and fair woman. Some have seen the beauties of Heaven in such a person. It is a vain thing to say they loved too much. I dare say there are ten thousand beauties in that creature which they have not seen. They loved it not too much but upon false causes. Nor so much upon false ones as only upon some little ones. They love a creature for sparkling eyes and curled hair, lily breasts and ruddy cheeks: which they should love moreover for being God's Image, Queen of the Universe, beloved by Angels, redeemed by Jesus Christ, an heiress of Heaven, and temple of the Holy Ghost: a mine and fountain of all virtues, a treasury of graces, and a child of God.

But these excellencies are unknown. They love her perhaps, but do not love God more: nor men as much: nor Heaven and Earth at all. And so, being defective to other things, perish by a seeming excess to that. We should be all Life and Mettle and Vigour and Love to everything: and that would poise us. . . . But God being beloved infinitely more, will be infinitely more our joy, and our heart will be more with Him, so that no man can be in danger by loving others too much, that loveth God as he ought.

THOMAS TRAHERNE (1637–1674)

English cleric and poet

One thing, however, marriage has done for me. I can never again believe that religion is manufactured out of our unconscious, starved desires and is a substitute for sex. For those few years H. and I feasted on love; every mode of it—solemn and merry, romantic and realistic, sometimes as dramatic as a thunderstorm, sometimes as comfortable and unemphatic as putting on your soft slippers. No cranny of heart or body remained unsatisfied. If God were a substitute for love we ought to have lost all interest in Him. Who'd bother about substitutes when he has the thing itself? But that isn't what happens. We both knew we wanted something besides one another—quite a different kind of something, a quite different kind of want. You might as well say that when lovers have one another they will never want to eat—or breathe.

C. S. LEWIS (1898–1963)
English novelist and Christian apologist

The virtue of man and woman is the same. For if the God of both is one, the master of both is also one; one church, one temperance, one modesty; their food is common, marriage an equal yoke; respiration, sight, hearing, knowledge, hope, obedience, love—all alike. And those whose life is common, have common graces and a common salvation; common to them are love and training.

CLEMENT OF ALEXANDRIA (150–220?)
Greek theologian and church father

There is one secret, the greatest of all—a secret which no previous religion dared, even in enigma, to allege fully—which is stated with the utmost distinctness by Our Lord and the Church. . . . I mean the doctrine of the Incarnation, regarded not as an historical event which occurred two thousand years ago, but as an event which is renewed in the body of every one who is in the way to the fulfillment of his original destiny. . . .

The spiritual body, into which the bodies of those who love and obey God perfectly are from time to time transfigured, is a prism. The invisible ray of the Holy Spirit, entering its candid substance, becomes divided, and is reflected in a triple and most distinct glory from its own surfaces. . . . this is the "bow in the cloud" of man's flesh; the pledge that he shall no more be overwhelmed by the deluge of the senses, which are killed for ever by this vision, as the flame of a tallow candle is killed by the electric light.

COVENTRY PATMORE (1823–1896)

English poet

Thy whole Body, pure and divine, blazes with the fire of Thy divinity, ineffably united to it. Thou has granted, Lord, that this corruptible temple—my human flesh—be united to Thy holy flesh, that my blood mingle with Thine; from henceforth I am a transparent and translucid member of Thy body. . . .

SIMEON THE NEW THEOLOGIAN (949–1022)

Byzantine saint, mystic, and spiritual writer

Abba Paul went to see Abba Basil and said to him, "Abba, as far as I can, I say my little office, I fast a little, I read and meditate, I live in peace and as far as I can, I purify my thoughts. What else can I do?" Then the old man stood up and stretched his hands towards heaven. His fingers became like ten lamps of fire and he said to him, "If you will, you can become all fire. You cannot be a monk unless you become like a consuming fire."

DESERT FATHERS (fourth–sixth centuries)

I said, "I cannot look at you, Father, because lightenings stream from your eyes. Your face has become more brilliant than the sun and my eyes cannot bear it."

Fr. Seraphim said:—"Do not be afraid, Lover of God, because you are now shining just as brightly as I am. You are now in the fullness of the Divine Spirit because, otherwise, you could not see me in that state." And inclining his head toward me he whispered quietly into my ear: "Thank the Lord God for his indescribable mercy to you. You saw I did not even cross myself but only prayed mentally in my heart to the Lord God saying: 'Lord, grant him clearly and with bodily eyes to see that descent of the Holy Spirit by which you honor those servants of yours to whom you appear in all your magnificent glory.' You see, Father, the Lord granted at once the humble request of the poor Seraphim. How much we must thank him for his indescribable gift to both of us. Rarely the Lord God manifests himself in this way, even to the greatest hermits. Divine Grace has condescended to console your sorrowful heart, like a fond mother, at the prayer of the Mother of God herself. Why do you not look me in the eyes? Look simply and be not afraid; the Lord is with us."

After these words I looked at his face and even greater respectful fear overcame me. Picture in the midst of the sun at its noonday brightest the face of the man who talks to you. You see the movement of his lips, the changing expression of his eyes. You hear his voice and feel that someone's hands are grasping your shoulders. But you do not see those hands, nor yourself, nor the body of the speaker but only the blinding light which spreads a good many meters, illuminating with a brilliant light the snow covering the meadow and the snow falling down on the great *staretz*. Picture my state then!

N. MOTOVILOV (c. 1831)
Disciple of St. Seraphim

There is nothing that befalls the soul in which the body does not take part. We receive impressions of this world, but also of the divine world partly through the body. . . .

Every sacrament is a gift of God, conferred on the soul by means of physical actions; the waters of baptism, the oil of chrism, the bread and wine of communion are all taken from the material world. We can never do either good or evil otherwise than in conjunction with our body. . . .

The body is not there only, as it were, for the soul to be born, mature and then to go, abandoning it; the body, from the very first day to the last, has been the co-worker of the soul in all things and is, together with the soul, the total man. It remains marked for ever, as it were, by the imprint of the soul and the common life they had together. Linked with the soul, the body is also linked through the sacraments to Jesus Christ himself . . . and the body is thus united in its own right with the divine world with which it comes into contact.

ANTHONY BLOOM (1914–)
Russian Orthodox monk and metropolitan of Sourozh

When we seek to keep watch over and correct our reason by a rigorous sobriety, with what are we to keep watch, if we do not gather together our mind, which has been dissipated abroad by the senses, and lead it back again into the interior, to the selfsame heart which is the seat of the thoughts? Where but in the heart, the controlling organ, the throne of grace, where the mind and all the thoughts of the soul are to be found?

Can you not see, then, how essential it is that those who have determined to pay attention to themselves in inner quiet should gather together the mind and enclose it in the body, and especially in that "body" most interior to the body, which we call the heart?

GREGORY PALAMAS (1296–1359)
Greek theologian and saint

After this our Lord revealed a sovereign spiritual loving in my soul. I was filled with an everlasting security that supported me completely, and I was without any fear. This feeling was so blessed that I experienced nothing but peace and rest, and there was nothing on earth that could have disturbed me.

Yet this lasted but a while, and I was abandoned again, alone with all the heaviness and weariness of life, and so burdened with myself that I barely had patience to live. There was no comfort then, nor ease: I believed in faith, and hope, and love, but truly I had no feeling of them. And then our blessed Lord gave me again comfort and rest in soul so blissful and so mighty that no fear, no sorrow, no bodily pain could have troubled me.

And then that pain returned again to my feeling, and then again the joy and the loving: now the one, now the other, again and again, perhaps twenty times. In the times of joy I might have said with St. Paul, "Nothing shall separate me from the love of Christ." And when in pain I might have cried out with Peter, "Lord, save me, for I perish."

This vision made me understand that every soul can derive great benefit from experiences such as these: sometimes to be comforted and consoled, other times to be abandoned and bereft. For

God wants us to know that he keeps us surely and loves us fully whether we be in sorrow or in joy.

JULIAN OF NORWICH (14th century)

English mystic and anchoress

Saint Teresa of Ávila also was subject to these vicissitudes, sometimes with a courage nothing could shake; sometimes with a timidity which was alarmed by the least pain; sometimes with fervor which seemed to be unchangeable; sometimes with a languor which seemed impossible to animate; at times with a disengagement which raised her easily above everything; at others with affections of debasing attachments which lowered her, as it were, beneath everything. Yet the surprising changes she not only experienced in herself, but had also observed in other holy souls served only to show her the weakness of human nature without discouraging her, and the strength of grace without creating pride.

The more frequent these changes were, the more sensible she was of the effect of these two objects which, as it were, balanced each other, and kept her in a right medium between excessive fear, and too much confidence. Knowing that day and night succeeded each other she was neither frightened by one, or dazzled by the other.

AMBROISE DE LOMBEZ (date of treatise: 1756)

French Capuchin theologian

Soon I found a withdrawing again of the Lord; then I knew a winter again, and the storms of the enemy; and not having yet learned the state of being contented in want, as well as in aboundings, I not only fell into a poor, wanting, murmuring state, but also into great trouble, in a sense of this change, and fears and doubts were ready to enter: I toiled in this night, but could catch nothing which administered any comfort that was lasting.

Here I was willing and running and striving, being in great fear and sorrow; and the more I toiled and labored, kindling sparks of my own, the more my sorrow was increased; for as yet I had not learned the state of resignation. And now, I was brought very low; and having mourned many days, in the sense of the withdrawings of the presence, love and power of my God, being in deep distress and amazement, Israel's travels in the wilderness were opened unto me; how the Lord tried them with want of bread and water, and that their happiness stood in their being content and resigned up to the will of God, and in the belief of the Lord's faithfulness, to have endured the trial. But they murmured and repined, and thereby grieved the Spirit of God; so did I.

Yet through the loving kindness of God, the state of resignation was opened unto me, in which man stood before he fell through transgression, into his own workings and willings. Now, when my understanding was thus opened, my soul cried unto the Lord my God,—Oh! preserve me in pure patience and passiveness, and in living, acceptable obedience, and I will trust in thee.

And as I believed in the light of the Lord, and thereby and therein was comprehended and resigned, his pure power, love and life broke in as formerly, which greatly refreshed; then the sun shined upon my tabernacle, and I bowed before the Lord, blessing and praising his holy, glorious name; then he instructed me, *and his pure Spirit and power opened in me the way of preservation, and that was, to center down into true humility.*

So then my soul began to be as the dove that found a place for the soles of her feet.

CHARLES MARSHALL (1637–1698)
English Quaker

The Holy Spirit occasionally withdraws so that he might be recalled more eagerly, or be more eagerly received and more alertly anticipated when he returns. He makes both frequent withdrawals from and visits to those in whom he indwells. Even with those who have become spiritual the Spirit alternates his presence and absence, visiting at dawn and suddenly testing them. The Holy Spirit withdraws whenever he wishes, according to the disposition of his hidden counsels, establishing and fixing in advance definite limits to a person's progress according to what the Spirit knows and wills.

Whoever lacks the Spirit will not recognize the Spirit's withdrawal.

GUIGO DE PONTE (d. 1297)
Carthusian monk and spiritual writer

A few days after Pascal's death, a manservant, arranging his clothes, noticed a curious bulge in his doublet. Opening the lining, he withdrew a folded parchment, written in Pascal's hand. Within the parchment was a scribbled sheet of paper, containing the words of the parchment, with some variations. These documents were the record of his mystical illumination, his two hours in the presence of God. For eight years he had worn them as an amulet, hiding them in his coat, sewing and unsewing them at need. . . .

On the night of November 23, 1654, Pascal was in his house on the rue Beaubourg in Paris when he had an experience which he regarded, ever after, as the most precious and significant of his life. He felt that he received a visit from God, a visit which—to use his words—completely absorbed him with "certitude, certitude, feeling, joy, peace."

FIRE is the word that appears in capital letters at the top of both of the documents—the feverishly scribbled paper, and the carefully penned parchment. Further down are the words, "Joy, joy, joy, tears of joy—"

Fire, the water of tears, and an overpowering sense of presence were the essential elements of his experience, but they followed a long period of numbness, dryness, separation. During this period he wrote to his sister, "It is a horrible thing to feel everything one possesses slip away," and "The eternal silence of these infinite spaces terrifies me." It was not only that he had lost all confidence in God's grace, but that he had ceased even to desire it. His sister wrote, "He found himself detached from all things in a way that he had never seen before, nor anything like it, but [he admitted] that also he was in such a great abandonment on God's part that he felt no attraction in that direction."

This lack of attraction was for Pascal a kind of terrible forgetfulness. It is no wonder, then, that when this state at last gave way to fire and tears of joy, he had a need to make a record of it.

How fitting, then, that the record of this experience—which was like having moved through the dryness of rock to water— should itself be carried like a hidden well or secret spring.

NOELLE OXENHANDLER (contemporary)
American writer and essayist

In one of the psalms it is written, "You, O Lord, are the same and your years will never end." My brothers and sisters, do our years never end? They slip away from us day by day. . . .

Nothing that exists remains constant. Even the human body is subject to a continual process of change; it has no permanence. Even the stars have no constancy: . . . they whirl through space, moving from east to west, and back again towards the east. They do not rest; they are not the same.

Nor is the human heart any more constant! Consider how many thoughts and distractions assail it. Consider the effect pleasure has upon us, how various cravings can wreak havoc inside us. The human mind is termed rational, but it too changes and possesses no stability. One moment we want something; the next moment we change our mind. One moment we are convinced of something; the next moment we are no longer so sure. One moment we remember; the next moment we forget. No one has an inner coherence of being. . . . It is important to allow all this frustration, these diseases, difficulties, troubles and pains, to humble us so that we return to the One who is always the same.

AUGUSTINE OF HIPPO (354–430)
Carthaginian saint, philosopher, and doctor of the church

O Thou who art unchangeable, Whom nothing changes! Thou art unchanged in love, precisely for our welfare not subject to any change: may we too will our welfare, submitting ourselves to the direction of Thy unchangeableness, so that we may, in unconditional obedience find our rest and remain at rest in Thy unchangeableness.

Thou art not like a man; if he is to preserve only some degree of constancy he must not permit himself too much to be moved nor by too many things. Thou, on the contrary, art moved and moved in infinite love, by all things, even that which we human beings call an insignificant trifle and pass by unmoved, the need of the sparrow, even this moves Thee; and what we so often scarcely notice, a human sigh, this moves Thee, O infinite Love!

But nothing changes Thee, O Thou Who are unchanging. O Thou who in infinite love dost submit to be moved, may this our prayer also move Thee to add Thy blessing, in order that there may be wrought such a change in him who prays as to bring him into conformity with Thy unchanging will, Thou who art unchangeable.

SØREN KIERKEGAARD (1813–1855)

Danish theologian

CYCLE TWO

THE LAW
OF BEARING

How is it possible to bear our neighbor? Why must we love our enemies? What will allow us to see our true relationship, and to recognize that we are all "members of the body of Christ"? What stands in the way of this vision? Catherine of Siena tells us, "You are your chief neighbor," giving us all a place to begin.

This cycle approaches the mystery of the Incarnation, the divine descent wherein "God is in the place where we are and gazes at us in a human being."

The whole person is a person who is on the one side open to God, and on the other side open to other human persons. . . . It has been said that there is no true person unless there are two entering into communication with one another. The isolated individual is not a real person. A real person is one who lives in and for others. And the more personal relationships we form with others, the more we truly realize ourselves as persons.

This idea of openness to God, openness to other persons, could be summed up under the word *love*. We become truly personal by loving God and by loving other humans. By love, I don't mean merely an emotional feeling, but a fundamental attitude. In its deepest sense, love is the life, the energy, of God Himself in us. . . .

We are not truly personal as long as we are turned in on ourselves, isolated from others. We only become personal if we face other persons, and relate to them.

KALLISTOS WARE (1934–)
Greek Orthodox archbishop

How can you grow in humility if there is no one against whom you can compare yourself? How can you demonstrate compassion when you are cut off from communion with your fellows? How can anyone grow in patience when there is no one to frustrate your wishes? If any claim to find the teaching of Holy Scripture quite sufficient to correct their character without anybody else's help, they are making themselves out to be like an architect who knows the theory of construction but is unable to put theory into practice, or like a smith who prefers not to practise his trade. To such as these are the words of the apostle addressed: "It is not the hearers of the Law who are righteous before God but the doers of the Law who shall be justified."

Our Lord, in loving every human being right to the end, did not limit himself to teaching us in words. In order to give us a precise and clear example of humility in the perfection of love, he took a towel and washed his disciples' feet. So what about you, living entirely on your own, how will you ever discover such humility? Whose feet will you wash? Whom will you care for? . . .

Living in community is like life in the arena: it is an inner journey, an experience of being continuously stretched as you strive to keep the commandments.

BASIL THE GREAT (330–379)
Doctor of the church, saint, and bishop of Caesarea

In the records of the Thebaid, of the strange ascetic monks of the Egyptian desert, followers of St. Anthony, the thing was put plainly enough.

A certain old man used to say, "It is right for a man to take up the burden for those who are near to him, whatsoever it may be, and, so to speak, to put his own soul in the place of that of his neighbor, and to become, if it were possible, a double man; and he must suffer, and weep, and mourn with him, and finally the matter must be accounted by him as if he himself had put on the actual body of his neighbor, and as if he had acquired his countenance and soul, and he must suffer for him as he would for himself."

. . . It is in small things that the practice could be begun—sleeplessness or anxiety or slight pains. It is between friends and lovers that the practice could be best begun; always remembering that in the end he whom holy Luck throws in our way is our neighbor—as much as (but perhaps not more than) he whom we go out of our way to seek. To begin the way in small things conveniently is better than to dream of the remote splendors of the vicarious life; not that they are likely in any case to seem very splendid when they come. To begin by practicing faith where it is easiest is better than to try and practice it where it is hardest. There is always somewhere where it can be done.

The doctrine of the Christian church has declared that the mystery of the Christian religion is a doctrine of co-inherence and substitution. . . . To love God and to love one's neighbor are but two movements of the same principle, and so are nature and grace; and the principle is the Word by whom all things were made and who gave himself for the redemption of all things. . . .

Humility, said the author of *The Cloud of Unknowing*, consists in seeing things as they are. If our lives are so carried by others and so depend upon others, it becomes impossible to think very highly of them. In the second place there arises within one a first faint sense of what might be called "loving from within." One no longer merely loves an object; one has a sense of loving precisely from the great web in which the object and we are both combined. There is, if only transitorily, a flicker of living within the beloved. Such sensations are, in themselves, of no importance. But they do for a moment encourage us, and they may assist us to consider still more intensely the great co-inherence of all life.

It is said (among other examples of substitution in the church) that the blessed Saint Seraphim of Sarov laid on a certain nun "the ascetic discipline of death, that she should die instead of her sick brother Michael, whose work was not yet done." . . .

Our chief temptation is to limit the operation [of this doctrine of co-inherence and substitution]. We can believe it happily of ourselves as regards our lovers and our friends; we can accept the idea, at least, as regards strangers; we cannot so easily as regards those of our "neighbors" who are, individually or nationally, inimical to us. We feel it as an outrage that we should be intimately interrelated, physically and spiritually, to those who have offended our pride or our principles; our very physical bodies revolt against it.

But the doctrine will not let us escape. It is not for us to make a division; that power our Lord explicitly reserved to himself. If we insist on it, we can, in his final judgment, *be* separated. That is hell. But only ourselves can put us there. . . .

CHARLES WILLIAMS (1886–1945)

English novelist, essayist, and poet

In the years of the [Russian] Civil War when the opposing armies were contending for power, conquering and losing ground in the course of three years, a small town fell into the hands of the Red Army which had been held by the remnants of the Imperial troops. A woman found herself there with her two small children, four and five years of age, in danger of death because her husband belonged to the opposite camp. She hid in an abandoned house hoping that the time would come when she would be able to escape.

One evening a young woman, Natalie, of her own age, in the early twenties, knocked at the door and asked her whether she was so-and-so. When the mother said she was, the young woman warned her that she had been discovered and would be fetched that very night in order to be shot. The young woman added, "You must escape at once." The mother looked at the children and said, "How could I?" The young woman, who thus far had been nothing but a physical neighbor, became at that moment the neighbor of the Gospel. She said, "You can, because I will stay behind and call myself by your name when they come to fetch you." "But you will be shot," said the mother. "Yes, but I have no children." And she stayed behind.

We can imagine what happened then. We can see the night coming, wrapping in darkness, in gloom, in cold and damp, this cottage. We can see there a woman who was waiting for her death to come and we can remember the Garden of Gethsemane. We can imagine Natalie asking that this cup should pass her by and being met like Christ by divine silence. We can imagine her turning in intention towards those who might have supported her, but who were out of reach. The disciples of Christ slept; and she could turn to no one without betraying. We can imagine that more than once she prayed that at least her sacrifice should not be in vain.

Natalie probably asked herself more than once what would happen to the mother and the children when she was dead, and there was no reply except the word of Christ, "No one has greater love than he who lays down his life for his friend." Probably she thought more than once that in one minute she could be secure! It was enough to open the door and the moment she was in the street she no longer was that woman, she became herself again. It was enough to deny her false, her shared identity. But she died, shot. The mother and the children escaped.

ANTHONY BLOOM (1914–)
Russian Orthodox monk and metropolitan of Sourozh

Our Lord was pleased to assume the likeness of every poor man and compared Himself to every poor man in order that no man who believes in Him should exalt himself over his brother, but, seeing the Lord in his brother, should consider himself less and worse than his brother, just as he is less than his Creator. And he should take the poor man in and honor him, and be ready to exhaust all his means in helping him.

A person is not saved by having once shown mercy to someone, although if he scorns someone but once he deserves eternal fire. For "I was hungry," and "I was thirsty" was said not just of one occasion, not of one day, but of the whole of life. In the same way "you gave me food," "you gave me drink," "you clothed me" and so on does not indicate one incident, but *a constant attitude to everyone.*

SIMEON THE NEW THEOLOGIAN (949–1022)
Byzantine saint, mystic, and spiritual writer

"Bear ye one another's burdens, and so fulfill the law of Christ" (Gal. 6:2). Thus the law of Christ is a law of bearing. Bearing means forbearing and sustaining. The brother is a burden to the Christian, precisely because he is a Christian. For the pagan the other person never becomes a burden at all. He simply sidesteps every burden that others may impose upon him.

The Christian, however, must bear the burden of a brother. He must suffer and endure the brother. It is only when he is a burden that another person is really a brother and not merely an object to be manipulated.

In bearing with men God maintained fellowship with them. It is the law of Christ that was fulfilled in the Cross. And Christians must share in this law. They must suffer their brethren, but, what is more important, now that the law of Christ has been fulfilled, they *can* bear with their brethren.

The Bible speaks with remarkable frequency of "bearing." It is capable of expressing the whole work of Jesus Christ in this one word. "Surely he hath borne our griefs, and carried our sorrows. . . . the chastisement of our peace was upon him" (Isa. 53:4–5). Therefore, the Bible can also characterize the whole life of the Christian as bearing the Cross. It is the fellowship of the Cross to experience the burden of the other. If one does not experience it, the fellowship he belongs to is not Christian.

It is, first of all, the *freedom* of the other person that is a burden to the Christian. The other's freedom collides with his own autonomy, yet he must recognize it. He could get rid of this burden by refusing the other person his freedom, by constraining him and thus doing violence to his personality, by stamping his own image upon him. But if he lets God create His image in him, he by this token gives him his freedom and himself bears the burden of this freedom of another creature of God. The freedom of the other person includes all that we mean by a person's nature, individuality, endowment. It also includes his weaknesses and oddities, which are such a trial to our patience, everything that produces frictions, conflicts, and collisions among us. To bear the burden of the other person means involvement with the created reality of the other, to accept and affirm it, and, in bearing with it, to break through to the point where we take joy in it.

This will prove especially difficult where varying strength and weakness in faith are bound together in a fellowship. The weak must not judge the strong, the strong must not despise the weak. The weak must guard against pride, the strong against indifference. None must seek his own rights. If the strong person falls, the weak one must guard his heart against malicious joy at his downfall. If the weak one falls, the strong one must help him rise again in all kindness. The one needs as much patience as the other.

DIETRICH BONHOEFFER (1906–1945)
German Lutheran pastor and theologian

Purely human love is continually in the process of flying away after, so to speak, or flying away with, the beloved's perfections. We say of a seducer that he steals a girl's heart, but of all purely human love, even when it is most beautiful, we must say that it has something thievish about it, that it really steals the beloved's perfections, whereas Christian love grants the beloved all his imperfections and weaknesses and in all his changes remains with him, loving the person it sees.

If this were not so, Christ would never have had a chance to love, for where would he have found the perfect person! Wonderful! What was it, namely, that for Christ was actually the obstacle to finding the perfect person? Was it not simply that he himself was the perfect one, which is to be recognized by his having boundlessly loved the person he saw! With regard to love, we continually speak, again and again, about the perfect person: with regard to love, Christianity, too continually speaks, again and again, about the perfect person—alas, but we human beings speak about finding the perfect person in order to love him, whereas Christianity speaks about being the perfect person who boundlessly loves the person he sees. We human beings want to look upward in order to look for the object of perfection (although the direction is continually toward the unseen), but in Christ perfection looked down to earth and loved the person it saw. We ought to learn from Christianity, because it is indeed true, in a far more universal sense than it is said, that no one ascends into heaven except the one who descends from heaven. However visionary this talk about soaring up to heaven, it is delusionary if you do not first Christianly descend from heaven. But Christianly to descend from heaven is boundlessly to love the person just as you see him.

Therefore if you want to be perfect in love, strive to fulfill this duty, in loving to love the person one sees, to love him just as you see him, with all his imperfections and weaknesses, to love him as you see him when he has changed completely, when he no longer loves you but perhaps turns away indifferent, or turns away to love another; to love him as you see him when he betrays and denies you.

SØREN KIERKEGAARD (1813–1855)
Danish theologian

[Samuel Johnson] loved the poor as I never yet saw anyone do, with an earnest desire to make them happy. What signifies, says someone, giving halfpence to common beggars? They only lay it out in gin or tobacco. "And why (says Johnson) should they be denied such sweeteners of their existence? It is surely very savage to refuse them every possible avenue to pleasure, reckoned too coarse for our own acceptance. Life is a pill which none of us can bear to swallow without gilding; yet for the poor we delight in stripping it still barer, and are not ashamed to show even visible displeasure, if ever the bitter taste is taken from their mouths." In consequence of these principles he nursed whole nests of people in his house, where the lame, the blind, the sick, and the sorrowful found a secure retreat from all the evils whence his little income could secure them.

HESTER LYNCH PIOZZI (1741–1821)
English writer

Dante says that directly a soul ceases to say "mine," and says "ours," it makes the transition from the narrow, constricted, individual life to the truly free, truly personal, truly creative spiritual life, in which all are linked together in one single response to the Father of all spirits, God. Here, all interpenetrate, and all, however humble and obscure their lives may seem, can and do affect each other. Every advance made by one is made for all.

Only when we recognize all this, and act on it, are we fully alive and taking our proper place in the universe of spirit; for life means the fullest possible give and take between the living creature and its environment: breathing, feeding, growing, changing. And spiritual life, which is profoundly organic, means the give and take, the willed correspondence of the little human spirit with the Infinite Spirit; its feeding upon Him, its growth towards perfect union with Him, its response to His attraction and subtle pressure.

That growth and that response may seem to us like a movement, a journey, in which by various unexpected and often unattractive paths, we are drawn almost in spite of ourselves—not as a result of our own over-anxious struggles—to the real end of our being, the place where we are ordained to be: a journey that is more like the inevitable movement of the iron flying to the great magnet that attracts it, than like the long and weary pilgrimage in the teeth of many obstacles from "this world to that which is to come."

Or it may seem like a growth from the childlike, half-real existence into which we are born into a full reality.

EVELYN UNDERHILL (1875–1941)

English writer on mysticism

Our Lord asks but two things of us: Love for Him and for our neighbor: this is what we must strive to obtain. . . . We cannot know whether we love God, although there may be strong reasons for thinking so, but there can be no doubt about whether we love our neighbor or no. Be sure that in proportion as you advance in fraternal charity you are increasing in your love of God. In this most important matter we should be most watchful in little things, and take no notice of the great works we plan during prayer. . . .

It is amusing to see souls who, while they are at prayer, fancy they are willing to be despised and publicly insulted for the love of God, yet afterwards do all they can to hide their small defects; if anyone unjustly accuses them of a fault, God deliver us from their outcries! . . .

The Law of Bearing

Prayer does not consist of such fancies.... No, our Lord expects works from us. Beg our Lord to grant you perfect love for your neighbor.... If someone else is well spoken of, be more pleased than if it were yourself; this is easy enough, for if you were really humble, it would vex you to be praised.... Force your will, as far as possible, to comply in all things with others' wishes although sometimes you may lose your own rights by doing so. Forget your self-interests for theirs, however much nature may rebel.

TERESA OF ÁVILA (1515–1582)

Spanish Carmelite saint and mystic

I would have you know that every virtue of yours and every vice is put into action by means of your neighbors. If you hate me, you harm your neighbors and yourself as well (for you are your chief neighbor), and the harm is both general and particular.

I say general because it is your duty to love your neighbors as your own self. In love you ought to help them spiritually with prayer and counsel, and assist them spiritually and materially in their need—at least with your good will if you have nothing else. If you do not love me you do not love your neighbors, nor will you help those you do not love. But it is yourself you harm most, because you deprive yourself of grace.

In loving me you will realize love for your neighbors, and if you love your neighbors you have kept the law. If you are bound by this love you will do everything you can to be of service wherever you are.

CATHERINE OF SIENA (1347–1380)

Italian Dominican mystic and saint

I always think that the best way to know God is to love many things. Love a friend, a wife, something—whatever you like—you will be on the way to knowing more about Him; that is what I say to myself. But one must love with a lofty and serious intimate sympathy, with strength, with intelligence; and one must always try to know deeper, better and more. That leads to God, that leads to unwavering faith.

One cannot always tell what it is that keeps us shut in, confines us, seems to bury us; nevertheless, one feels certain barriers, certain gates, certain walls. Is all this imagination, fantasy? I don't think so. And one asks, "My God! is it for long, is it forever, is it for all eternity?"

Do you know what frees one from this captivity? It is every deep, serious affection. Being friends, being brothers, love, that is what opens the prison by some supreme power, by some magic force. Without this, one remains in prison. Where sympathy is renewed, life is restored.

VINCENT VAN GOGH (1853–1890)

Dutch painter

To be no part of any body, is to be nothing. At most, the greatest persons are but great wens, and excrescences; men of wit and delightful conversation, but as moles for ornament, except they be so incorporated into the body of the world that they contribute something to the sustentation of the whole.

JOHN DONNE (1572–1631)

English poet and dean of St. Paul's Cathedral, London

Worship does not consist in achieving a mental state of concentrated isolation from one's fellows. But in the depth of common worship it is as if we found our separate lives were all one life, within whom we live and move and have our being. Communication seems to take place sometimes without words having been spoken. In the silence we received an unexpected commission to bear in loving intentness the spiritual need of another person sitting nearby. And that person goes away, uplifted and refreshed. Sometimes in that beautiful experience of living worship which the Friends have called "the gathered meeting," it is as if we joined hands and hearts, and lifted them together toward the unspeakable glory. Or it is as if that light and warmth dissolved us together into one. Tears are not to be scorned, then, for we stand together in the Holy of Holies.

THOMAS RAYMOND KELLY (1893–1941)
American Quaker

Jesus says to us, "As you did it to one of the least of these my brethren, you did it to me." How often we have heard this statement and used it in pious, edifying talk. But suppose we ask ourselves how Jesus could really say that. Is it not really just a juridical fiction: I give you credit for it, as though you had done to me personally what you have done to the least of these other human beings?

No, this saying of Jesus is not a legal fiction, a moral make-believe, a kind of compensation. It is truly the case that we meet the incarnate Word of God in the other human being, because God himself really is in this other. If we love him, if we do not as it were culpably impede the dynamism of this love and fundamentally turn it back towards ourselves, then there occurs precisely the divine descent into the flesh of man, so that God is in the place where we are and gazes at us in a human being.

This divine descent continues through us and it then happens that we, because God loves us, love our neighbor and have already loved God by the very fact of loving our neighbor. For, of course, we cannot achieve this love at all except on the basis of that divine love for us which in fact made itself our brother.

The Christological side, if I may so call it, of our brotherly love would have to be taken really seriously and really realized in life. Where the other human being confronts me, there Christ really is, asking me whether I will love him, the incarnate Word of God, and if I say yes, he replies that he is in the least of his brethren.

That is difficult. It is the ultimate reality and the hardest task of our lives. We can be deceived about it time and time again. But if we have turned in love from self to our neighbor, we have come to God, not by our strength but by God's grace. God who, as John says, had loved us so that we might love our neighbor, has truly laid hold of us, has torn us as it were from self and has given us what in conjunction constitutes our eternity, a personal union with others in which we are also united to God.

KARL RAHNER (1904–1984)
German Jesuit theologian

The divine humility shows itself in rendering service. He who is entitled to claim the service of all his creatures chooses first to give his service to them. "The Son of Man came not to receive service but to give it." But our humility does not begin with the giving of service; it begins with the readiness to receive it. For there can be much pride and condescension in our giving of service. It is wholesome only when it is offered spontaneously on the impulse of real love; the conscientious offer of it is almost sure to "have the nature of sin," as almost all virtue has of which the origin is in our own deliberate wills. For unless the will is perfectly cleansed, its natural or original sin—the sin inherent in it of acting from the self instead of God as center—contaminates all its works.

So our humility shows itself first in the readiness to receive service from our fellow-men and supremely from God. To accept service from others is to acknowledge a measure of dependence on them. It is well for us to stand on our own feet: to go through life in parasitic dependence on others, contributing nothing, is contemptible; but those who are doing their share of the world's work should have no hesitation in receiving what the love or generosity or pity of others may offer. The desire "not to be beholden to anybody" is completely unchristian. . . .

But it is the service of God which we must above all be ready to accept. . . . Our first thought must never be "What can I do for God?" The answer to that is, Nothing. The first thought must always be "What would God do for me?"

WILLIAM TEMPLE (1881–1944)
English archbishop of Canterbury

In things that belong to action, to works, to charity, there is nothing perfect there neither. I would be loath to say that every good is a sin; it is not utterly so; not so altogether; but it is so much toward it that there is no work of ours so good that we can look for thanks to God's hand for that work; no work that has not so much ill mingled with it, as that we need not cry God mercy for that work.

There was so much corruption in the getting, or so much vainglory in the bestowing, as that no man builds a Hospital, but his soul lies, though not dead, yet lame in that Hospital; no man mends a highway, but he is, though not drowned, yet mired in that way; no man relieves the poor, but he needs relief for that relief.

In all those works of Charity, the world that has benefit by them is bound to confess and acknowledge a goodness, and to call them good works; but the man that does them, and knows the weaknesses of them, knows they are not good works.

JOHN DONNE (1572–1631)
English poet and dean of St. Paul's Cathedral, London

The sign of childishness is to say: *"Me wants, me-me";* the sign of youth is to say: *"I"*—and *"I"*—and *"I";* the sign of maturity and the introduction to the eternal is the will to understand that this *"I"* signifies nothing if it does not become the "thou" to whom eternity unceasingly speaks, and says: "Thou *shalt,* thou shalt, thou shalt."

The youth wishes to be the only *"I"* in the whole world; maturity consists in understanding this "thou" for itself, even if it is not said to any other man. Thou shalt, thou shalt love thy neighbor.

SØREN KIERKEGAARD (1813–1855)
Danish theologian

We go to church for love, for the new love of Christ himself, which is granted to us in our unity. We go to church so that this divine love will again and again be "poured into our hearts," so that again and again we may "put on love" so that, constituting the body of Christ, we can abide in Christ's love and manifest it in the world.

But that is why our contemporary, utterly "individualized" piety, in which we egotistically separate ourselves from the gathering, is so grievous, so contradictory to the age-old experience of the Church. Even while standing in the church, we continue to sense some people as "neighbors" and others as "strangers"—a faceless mass that "has no relevance" to us and to our prayer and disturbs our "spiritual concentration." How often do seemingly "spiritually" attuned and "devout" people openly declare their distaste for crowded gatherings, which disturb them from praying, and seek empty and quiet chapels, secluded corners, separate from the "crowds." In fact, such individual "self-absorption" would hardly be possible in the church assembly—precisely because this is not the purpose of the assembly and of our participation in it.

Concerning this individual prayer the gospels say: "When you pray, go into your room and shut the door and pray . . ." Does not this mean that the *assembling as the Church* has another purpose, already contained in the very word "assembly"? Through it the Church fulfills herself, accomplishes our communion with Christ and with his love, so that in participating in it, we comprise "out of many, one body."

PAUL EVDOKIMOV (1901–1970)
Russian Orthodox theologian

Advice from a senior devil to his junior charge:

My dear Wormwood,

I note with grave displeasure that your patient has become a Christian. Do not indulge the hope that you will escape the usual penalties; indeed, in your better moments, I trust you would hardly even wish to do so. In the meantime we must make the best of the situation. There is no need to despair; hundreds of these adult converts have been reclaimed after a brief sojourn in the Enemy's camp and are now with us. All the *habits* of the patient, both mental and bodily, are still in our favour.

One of our great allies at present is the Church itself. Do not misunderstand me. I do not mean the Church as we see her spread out through all time and space and rooted in eternity, terrible as an army with banners. That, I confess, is a spectacle which makes our boldest tempters uneasy. But fortunately it is quite invisible to these humans. All your patient sees is the half-finished, sham Gothic erection on the new building estate. When he goes inside, he sees the local grocer with rather an oily expression on his face bustling up to offer him one shiny little book containing liturgy which neither of them understands, and one shabby little book containing corrupt texts of a number of religious lyrics, mostly bad, and in very small print. When he gets to his pew and looks round him he sees just that selection of his neighbours whom he has hitherto avoided. You want to lean pretty heavily on those neighbours. Make his mind flit to and fro between an expression like "the body of Christ" and the actual faces in the next pew. It matters very little, of course, what kind of people that next pew really contains. You may know one of them to be a great warrior on the Enemy's side. No matter. Your patient, thanks to Our Father below, is a fool. Provided that any of those neighbours sing out of tune, or have boots that squeak, or double chins, or odd clothes, the patient will quite easily believe that their religion must therefore be somehow ridiculous. At his present stage, you see, he has an idea of "Christians" in his mind which he supposes to be spiritual but which, in fact, is largely pictorial. His mind is full of togas and sandals and armour and bare legs and the mere fact that the other people in church wear modern clothes is a real—though of course uncon-scious—difficulty to him. Never let it come to the surface; never let him ask what he expected them to look like. Keep everything hazy in his mind now, and you will have an eternity wherein to amuse yourself by producing in him the peculiar kind of clarity which Hell affords.

Work hard, then, on the disappointment or anti-climax which is certainly coming to the patient during his first few weeks as a churchman. The enemy allows this disappointment to occur on the threshold of every human endeavour. It occurs when the boy who has been enchanted in the nursery by *Stories from the Odyssey* buckles down to really learning Greek. It occurs when lovers have got married and begin the real task of learning to live together. In every department of life it marks the transition from dreaming aspiration to laborious doing. The Enemy takes this risk because He has a curious fancy of making all these disgusting little human vermin into what he calls His "free" lovers and servants— "sons" is the word He uses, with his inveterate love of degrading the whole spiritual world by unnatural liaisons with the two-legged animals. Desiring their freedom, He therefore refuses to carry them, by their mere affections and habits, to any of the goals which He sets before them: He leaves them to do it "on their own." If once they get through this initial dryness success-fully, they become much less dependent on emotion and therefore much harder to tempt.

I have been writing hitherto on the assumption that the people in the next pew afford no *rational* ground for disappointment. Of course if they do—if the patient knows that the woman with the absurd hat is a fanatical bridgeplayer or the man with squeaky boots a miser and an extortioner—then your task is so much the easier. All you then have to do is to keep out of his mind the question "If I, being what I am, can consider that I am in some sense a Christian, why should the different vices of those people in the next pew prove that their religion is mere hypocrisy and convention?" You may ask whether it is possible to keep such an obvious thought from occurring even to a human mind. It is, Wormwood, it is! Handle him properly and it simply won't come into his head. He has not been anything like long enough with the Enemy to have any real humility yet. What he says, even on his knees, about his own sinfulness is all parrot talk. At bottom, he still believes he has run up a very favourable credit-balance in the Enemy's ledger by allowing himself to be converted, and thinks that he is showing great humility and condescension in going to church with these "smug," commonplace neighbours at all. Keep him in that state of mind as long as you can,

> Your affectionate uncle,
>
> *Screwtape*

C. S. LEWIS (1898–1963)
English novelist and Christian apologist

And who is the robber of whom Christ spoke? It is the unspeakably harmful tendency to pass judgment upon our neighbor. This tendency is deeply rooted in human nature and many people are guilty of it. It is an evil inclination that makes a man willing to always judge others without ever attempting to judge himself.

So-and-so, he will say, talks too much; another too little. One man eats too much, another not enough; this one weeps too much, that one ought to weep more. In all circumstances we encounter this destructive judging, and this again gives rise to a deep contempt which shows itself in a person's behavior and speech. Thus one inflicts on one's neighbor the same wound which one bears oneself, by passing the evil judgment on to him. And finally a mortal blow is inflicted on him when all this comes to his hearing.

What do you really know about your neighbor? Do you know what God has willed for him, or to what destiny he has been called?

JOHANNES TAULER (1300–1361)
German Dominican contemplative

When I think of the way in which people talk of each other, there is nothing that seems to me more horrible. The low, the worse than unkind way in which we are accustomed to look at others, and criticise their disposition, judging them in the lowest possible court of the mind.

There is no remedy for this like praying for one another. If it is your habit to pray to God concerning your neighbors, to think of their plight as that of immortal creatures, to consider that they are journeying to heaven like yourself, and that their faults are impediments in their way to be removed, and transgressions to be forgiven, and for the forgiveness of which you plead with God—if you are in the habit, in other words, of dissecting those persons' history in the light of God's countenance, and striving to obtain God's forgiveness in their behalf, then, in the solemnity of such circumstances, you will sympathize with them and refrain from speaking of them in a damaging way.

The habit of taking each other before God in prayer, familiarly and by name, is eminently beneficial. It will cleanse you. It will sweeten your disposition. It will take away from you every particle of the raven, that loves to feed on carrion.

HENRY WARD BEECHER (1813–1887)
American Congregational minister

What about the men who run about the countryside painting signs that say "Jesus saves" and "Prepare to meet God!" Have you ever seen one of them? I have not, but I often try to imagine them, and I wonder what goes on in their minds. Strangely, their signs do not make me think of Jesus, but of *them*. Or perhaps it is "their Jesus" who gets in the way and makes all thought of Jesus impossible. They wish to force *their* Jesus upon us, and He is perhaps only a projection of themselves. They seem to be at times threatening the world with judgment and at other times promising it mercy. But are they asking simply to be loved and recognized and valued, for themselves? In any case, their Jesus is quite different from mine. But because their concept is different, should I reject it in horror, with distaste? If I do, perhaps I reject something in my own self that I no longer recognize to be there. And in any case, if I can tolerate their Jesus then I can accept and love *them*. Or I can at least conceive of doing so. Let not their Jesus be a barrier between us, or *they* will be a barrier between us and Jesus.

THOMAS MERTON (1915–1968)
American Cistercian monk

Human love is directed to the other person for his own sake, spiritual love loves him for Christ's sake. Therefore, human love seeks direct contact with the other person; it loves him not as a free person but as one whom it binds to itself. It wants to gain, to capture by every means; it uses force. It desires to be irresistible, to rule.

Human love has little regard for truth. It makes the truth relative, since nothing, not even the truth, must come between it and the beloved person. Human love desires the other person, his company, his answering love, but it does not serve him. On the contrary, it continues to desire even when it seems to be serving. There are two marks, both of which are one and the same thing, that manifest the difference between spiritual and human love: Human love cannot tolerate the dissolution of a fellowship that has become false for the sake of genuine fellowship, and human love cannot love an enemy, that is one who seriously and stubbornly resists it. Both spring from the same source: human love is by its very nature desire—desire for human community. So long as it can satisfy its desire in some way, it will not give it up, even for the sake of truth, even for the sake of genuine love for others. But where it can no longer expect its desire to be fulfilled, there it stops short—namely, in the face of an enemy. There it turns into hatred, contempt, and calumny.

Right here is the point where spiritual love begins. This is why human love becomes personal hatred when it encounters genuine spiritual love, which does not desire but serves. Human love makes itself an end in itself. It creates of itself an end, an idol which it worships, to which it must subject everything. Spiritual love, however, comes from Jesus Christ, it serves him alone; it knows that it has no immediate access to other persons.

◆

Spiritual love proves itself in that everything it says and does commends Christ. It will not seek to move others by all too personal, direct influence, by impure interference in the life of another. It will not take pleasure in pious, human fervor and excitement. It will rather meet the other person with the clear Word of God and be ready to leave him alone with this word for a long time, willing to release him again in order that Christ may deal with him. It will respect the line that has been drawn between him and us by Christ, and it will find full fellowship with him in the Christ who alone binds us together.

DIETRICH BONHOEFFER (1906–1945)
German Lutheran pastor and theologian

That which I am and the way that I am, with all my gifts of nature and grace, you have given to me, O Lord, and you are all this. I offer it all to you, principally to praise you and to help my fellow Christians and myself.

UNKNOWN ENGLISH MYSTIC (14th century)
The Book of Privy Counseling

One fine summer night in June 1933 I was sitting on a lawn after dinner with three colleagues, two women and one man. We liked each other well enough but we were certainly not intimate friends, nor had any one of us a sexual interest in another. Incidentally, we had not drunk any alcohol. We were talking casually about everyday matters when, quite suddenly and unexpectedly, something happened. I felt myself invaded by a power which, though I consented to it, was irresistible and certainly not mine. For the first time in my life I knew exactly—because, thanks to the power, I was doing it—what it means to love one's neighbor as oneself. I was also certain, though the conversation continued to be perfectly ordinary, that my three colleagues were having the same experience. (In the case of one of them, I was able later to confirm this.) My personal feelings towards them were unchanged—they were still colleagues, not intimate friends—but I felt their existence as themselves to be of infinite value and rejoiced in it.

I recalled with shame the many occasions on which I had been spiteful, snobbish, selfish, but the immediate joy was greater than the shame, for I knew that, so long as I was possessed by this spirit, it would be literally impossible for me deliberately to injure another human being. I also knew that the power would, of course, be withdrawn sooner or later and that, when it did, my greed and self-regard would return. The experience lasted at its full intensity for about two hours when we said good-night to each other and went to bed. When I awoke the next morning, it was still present, though weaker, and it did not vanish completely for two days or so. The memory of the experience has not prevented me from making use of others, grossly and often, but it has made it much more difficult for me to deceive myself about what I am up to when I do. And among the various factors which several years later brought me back to the Christian faith in which I had been brought up, the memory of this experience and asking myself what it could mean was one of the most crucial, though, at the time it occurred, I thought I had done with Christianity for good.

W. H. AUDEN (1907–1973)

English poet

Father Zossima: If the evil doings of men move you to indignation and overwhelming distress, even to a desire for vengeance on the evildoers, shun above all things that feeling. Go at once and seek suffering for yourself, as though you were yourself guilty of that wrong. Accept that suffering and bear it and your heart will find comfort, and you will understand that you too are guilty, for you might have been a light to the evildoers and were not a light to them. If you had been a light, you would have lightened the path for others too, and the evildoer might perhaps have been saved by your light.

You are working for the whole, you are acting for the future. Seek no reward, for great is your reward on this earth: the spiritual joy which is only vouchsafed to the righteous man. Fear not the great nor the mighty, but be wise and ever serene. Know the measure, know the times, study that. When you are left alone, pray. Love to throw yourself on the earth and kiss it. Kiss the earth and love it with an unceasing, consuming love. Love all men, love everything. Seek that rapture and ecstasy. Water the earth with the tears of your joy and love those tears. Don't be ashamed of that ecstasy, prize it, for it is a gift of God and a great one; it is not given to many but only to the elect.

FYODOR DOSTOYEVSKY (1821–1881)

Russian novelist

The thorough-going acceptance of the truth of the Gospel right through to the end, an agreement to bring it to effective realization, would lead to the destruction of states, civilizations, and societies which are organized according to the law of this world. It would lead to the perishing of the world which is in every respect opposed to the truth of the Gospel.

And so people and nations have amended the Gospel. They have filled it up with "truths" that belong to this world, "truths" which were really pragmatic because they were a lie and an adjustment to a lie.

NICHOLAS BERDYAEV (1874–1948)
Russian Orthodox theologian

Most people really believe that the Christian commandments (such as, to love one's neighbor as oneself) are intentionally a little too severe—like putting the clock ahead a half an hour to make sure of not being late in the morning.

SØREN KIERKEGAARD (1813–1855)
Danish theologian

CYCLE THREE

THE TRUE HUMAN PERSON

Sin may seem to many to be a disagreeable relic of an unenlightened past, but it is truly the out-of-balance, upside-down, egocentric state in which we pass most of our lives. Sin is both the mark of our servitude and the emblem of our freedom; an awareness of the state of sin is shown here to be where we find our need for liberation and fulfillment.

The first Light which shined in my Infancy in its primitive and innocent clarity was totally eclipsed: so much that I had to learn all again. If you ask me how it was eclipsed? Truly by the customs and manners of men, which like contrary winds blew it out: by an innumerable company of other objects, rude, vulgar, and worthless things, that like so many loads of earth and dung did overwhelm and bury it: by the impetuous torrent of wrong desires in all others whom I saw or knew that carried me away and alienated me from it: by a whole sea of other matters and concernments that covered and drowned it: finally by the evil influence of a bad education that did not foster and cherish it.

All men's thoughts and words were about other matters. They all prized new things which I did not dream of. I was a stranger and

unacquainted with them; I was little and reverenced their authority; I was weak, and easily guided by their example: ambitious also,
and desirous to approve myself unto them. And finding not one
syllable in any man's mouth of those things, by degrees they vanished, my thoughts (as indeed what is more fleeting than a
thought?) were blotted out; and at last all the celestial, great, and
stable treasures to which I was born, as wholly forgotten, as if they
had never been.

THOMAS TRAHERNE (1637–1674)

English cleric and poet

They are miserable and mistaken persons who, since Adam planted
thorns round about paradise, are more in love with that hedge
than all the fruits of the garden. . . . Tell them they have lost a
bounteous friend, a rich purchase, a fair farm, and you dissolve
their patience; it is an evil bigger than their spirit can bear; it brings
sickness and death; they can neither eat nor sleep with such a sorrow. But if you represent to them the enemy of a vicious habit, and
the dangers of a state of sin; if you tell them they have displeased
God, and interrupted their hopes of heaven; it may be that they
will be so civil as to hear it patiently, and to treat you kindly,
first to commend, and then forget your story, because they prefer
the world with all its sorrows before the pure unmingled felicities
of heaven.

But it is strange that any man should be so passionately in love
with the thorns which grow on his own ground, that he should
wear them for armlets, and knit them in his shirt, and prefer them
before the kingdom and immortality. No man loves this world the
better for being poor; but men that love it because they have great

possessions, love it because it is troublesome and chargeable, full of noise and temptation, because it is unsafe and ungoverned, flattered and abused; and he that considers the troubles of an overlong garment and of a crammed stomach, a trailing gown and a loaden table, may justly understand all that for which men are so passionate, is their hurt and their objection, that which a temperate man would avoid, and a wise man cannot love.

JEREMY TAYLOR (1613–1667)

English bishop and writer

Celia is always telling you how provoked she is, what intolerable shocking things happen to her, what monstrous usage she suffers, and what vexations she meets with everywhere. She tells you that her patience is quite wore out, and there is no bearing the behavior of people.

Every assembly that she is at sends her home provoked; something or other has been said or done that no reasonable, well-bred person ought to bear. Poor people that want her charity are sent away with hasty answers, not because she has not a heart to part with any money, but because she is too full of some trouble of her own to attend to the complaints of others.

Celia has no business upon her hands but to receive the income of a plentiful fortune; but yet by the doleful turn of her mind you would be apt to think that she had neither food nor lodging. If you see her look more pale than ordinary, if her lips tremble when she speaks to you, it is because she is just come from a visit where Lupus took no notice at all of her, but talked all the time to Lucinda, who has not half her fortune. When cross accidents have so disordered her spirits that she is forced to send for the doctor to make her able to eat, she tells him in great anger at Providence that she never was well since she was born, and that she envies every beggar that she sees in health.

This is the disquiet life of Celia, who has nothing to torment her but her own spirit. If you could inspire her with Christian humility, you need do no more to make her as happy as any person in the world, and her blood would need nothing else to sweeten it.

WILLIAM LAW (1686–1761)
English contemplative and cleric

Every man is under that complicated disease, and that riddling distemper, not to be content with the most, and yet to be proud of the least thing he has; that when he looks upon men, he despises them, because he is some kind of officer, and when he looks on God, he murmurs at Him, because He made him not a king.

JOHN DONNE (1572–1631)
English poet and dean of St. Paul's Cathedral, London

What is at the source of what we call sin? Compared to the source, the action is only an excrescence—something that bursts through from an undercurrent which is always acting in human beings. . . .

If we were to stop all our outer and inner movements at a given moment, we would nearly always feel a tendency which has about it something narrow, something with a negative aspect that tends to be egoistic. All that is usually going on unseen. But if we try to awaken to what is going on in ourselves, we will be able to witness, in addition to what could be called the "coarse" life in us, another life of another quality—much subtler, much higher, lighter. . . .

If we let our attention be taken by our automatic tendencies, it deprives us of contact with that other source of life. It could be said that there is a continual tendency to sin, in that sense. When these sins are spoken of as deadly, it means that these tendencies—if they are allowed to rule—at every moment deprive the human being of the possibility of turning towards this real life. . . .

One can feel these tendencies as inescapable parts of one's nature which to a certain extent bring data about oneself and the external world. Many demands come to me from external life and I must sustain my outer life with the ego—as I am, I have nothing else. So it is through these tendencies that the ego is informed.

Take anger, for example. With a little vigilance, it is possible at the beginning of a movement of anger to surprise in oneself the sudden, sharp upsurge of an instinctive impulse that tends to immediately reject whatever is irritating us, making us suffer. This impulse is necessary—how could we get along without it? We would be inert: we could let our hand stay in a fire without reacting.

And pride—don't we teach a child to be proud of his successes, of his strength? Lacking this pride, he wouldn't respect himself and wouldn't make himself respected by others. . . .

On the portals of certain cathedrals, one can see statues representing the vices, and above them, the virtues. But between the vices and the virtues there is something intermediary. What remains hidden in the middle is the wish to be sincere, to try to understand the meaning of one's life. A human being has to stand in between and not allow himself to be taken by these tendencies; not to let them raise opposition and justification. We must not let them make us forget the one and only thing important for us.

PAULINE DE DAMPIERRE (contemporary)
French exponent of Gurdjieff teaching

Know that the impulse to wrong is never without use and benefit to the just person. Let us notice that there are two sorts of people involved. One is so constituted that he has little or no impulse to do wrong, whereas the other is often strongly tempted. His outward self is easily swayed by whatever is at hand—swayed to anger, pride, sensuality or whatever, but his better nature, his higher self, remains unmoved and will not do wrong, or be angry, or sin in any way. He therefore fights hard against whichever vice is most natural to him, as people must who are by nature choleric, proud, or otherwise weak and who will not commit the sin to which they are liable. These people are more to be praised than the first kind. Their reward is also greater and their virtue of much higher rank. For the perfection of virtue comes of struggle, or, as St. Paul says, "Virtue is made perfect in weakness."

The impulse to sin is not sin but to consent to sin, to give way to anger, is indeed sin. Surely, if a just person could wish such a thing, he would not wish to be rid of the impulse to sin, for without it he would be uncertain of everything he did, doubtful about what to do, and he would miss the honor and reward of struggle and victory.

MEISTER ECKHART (1260–1327)
German Dominican mystic and theologian

As fruits ungrateful to the planter's care
On savage stocks inserted learn to bear;
The surest Virtues thus from Passions shoot,
Wild Nature's vigor working at the root.
What crops of wit and honesty appear
From spleen, from obstinacy, hate, or fear!

See anger, zeal and fortitude supply;
Ev'n av'rice, prudence; sloth, philosophy;
Lust, thro' some certain strainers well refin'd,
Is gentle love, and charms all womankind:
Envy, to which th'ignoble mind's a slave,
Is emulation in the learn'd or brave:
Nor Virtue, male or female, can we name,
But what will grow on Pride, or grow on Shame.

ALEXANDER POPE (1688–1744)

English poet

Humanity is in a state of servitude. We frequently do not notice that we are slaves, and sometimes we love it. But humanity also aspires to be set free. It would be a mistake to think that the average person loves freedom. A still greater mistake would be to suppose that freedom is an easy thing. Freedom is a difficult thing. It is easier to remain in slavery. Love of freedom and aspiration towards liberation are an indication that some upward progress has already been achieved. They witness to the fact that inwardly a person is already ceasing to be a slave. There is a spiritual principle within which is not dependent upon the world and is not determined by the world. The liberation of humanity is the demand, not of nature, nor of reason, nor of society, as is often supposed, but of spirit. Spirit is freedom, and freedom is the victory of spirit.

But it would be a mistake to think that our slavery is always the outcome of the power of the animal and material side of our natures. On the spiritual side itself there may be grievous loss of health, division, exteriorization, there may be self-estrangement of spirit, loss of freedom, captivity of spirit. In this lies all the complexity of the problem of freedom and slavery. The spirit is exteriorized, thrown out into the external, and acts upon man as necessity—and it returns to itself within, that is, to freedom. One who is free should feel himself to be not on the circumference of the objectivized world, but at the center of the spiritual world. Liberation is being present at the center, and not at the circumference, in real subjectivity and not in ideal objectivity.

NICHOLAS BERDYAEV (1874–1948)
Russian Orthodox theologian

In a sense, God had to take the risk: if He wanted there to be love, He had to give us freedom. And by giving us freedom, He gave us the possibility of rejecting His love. Freedom therefore implies the possibility of doing evil. The world was not created evil. But God took the risk because He wished there to be love. This is the true meaning of the Christian doctrine of Hell, which is so widely misunderstood.

God does not condemn us to Hell; God wishes all humans to be saved. He will love us to all eternity, but there will exist the possibility that we do not accept that love and do not respond to it. And the refusal to accept love, the refusal to respond to it, that precisely is the meaning of Hell. Hell is not a place where God puts us; it's a place where we put ourselves. The doors of Hell, insofar as they have locks, have locks on the inside.

KALLISTOS WARE (1934–)
Greek Orthodox archbishop

Insensitivity is deadened feeling in body and spirit, and comes from long sickness and carelessness. . . .

The insensitive man is a foolish philosopher, a blind man teaching sight to others. He talks about healing a wound and does not stop making it worse. He complains about what has happened and does not stop eating what is harmful. He prays against it but carries on as before, doing it and being angry with himself. And the wretched man is in no way shamed by his own words. "I'm doing wrong," he cries, and zealously continues to do so.

His lips pray against it and his body struggles for it. He talks profoundly about death and acts as if he will never die. He groans over the separation of soul and body, and yet lives in a state of somnolence as if he were eternal. He has plenty to say about self-control and fights for a gourmet life. He reads about the judgment and begins to smile, about vainglory and is vainglorious while he is reading. He recites what he has learnt about keeping vigil, and at once drops off to sleep. Prayer he extols, and runs from it as if from a plague. Blessings he showers on obedience, and is the first to disobey. Detachment he praises, and he shamelessly fights over a rag.

When he is angry he gets bitter, and then his bitterness makes him angry, so that having suffered one defeat he fails to notice that he has suffered another. He gorges himself, is sorry, and a little later is at it again. He blesses silence and cannot stop talking about it. He teaches meekness and frequently gets angry while he is teaching it. Having come to his senses, he sighs and shaking his head embraces his passion once more. He denounces laughter, and while lecturing on mourning he is all smiles. In front of others he criticizes himself for being vainglorious, and in making the admission he is looking for glory. . . . In everything he shows himself up for what he is, and does not come to his senses, though I would not say he was incapable of doing so.

I have seen such men weep as they hear of death and the dread judgment, and with the tears still in their eyes they rush off to dinner.

JOHN CLIMACUS (520–603)
Father of the Eastern church

The swine of gluttony has piglets with these names. Too Early is the name of the first, the next Too Fastidiously, the third, Too Freely; the fourth is called Too Much, the fifth Too Often. These piglets are more often born through drink than food.

I talk about them only briefly, because I have no fear that you feed them.

THE ANCHORESS'S RULE (c. 1220)
English

Our ordinary waking life is a bare existence in which, most of the time, we seem to be absent from ourselves and from reality because we are involved in the vain preoccupations which dog the steps of every living man. But there are times when we seem suddenly to awake and discover the full meaning of our own present reality. Such discoveries are not capable of being contained in formulas or definitions. They are a matter of personal experience, of incommunicable intuition. In the light of such an experience it is easy to see the futility of all the trifles that occupy our minds. We recapture something of the calm and the balance that ought always to be ours, and we understand that life is far too great a gift to be squandered on anything less than perfection.

In the lives of those who are cast adrift in the modern world, with nothing to rely on but their own resources, these moments of understanding are short-lived and barren. For, though man may get a glimpse of the natural value of his spirit, nature alone is incapable of fulfilling his spiritual aspirations.

THOMAS MERTON (1915–1968)

American Cistercian monk

Christian ascesis is only a method in the service of life, and it will seek to adapt itself to the new needs. In present conditions, under the burden of overwork and the wear on nerves, sensibility is changing. At Thebaid, extreme fasts and constraints were imposed; today the combat is not the same. Man has no need of supplementary pain; hair shirts, chains, flagellations would run the risk of uselessly breaking him.

[Today] mortification could be the liberation from every kind of opiate—speed, noise, alcohol, and all kinds of stimulants. Rather, the ascesis could be necessary rest, the discipline of regular periods of calm and silence, when man could regain his ability to stop for prayer, and contemplation, even in the heart of all the noises of the world; and he could then listen to the presence of others. The fast, as opposed to the maceration of flesh inflicted on himself, could be his renunciation of the superfluous, his sharing with the poor, and his smiling equilibrium.

PAUL EVDOKIMOV (1901–1970)

Russian Orthodox theologian

Now tell me why is wealth an object of ambitions? To the majority of those who are afflicted with this grievous malady it seems to be more precious than health and life, and public reputation, and good opinion, and country, and household, and friends, and kindred and everything else. Moreover the flame has ascended to the very clouds: and this fierce heat has taken possession of land and sea. Nor is there any one to quench this fire: but all people are engaged in stirring it up, both those who have been already caught by it, and those who have not yet been caught, in order that they may be captured.

And you may see everyone, husband and wife, household slave, and freeman, rich and poor, each according to his ability carrying loads which supply much fuel to this fire by day and night: loads not of wood (for the fire is not of that kind), but loads of souls and bodies, of unrighteousness and iniquity. Those who have riches place no limit anywhere to this monstrous passion, even if they compass the whole world: and the poor press on to get in advance of them, and a kind of incurable craze, and unrestrainable frenzy, and irremediable disease possesses the souls of all.

This love of money has conquered every other kind: neither friends nor kindred are taken into account: and why do I speak of friends and kindred? not even wife and children are regarded, and what can be dearer to man than these? but all things are dashed to the ground and trampled underfoot, when this savage and inhuman mistress has laid hold of the souls.

JOHN CHRYSOSTOM (345–407)
Father of the Eastern church, saint, and bishop of Constantinople

We cannot find a better means of growing in spirituality than through our everyday life. There are the long monotonous hours of work, for which often no recognition is given, the continuous and painful struggle which receives little reward, disappointment and failure, adversity and misunderstanding. There are the many wishes denied to us, the many small humiliations. There are such things as physical discomfort, the inclemency of the elements, the friction of human contacts. Through these and a thousand other trials in which everyday life abounds, a man can learn to become calm and unselfish, if he only understands these task-masters, mundane and yet providential. He must willingly accept them, rather than try to ward them off. . . .

In this way, we can use everyday life to fight our selfishness, slowly but certainly, since the guidance showered upon us by God in daily life is always certain and sure. In this way, the love of God will grow of itself in our hearts, a love both calm and chaste. In everyday life we can mortify ourselves without vanity and without ostentation. Nobody will notice our efforts, and we ourselves will be scarcely aware of our mortification; yet, through the myriad occupations of our daily life, one defense after another will be thrown down, behind each of which our selfishness had entrenched itself. At last, when we have ceased to put up new defenses, when we have learnt to accept our precarious human situation and rely on the grace of God, we will notice suddenly and almost cheerfully, that those defenses were quite unnecessary. . . .

Through everyday life, we are taught that we become rich in giving, that we advance spiritually through holy resignation, that we are blessed in sacrifice and that we find love when we give love to others. Thus a man becomes unselfish and free. . . .

It is of supreme importance that we should achieve this conquest of our everyday life, because otherwise we allow ourselves to be dragged down to its level. Nothing can free us so much as this conquest. If we succeed, the love thus engendered will suffuse all the things of this world with the infinity of God, through a holy desire to exalt all the humdrum activities of daily life unto a hymn of praise to the glory of God. The cross of everyday life is the only means by which our selfishness can die, because in order to be utterly destroyed our selfishness must be ceaselessly crucified. This fruit of that cross will be a love born from the death of our selfishness.

Thus, through love, fidelity, faith, preparedness, and surrender to God, our everyday actions are transformed into lived prayer. . . . All our interests are unified and exalted by the love of God; our scattered aims are given a specific direction towards God; our external life becomes the expression of our love of God. Thus, our life takes on new meaning in the light of our eternal destiny.

KARL RAHNER (1904–1984)
German Jesuit theologian

Mortification means killing the very roots of self-love, pride and possessiveness, anger and violence, ambition and greed in all their disguises, however respectable those disguises may be, whatever uniforms they wear. In fact, it really means the entire transformation of our personal, professional and political life into something more consistent with our real situation as small, dependent, fugitive creatures; all sharing the same limitations and inheriting the same half-animal past. That may not sound very impressive or unusual; but it is the foundation of all genuine spiritual life, and sets a standard that is not peculiar to orthodox Christianity.

Those who are familiar with Blake's poetry will recognize that it is all to be found there. Indeed, wherever we find people whose spiritual life is robust and creative, we find that in one way or another this transformation has been erected, and this price has been paid.

EVELYN UNDERHILL (1875–1941)

English writer on mysticism

We must let our heart go its own way, towards its own deepest desire, which it knows is different from all others. This desire is different from all others not necessarily because it is more strongly felt, but because it comes from further off, from what is deepest in us. It is not simply an act of our free will, but something which is in our deepest being and which involves all that we are. It is something quite simple but inseparable fundamentally from our self-awareness and open to a limitless beyond. God reveals himself to us in this awareness that we are essentially a cry for him.

Our inner atmosphere is not made up only of what we are clearly conscious of and can be precisely expressed. It is also composed of all that is living in our inmost depths. This is what makes us realize what we fundamentally are. It is always there.

Throughout the day we are a succession of social personalities, sometimes unrecognizable to others or even to ourselves. And when the time comes to pray and we want to present ourselves to God we often feel lost because we do not know which of these social personalities is the true human person, and have no sense of our own true identity. The several successive persons that we present to God are not ourselves. There is something of us in each of them but the whole person is missing. And that is why a prayer which could rise powerfully from the heart of the true person cannot find its way between the successive men of straw we offer to God. . . .

It is extremely important that we find our unity, our fundamental identity. Otherwise we cannot encounter the Lord in truth. We should be on the watch all the time to see that none of our words and actions are incompatible with the fundamental integrity we are seeking. We must try and discover the real person we are, the secret person, the core of the person to come and the only eternal reality which is already in us.

This discovery is difficult because we have to cast aside all the men of straw. From time to time something authentic shows through, when we forget ourselves our deep reality may take over, in moments when we are carried away by joy so that we forget who might be looking at us, forget to stand aside and look at ourselves, or when we are unselfconscious in moments of extreme pain, moments when we have a deep sense of sadness or of wonder. At these moments we see something of the true person that we are. But no sooner have we seen, than we often turn away because we do not want to confront this person face to face. We are afraid of him, he puts us off. Nevertheless this is the only real person there is in us. And God can save this person, however repellent he may be, because it is a true person.

God cannot save the imaginary person that we try to present to him, or to others or ourselves. As well as seeking the real person in us, through these chance manifestations, we must also seek constantly the person we are to God. We must seek for God in us and ourselves in God. This is a work of meditation which we should engage in every day all through our lives.

ANTHONY BLOOM (1914–)
Russian Orthodox monk and metropolitan of Sourozh

There is a warning conscience, and a gnawing conscience. The warning conscience cometh before sin; the gnawing conscience followeth after sin. The warning conscience is often lulled asleep; but the gnawing conscience awakeneth her again.

HENRY SMITH THE SILVER-TONGUED (1550–1600)
English clergyman

When first we turn to God in the actual history of our lives, our repentance is mixed with all kinds of imperfect views and feelings. Doubtless there is in it something of the true temper of simple submission, but the wish of appeasing God on the one hand, or a hard-hearted insensibility about our sins on the other, mere selfish dread of punishment, or the expectation of a sudden easy pardon, these, and such-like principles, influence us, whatever we may say or may think we feel.

It is, indeed, easy enough to have good words put into our mouths, and our feelings roused, and to profess the union of utter self-abandonment and enlightened sense of sin; but to claim is not really to possess these excellent tempers. Really to gain these is a work of time. . . . When the Christian by experience knows how few and how imperfect are his best services . . . he acknowledges and adopts, as far as he can, St. Paul's words, and nothing beyond them, "This is a faithful saying, and worthy of all acceptation, that Christ Jesus came into the world to save sinners, of whom I am chief."

JOHN HENRY NEWMAN (1801–1890)
English Roman Catholic cardinal

Discipline (or mortification) puts back in its place that something in us which should serve but wants to rule. It puts reason back again as the rule of life; it makes us calm and reasonable. If it does not tend to do this, then it is stupid and pointless.

Mortification of the body is above all a symbol. It stands for that chastisement which the will should have the courage to inflict on all the powers of the soul, in order to submit them, along with itself, to God, and so re-establish in Him that shattered unity of our human nature. That is the goal, most sublime and blessed, of all our efforts: a goal which is well worth the journeying, however hard it may be.

ANONYMOUS CARTHUSIAN MONK (contemporary)

I think you would find it easier to read the spiritual meaning behind ordinary expressions if I explained certain terms commonly used in reference to contemplative work. This may give you greater confidence in discerning accurately when you are dealing with things exterior and beneath yourself, with those interior and equal to yourself, and with those transcending yourself though still beneath God.

Beneath you and external to you lies the entire created universe. Yes, even the sun, the moon, and the stars. They are fixed above you, splendid in the firmament, yet they cannot compare to your exalted dignity as a human being.

The angels and the souls of the just are superior to you inasmuch as they are confirmed in grace and glorious with every virtue, but they are your equals in nature as intelligent creatures. You are gifted with three marvelous spiritual faculties, *Mind, Reason,* and

Will, and two secondary faculties, *Imagination* and *Feeling.* There is nothing above you except God himself.

When you are reading books about the interior life and come across any references to *yourself,* understand it to mean your whole self as a human being of spiritual dignity and not merely your physical body. As man you are related to everything in creation through the medium of your faculties.

If you understand all this about the hierarchy of creation and your own nature and place in it, you will have some criteria for evaluating the importance of each of your [inner and outer] relationships.

UNKNOWN ENGLISH MYSTIC (14th century)

The Cloud of Unknowing

The primary mystery is the mystery of the birth of God in man (who includes the world in himself) and the birth of man in God. In our imperfect language this means that there is in God a need for a responsive creative act on the part of man. Man is not merely a sinner; the consciousness of sin is but an experience which moves him as he treads his path; man is also a creator. The human tragedy from which there is no escape, the dialectic of freedom, necessity and grace finds its solution within the orbit of the divine Mystery, within the Deity, which lies deeper than the drama between Creator and creature, deeper than representations of heaven and hell.

Here the human tongue keeps silence. The eschatological outlook is not limited to the prospect of an indefinable end of the world, it embraces in its view every moment of life. At each moment of one's living, what is needed is to put an end to the old world and to begin the new. In that is the breath of the Spirit.

NICHOLAS BERDYAEV (1874–1948)

Russian Orthodox theologian

O Lord, I most humbly acknowledge and confess that I have understood sin by understanding thy laws and judgments, but have done against thy known and revealed will.

Thou hast set up many candlesticks, and kindled many lamps in me, but I have either blown them out, or carried them to guide me in by forbidden ways.

Thou hast given me a desire of knowledge, and some means to it, and some possession of it, and I have armed myself with thy weapons against thee. Yet, O God, have mercy upon me, for thine own sake, have mercy upon me. Let not sin and me be able to defraud thee, nor to frustrate thy purposes. . . .

JOHN DONNE (1572–1631)

English poet and dean of St. Paul's Cathedral, London

CYCLE FOUR

THE SACRAMENT
OF PRESENCE

Discontent with ordinary life is said to be necessary before a deeper need is awak-
ened. Beginning at this awakening, Cycle Four searches out the ground and grace
of the present moment. And it leads us to understand the significance of Abba
Dorotheus's advice in the sixth century: "Everything you do, be it great or small,
is but one-eighth of the problem, whereas to keep your state undisturbed, even if
thereby you should fail to accomplish the task, is the other seven-eighths."

It was on a day when I was preparing a speech to be delivered in
praise of the Emperor; there would be a lot of lies in the speech,
and they would be applauded by those who knew they were lies.
My heart was all wrought up with the worry of it all and was boil-
ing in a kind of fever of melting thoughts.

I was going along one of the streets of Milan when I noticed a
poor beggar; he was fairly drunk, I suppose, and was laughing and
enjoying himself. It was a sight that depressed me, and I spoke to
the friends who were with me about all the sorrows that come to
us because of our own madness . . . and it seemed to me that the
goal of this and all such endeavors was simply to reach a state of

happiness that was free from care; the beggar had reached this state before us, and we, perhaps, might never reach it at all. . . .

And undoubtedly he was happy while I was worried; he was carefree while I was full of fears. . . . The beggar would sleep off his drunkenness that very night; but I had gone to bed with mine and woken up with it day after day after day and I should go on doing so. Yes, and so without any doubt he was the happier. . . .

I said much along these lines to my intimate friends at the time, and I often noticed that it was the same with them as it was with me, and I found that things were not at all well with me.

AUGUSTINE OF HIPPO (354–430)
Carthaginian saint, philosopher, and doctor of the church

Now, I will suppose your distressed state to be as you represent it: inwardly, darkness, heaviness, and confusion of thoughts and passions; outwardly, ill usage from friends, relations, and all the world, unable to strike up the least spark of light or comfort by any thought or reasoning of your own.

O happy famine, which leaves you not so much as the husk of one human comfort to feed upon! For this is the time and place for all that good and life and salvation to happen to you which happened to the Prodigal Son. Your way is as short and your success as certain as his was. You have no more to do than he had; you need not call out for books or methods of devotion; for in your present state much reading and borrowed prayers are not your best method.

All that you are to offer to God, all that is to help you to find Him to be your Saviour and Redeemer, is best taught and expressed by the distressed state of your heart. Only let your present and past distress make you feel and acknowledge this twofold great truth: first, that in and of yourself you are nothing but darkness, vanity, and misery; secondly, that of yourself you can no more help yourself to find comfort than you can create an angel.

WILLIAM LAW (1686–1761)
English contemplative and cleric

We see that we cannot partake deeply of the life of God unless we change profoundly. It is therefore essential that we should go to God in order that he should transform and change us, and that is why, to begin with, we should ask for conversion. Conversion in Latin means a turn, a change in the direction of things. The Greek word *metanoia* means a change of mind.

Conversion means that instead of spending our lives in looking in all directions, we should follow one direction only. It is a turning away from a great many things which we value solely because they were pleasant or expedient for us. The first impact of conversion is to modify our sense of values: God being at the center of all, everything acquires a new position and a new depth. All that is God's, all that belongs to him, is positive and real. Everything that is outside him has no value or meaning.

But it is not a change of mind alone that we can call conversion. We can change our minds and go no farther; what must follow is an act of will and unless our will comes into motion and is redirected Godwards, there is no conversion; at most there is only an incipient, still dormant, and inactive change in us.

ANTHONY BLOOM (1914–)
Russian Orthodox monk and metropolitan of Sourozh

Of one thing we can be certain. He who has honestly resolved to seek the love of God, may be said to possess that love already in his heart. For that very resolution is a proof that the grace of God has descended into the depths of his heart to kindle there a longing for God's love. . . .

We often feel that our heart is stony, and that we have no power to warm it with love. There is, however, one thing we can all do: we can heed the first feeble stirrings of a love for God, the first timid longing of our restless hearts for God. The busy cares of life make us dusty and tired, so that even life's joys may become insipid. There are times when we feel cold and alone, our friends become as strangers to us, and even the love of our dearest fails to satisfy a deep longing in our innermost soul. Our world seems a meaningless tangle of empty hurryings to and fro. . . . in addition, there is all the bitterness that can fill the heart—desolation, grief, distress, and suffering both of body and of soul.

Grace comes when we are made to realize the futility and ephemeral nature of all things under the sun, and it is typical of human nature to resist this realization. When one thing turns to dust and ashes for us, we turn from it hopefully to something else, and so the restless search goes on. This seed of restlessness placed in the human heart, though at first sight it may appear an unwholesome thing, is in reality a great blessing. For when a man has discovered that all his fevered searching leads only to blank walls of disillusion, he begins to experience a new realization which makes a way for the love of God in his heart.

God alone can possess us fully and satisfy us entirely. Hence, that disillusionment which makes the heart cry out its "vanity of vanities" over all earthly things, is essential to all Christians. Reeling under the impact of this disillusion, yet neither despairing nor blinding ourselves with any deception, we begin to grope towards the love of God which comes to us as "something else" about which we are as yet vague and uncertain, but which we know this world cannot give us.

KARL RAHNER (1904–1984)
German Jesuit theologian

This was not the man they had known, but they had scarcely expected to be confronted with *him*; this was, in a sense deeper than questions of fact, the man they had not known, and the man they had not known may have been the real one. The real man, whoever he had been, had suffered and now he was dead: this was all that was sure and all that mattered now. Every man in the chapel hoped that when his hour came he, too, would be eulogized, which is to say forgiven, and that all of his lapses, greeds, errors and strayings from the truth would be invested with coherence and looked upon with clarity. This was perhaps the last thing human beings could give each other and it was what they demanded, after all, of the Lord. Only the Lord saw the midnight tears, only He was present when one of His children, moaning and wringing hands, paced up and down the room. . . . it was better not to judge the man who had gone down under an impossible burden. It was better to remember: *Thou knowest this man's fall; but thou knowest not his wrassling.*

JAMES BALDWIN (1924–1987)
American novelist, playwright, and essayist

Since about my thirtieth year, and more and more clearly as the years go by, and despite intervals of sterility caused by suffering, bad luck, drunkenness, over-eating, sluggishness of soul, lassitude of heart: suddenly, in the midst of anguish or distress, it is there: gratitude. The response to my often unconscious but tireless interior allocution—continued probably during sleep also; the response which is not inspiration or idea or anything else but this, wholly, simply, uniquely: gratitude. . . .

Last year, I found myself stopping halfway down the stairs, one foot on one step, the other on the next. This month, I found myself, and above all was found by joy, in the act of taking off my spectacles. The time it takes for the hand to be lowered, with the spectacle in the finger: and that was when the grace of gratitude welled up within me, interflowing with the response I was seeking. . . .

My own humble experience is not that of ecstasy. I do not levitate, I am not transported, I am not somewhere else, nor outside myself, nor with God—nothing of that. Just a poor brute suddenly stopping halfway down the stairs, or slowly taking off his glasses. But those two or three minutes in the life of a man, are the reason why I shall not have lived in vain.

PETRU DUMITRIU (1924–)
Romanian novelist and poet

Remember, you said you could not control your thoughts, and then you wrote how I was ruining you with what I was saying, that everything had been better for you previously, but once you began to scrutinize yourself under my direction, you saw only disorder; your thoughts, feelings, and desires were all in disarray, and you had no strength to put them in any kind of order. Here is the solution to the problem of why it is that way: *You have no center.*

And you have no center because you have still not decided through your own consciousness and free choice which way you will go. Up to this point, the grace of God has instilled in you a feasible order, and this order has been and still is within you. From this point, however, the grace of God will not act on its own, but will instead await your decision. If you, through your own choice and decision, do not choose grace, then it will abandon you completely, and leave you in the hands of your self-will.

You will be shunted off to the opposite side, and maybe your heart will even choose it; but do not expect that your inner disorder will abate by taking this direction. No, an even greater confusion and disorder will be created. Inner regulation begins only when you choose the side of grace, and make the ways of life in the spirit of grace the inviolable rule of your life.

From that moment, as the decision is forming inside you, a center will also form within you, a powerful center, which will begin more and more forcefully to draw you toward itself. In this center will be grace, which has taken hold of your consciousness and free will (or, your consciousness and free will, combined with grace). This is the same thing which was previously called the resurrection or restoration of the spirit. Then the grace of God will begin to draw toward this center all of the other forces of your nature, both intellectual and spiritual, and govern their entire action, retaining within them that which is good, and destroying that which is bad.

This drawing of everything to one center and directing of all to one goal is the inner rebirth which you have so fervently desired. Once this rebirth has been accomplished, then everything both great and small will proceed from this one center, and within you will be established the most perfect harmony, and the peace of

God, which surpasses all understanding, will overshadow the inner temple of your nature.

May the God of peace be with you!

THEOPHAN THE RECLUSE (1815–1894)
Russian Orthodox monk and saint

It is very important to recognize that we will never succeed in keeping any of the commandments, in loving God or our neighbor, if our minds are perpetually distracted. For it is impossible to gain any accurate knowledge, be it in art or science, if one is always flitting from one subject to the next. It is impossible to master something without being prepared to persevere to the end. Our activity must correspond with our aims since nothing in this life is achieved by inappropriate methods. You cannot become an expert smith if you persist in doing pottery; athletes' wreaths are not won by practicing the flute! For each end a proper and necessary effort is required.

Thus, we must practice the art of being well-pleasing to God according to Christ's Gospel, by disengaging from mundane preoccupations and by fostering a determined attention of the mind. . . .

Anyone who truly wishes to follow God must be free from the fetters that attach us to this world. We need to make a complete break with our former way of life. For example, unless we avoid all obsession with the body and the concerns of this world, we will never succeed in pleasing God. Our minds must be trained to another pattern of thinking; for as the apostle Paul says: "Our citizenship is in heaven." Indeed, the Lord has stated quite clearly, "Unless you renounce everything you possess, you cannot be my disciple."

Having done this, it is vital that we be vigilant to ensure that we never distance ourselves from God, or obscure our memory of his wonders with our distracted imagination. It is important to cherish a pure thought of God, consciously imprinting it upon our memory as if it were an indelible seal. In this way we grow in love for God: it stirs us to fulfill his commandments and in so doing, the love of God in us is nurtured in perpetuity.

BASIL THE GREAT (330–379)
Doctor of the church, saint, and bishop of Caesarea

[The] true possession of God depends on the disposition, and on an inward directing of the reason and intention toward God, not on a constant contemplation in an unchanging manner, for it would be impossible to nature to preserve such an intention, and very laborious, and not the best thing either. A man ought not to have a God who is just a product of his thought, nor should he be satisfied with that, because if the thought vanished, God too would vanish. But one ought to have a God who is present, a God who is far above the notions of men and of all created things. That God does not vanish, if a man does not willfully turn away from him.

The man who has God essentially present to him grasps God divinely, and to him God shines in all things; for everything tastes to him of God, and God forms himself for the man out of all things. God always shines out in him, in him there is a detachment and a turning away, and a forming of his God whom he loves and who is present to him. It is like a man consumed with a real and burning thirst, who may well not drink and may turn his mind to other things. But whatever he may do, in whatever company he may be, whatever he may be intending or thinking of or working at, still the idea of drinking does not leave him, so long as he is thirsty. The more his thirst grows, the more the idea of drinking grows and intrudes and possesses him and will not leave him. Or if a man loves something ardently and with all his heart, so that nothing else has savor for him or touches his heart but that, and that and nothing but that is his whole object: Truly, wherever he is, whomever he is with, whatever he may undertake, whatever he does, what he so loves never passes from his mind, and he finds the image of what he loves in everything, and it is the more present to him the more his love grows and grows. He does not seek rest, because no unrest hinders him.

MEISTER ECKHART (1260–1327)
German Dominican mystic and theologian

The present moment is like an ambassador announcing the policy of God; the heart declares "Thy will be done," and souls, traveling at full speed, never stopping, spread the news far and wide. For them everything without exception is an instrument and means of sanctification, providing that the present moment is all that matters.

It is no longer a question of supplication or silence, reticence or eloquence, reading or writing, ideas or apathy, neglect or study of spiritual books, affluence or destitution, sickness or health, life or death. All that matters is what the will of God ordains each moment. This is the casting off, the withdrawal from, the renunciation of, the world, not actually but in effect, to be nothing by or for ourselves, to belong totally to God, to please him, making our sole happiness to look on the present moment as though nothing else in the world mattered.

JEAN PIERRE DE CAUSSADE (1675–1751)
French Jesuit

I know a person who for forty years has practiced the "presence of God" to which he gives several other names. At one time, he calls it a clear and distinct knowledge of God, sometimes a confused or general and loving regard of God, and recollection of God. At other times, he calls it attentiveness to God or silent conversation with God, or confidence in God, or the life and peace of the soul. Finally, this person said to me that all these ways of expressing the presence of God are only synonyms. They signify one and the same thing and the presence to him is now as something natural. This is how it works:

This person says that as a consequence of acts and of often recalling his spirit into the presence of God, the habit of doing so was formed in such a way that as soon as his mind was free from his external occupations, and also even when he was the busiest, the peak of his spirit, or the highest part of his soul, rises up without urging from him and remains as if suspended and instantly fixed in God. Over and above all things, as in his center and in his place of repose, he almost always felt his spirit in this suspension accompanied by faith, which to him was sufficient. That is what this person called the actual presence of God. . . . it is fitting to know that this conversation with God is held in the depths and in the center of the soul. It is there that the soul speaks with God, heart to heart, and always in a grand and profound peace in which the soul finds joy in God. To the soul all that happens outside is like but a fire of straw that goes out as soon as it blazes up and almost never, or very seldom, reaches the point of troubling its inner peace. . . .

The presence of God is, then, the life and food of the soul. It can be acquired with the grace of the Lord. Here are the means to do this.

The first means is a great purity of life.

The second is a strong fidelity to the practice of this presence and to the interior regard of God in oneself. This should always be done gently, humbly, and lovingly, allowing oneself to go to no trouble whatsoever.

It is necessary to take special care that this interior regard, although it precedes for an instant your exterior actions, should from time to time accompany them and you should finish them all in that way. As time and much work are needed to acquire this practice, one must not be discouraged when one fails therein. The habit is not formed except with difficulty, but when it becomes formed, all will be accomplished with pleasure.

The heart is the first (organ of the body) to have life and the one that dominates the other members. . . . It is at this particular place that we ought to take care to bring about this small interior regard. It is this that is required to render the exercise easier. . . .

This practice of the presence of God, somewhat troublesome in the beginning, carried out with fidelity operates marvelous effects secretly in the soul and draws in abundance the graces of the Lord and leads it imperceptibly to this simple regard, to this lovely vision of God present everywhere. This is the most holy, most solid, easiest and most effective manner of performing prayer. . . .

The further it advances, the more alive its faith becomes. Finally, it becomes so penetrating that one can almost say, "I no longer believe, but I see and experience."

The presence of God breathes into the will a spirit of contempt for creatures and kindles a fire of sacred love. Being always with God, who is a consuming fire, it reduces to ashes whatever can be in opposition to it. This soul thus aflame can no longer live except in the presence of its God, a presence that produces in its heart a holy ardor, a sacred eagerness and a fierce desire to see God loved, known, served, and adored by all creatures.

In the presence of God, and through interior regard, the soul becomes familiar with God in such a manner that it spends almost its whole life in continual acts of love, adoration, contrition, thanksgiving, offerings, petitions, and of all the most excellent virtues. Sometimes it even becomes a single act that ceases to act because the soul is always in continual exercise of this divine presence.

I know that few persons are found who reach this stage. It is a grace with which God favors only a few souls, since after all, this simple regard is a gift from His generous hand. Yet I would say, for the consolation of those who desire to undertake this holy practice, that He gives it ordinarily to souls that are disposed to accept it, and if He does not give it, one can at least with the help of His ordinary graces acquire by the practice of the presence of God a manner and a state of prayer and closely approach this simple regard.

BROTHER LAWRENCE (1614–1691)
Lay brother among Carmelites in Paris

Internal prayer is so weighty a point that one may call it the only means to attain perfection in this life and to kindle pure and disinterested love in our hearts. All Christians (who indeed wish to be such) are called to this state of pure love, and by the power of this call have the necessary grace offered to them to attain such a state. This inward prayer suits all persons, even the most simple and ignorant, who are also capable of performing this order or manner of prayer. . . .

Now remains only to show that this is a prayer which may be performed at all times and in all places, which can be interrupted only by sin and unfaithfulness.

This inward prayer is performed in the spirit of the inward man through faith and love, and therefore is justly called the Prayer of Faith and Love.

This Prayer of Faith is simple, pure, universal, and obscure, without words, and as nothing can put bounds to its vast extent, so is nothing able to interrupt it or to make it cease. And the Prayer of Divine Love, which consists in the entire inclination of the heart towards the Supreme Good, which is God, can be even less easily interrupted, since the heart is never weary of loving.

This incessant prayer consists in an everlasting inclination of the heart to God, which inclination flows from Love. This love draws the presence of God into us; so that, as by the operation of divine grace the love of God is generated in us, so is also the presence of grace increased by this love, that such prayer is performed in us, without us or our thinking about it.

It is the same as with a person living in the air and drawing it in with his breath without thinking that by it he lives and breathes, because he does not reflect upon it. Wherefore this way is called a Mystical Way—that is, a secret and incomprehensible way.

In one word, the prayer of the heart may be performed at all times, though the heart cannot think or speak at all times.

JOHANNES KELPIUS (1673–1708)
German recluse, mystic, and teacher

Simplicity is an uprightness of soul that cuts off all useless reflections on self and on one's actions. It is different from sincerity.

There are many people who are sincere without being simple: they say nothing which they do not believe to be true; they would only be seen for what they are; but they are ever afraid of being seen for what they are not; they are always musing over all their words and thoughts and thinking about what they have done, in fear of having done or said too much. These people are sincere, but they are not simple: they are not at their ease with others, and other people are not at ease with them. There is nothing easy about them, nothing free, spontaneous or natural. People who are imperfect, less regular, less masters of themselves, are more lovable. This is how men find them, and it is the same with God.

To be always taken up with creatures without ever returning to oneself is the blind state of people caught up in their surroundings and in sensuous things: this is the extreme opposite of simplicity. To be always taken up with oneself in whatever one does is the other extreme, which makes a person wise in his own eyes, always reserved, full of self, disturbed by the least thing which troubles his good opinion of himself. . . .

If a man wants his friend to be free and easy with him, to forget himself in the exchanges of friendship, how much more does God, who is the true friend, desire the soul to be free from self-consciousness, worry, care, anxiety, and reserve, in that sweet and gentle intimacy which he has prepared for this soul.

The great obstacle to this blessed simplicity is the foolish wisdom of the world, which will not leave anything to God but wants to do everything through its own effort, to arrange everything itself, and to be for ever involved in these works. . . .

The cessation of anxious, burdened reflections on self leaves the soul in ineffable peace and freedom: this is simplicity. It is like being a little child on its mother's breast, no longer wanting anything, no longer afraid of anything. With this purity of heart it no longer matters what others think of us, provided we have the charity to avoid scandalizing anyone: one just does all one's actions in the present moment as well as possible with gentle, free, cheerful attentiveness, and without being anxious for success.

FRANÇOIS FÉNELON (1651–1715)
French Roman Catholic archbishop of Cambrai

Many persons think of divine grace as a species of impersonal, featureless life, which can be stored up and even "increased" by appropriate action, in the way a water-level can be raised by building a dam, or as a fortune can be amassed through the exercise of thrift. But such a view leaves no room for the freedom of the light of grace, which never behaves like the Enlightenment's "light of reason" or "light of nature." This light of nature is always there; it will shine in the heavens as long as human beings exist; it is utterly dependable. Pervading everything human, it has no real center. But the "true light" (Jn. 1:9) without which this all-pervading light would be illusory, always shines forth in complete freedom. "The light is with you for a little longer. Walk while you have the light." (Jn. 12:35). Otherwise it would not be the Word, who is God, Person and Son, Lord of all those who are "created in him."

If we want to live in his light, we must listen to his word, which always addresses us personally, which is always new since it is always free. It is impossible to deduce this word from some prior word that we have already understood and put into store: clear and fresh, it pours forth from the wellspring of absolute, sovereign freedom. The word of God can require something of me today that it did not require yesterday; this means that, if I am to hear this challenge, I must be fundamentally open and listening. It is true that no relationship is more intimate, more rooted in being than that between the recipient of grace and the grace-giving Lord, between the head and the body, the vine and the branches.

HANS URS VON BALTHASAR (1905–1988)
Swiss Roman Catholic theologian

Over whatever you have to do, even if it be very urgent and demands great care, I would not have you argue or be agitated. For rest assured, everything you do, be it great or small, is but one-eighth of the problem, whereas to keep one's state undisturbed even if thereby one should fail to accomplish the task, is the other seven-eighths.

So if you are busy at some task and wish to do it perfectly, try to accomplish it—which, as I said, would be one-eighth of the problem—and at the same time to preserve your state unharmed, which constitutes seven-eighths. If, however, in order to accomplish your task you would inevitably be carried away and harm yourself or another by arguing with him, you should not lose seven for the sake of preserving one-eighth.

ABBA DOROTHEUS (sixth century)
Saint, ascetical writer, and founder of a Palestinian monastery

The origin and cause of thoughts lies in the splitting up, by man's transgression, of his single and simple memory, which has thus lost the memory of God, and, becoming multiple instead of simple, and varied instead of single, has fallen prey to its own forces.

To cure this original memory of the deceitful and harmful memory of thoughts means to bring it back to its ancient simplicity. . . . Memory can be cured by a constant memory of God, consolidated by the action of prayer.

ST. GREGORY THE SINAITE (1255–1346)
Monk of Sinai and Mt. Athos

Memory is corrupted and ruined by a crowd of "memories." If I am going to have a true memory, there are a thousand things that must first be forgotten. Memory is not fully itself when it reaches only into the past. A memory that is not alive to the present does not "remember" the here and now, does not "remember" its true identity, is not memory at all. He who remembers nothing but facts and past events, and is never brought back into the present, is a victim of amnesia.

THOMAS MERTON (1915–1968)
American Cistercian monk

The solitude so necessary to a sweet and familiar converse with God consists in the silence of the soul, rather than in an exterior solitude which in itself is not capable of making us recollected. The noise which arises in ourselves, and disturbs the powers of the mind on which God desires to act, distracts us much more than that which comes from without and strikes only the ear.

One may be palpably touched with the presence of God and be entirely recollected in the midst of a tumult of creatures. . . . but one can scarcely be recollected in the tumults of thought, in the emotions of passion and confusion of the soul. Besides, God does not say He will lead us in solitude to speak to our ears, but to our hearts. Therefore, He requires of us an interior solitude.

AMBROISE DE LOMBEZ (date of treatise: 1756)

French Capuchin theologian

I turn over my little omelet in the frying pan for the love of God. When it is done, if I have nothing to do, I bow down to the ground and adore God from whom has come the grace to make it. Then I straighten up, more contented than a king. When there is nothing more that I can do, it is enough to pick up a straw from the floor for the love of God.

People look for methods for learning to love God. They desire to arrive by I don't know how many different practices. They take great pains to remain in the presence of God by a quantity of means. Is it not much shorter and more direct to do everything for the love of God, to use all the tasks of one's situation, to give testimony of it, and to maintain His presence within us by this communication of the heart with Him? He has no fancy ways for this. One has only to go plainly and simply to Him.

BROTHER LAWRENCE (1614–1691)

Lay brother among Carmelites in Paris

We do distinguish between the certain knowledge of God, and the uncertain; between the spiritual knowledge, and the literal; the saving heart-knowledge, and the soaring airy head-knowledge. The last, we confess, may be divers ways obtained; but the first, by no other way than the inward immediate manifestation and revelation of God's Spirit, shining in and upon the heart, enlightening and opening the understanding.

ROBERT BARCLAY (1648–1690)

Scottish Quaker

[God] creates minds to share in himself, gives them life, so that they may experience him, causes them to desire him, enlarges them to grasp him, justifies them so that they may deserve him, stirs them to zeal, ripens them to fruition, directs them to equity, forms them in benevolence, moderates them to make them wise, strengthens them to virtue, visits them to console, enlightens them with knowledge, sustains them to immortality, fills them with happiness, surrounds them with safety.

BERNARD OF CLAIRVAUX (1091–1153)

Cistercian abbot, saint, and theologian

An inner, secret turning to God can be made fairly steady over weeks and months and years of practice, and lapses and failures and returns. It is as simple an art as Brother Lawrence found it, but it may be long before we achieve any steadiness in the process. Begin now, as you read these words, as you sit in your chair, to offer your whole selves, utterly and in joyful abandon, in quiet, glad surrender to Him who is within. In secret ejaculations of praise, turn in humble wonder to the Light, faint though it may be. Keep contact with the outer world of sense and meanings. Here is no discipline in absent-mindedness. Walk and talk and work and laugh with your friends. But behind the scenes, keep up the life of simple prayer and inward worship. Keep it up throughout the day. Let inward prayer be your last act before you fall asleep and the first act when you awake. And in time you will find as did Brother Lawrence, that "those who have the gale of the Holy Spirit go forward even in sleep."

The first signs of simultaneity are given when at the moment of recovery from a period of forgetting there is a certain sense that we have not completely forgotten Him. It is as though we are only coming back into a state of vividness which had endured in dim and tenuous form throughout. What takes place now is not reinstatement of a broken prayer but return to liveliness of that which had endured, but mildly. The currents of His love have been flowing, but whereas we had been drifting in Him, now we swim. It is like the background of a picture which extends all the way across behind a tree in the foreground. It is not that we merely know intellectually that the background of the picture has unbroken extension; we experience aesthetically that it does extend across. Again, it is like waking from sleep yet knowing, not by inference but by immediate awareness, that we have lived even while we were asleep. For sole preoccupation with the world is sleep, but immersion in Him is life.

There is a total Instruction as well as specific instructions from the Light within. The dynamic illumination from the deeper level is shed upon the judgments of the surface level, and lo, "former things are passed away, behold, they are become new."

Paradoxically, this total Instruction proceeds in two opposing directions at once. We are torn loose from earthly attachments and ambitions—*contemptus mundi.* And we are quickened to a divine but painful concern for the world—*amor mundi.* He plucks the world out of our hearts, loosening the chains of attachment. And He hurls the world into our hearts, where we and He together carry it in infinitely tender love.

THOMAS RAYMOND KELLY (1893–1941)
American Quaker

See, the bridegroom cometh; go out to meet him.

Now Christ says spiritually within the one devoted to Him: "See." There are three points that make one seeing in inner practice. The first is the interior illumination of God's grace. The grace of God in the soul is like a candle in a lantern or a glass vessel; for it warms and illuminates and shines through the vessel, that is, the good person. And it reveals itself to the person who has this grace within, if he is observing himself in an inner manner, and reveals itself to others through him, in virtue and in good example.

The interior flash of God's grace suddenly stirs and moves a person from within, and that swift movement is the first point which makes us seeing.

Out of this swift movement by God comes the second point on the part of the person, namely, a gathering of all the faculties within and without in Unity of spirit, in the bond of love.

The third point is freedom, so that a person could turn within himself, imageless and unhindered, as often as he wishes and as often as he thinks on his God. That is, that a person can be undisturbed by weal and woe, by profit or loss, by exaltation or by oppression, by alien cares, by joy and by fear. These three points make a person seeing in inward practice. If you have these three points, then you have a foundation and a beginning of inner practice and of inner life.

JAN VAN RUUSBROEC (1293–1381)

Flemish mystic and theologian

PREPARING THE GROUND

We have long been told to be "quick to listen and slow to speak," but what is the urgent need behind this injunction? "The greatest necessity of all is to control and curb our tongue," says Nicodemus of the Holy Mountain, but why is this so? What is at the root of wanting to talk about everything, and to criticize and pass judgment on everything, and what is in peril when this is going on within us?

Christian and his friend Faithful met another traveler on their journey.

Now Faithful began to wonder at their companion; and said to Christian, "What a brave companion we've got! Surely this man will make a very excellent pilgrim."

At this Christian modestly smiled, and said, "This man, with whom you are so taken, will beguile with that tongue of his twenty of those who don't know him."

"Do you know him then?"

"Know him! Yes—better than he knows himself."

"Pray, who is he?"

"His name is Talkative: he dwells in our town. Notwithstanding his fine tongue, he is a sorry fellow."

"Well, he *seems* to be a very fine man."

"That he is," replied Christian, "to those who don't know him well. He is best abroad; near home, he is ugly enough. . . ."

"But I am ready to think you jest, for you are smiling."

"God forbid that I should jest in this matter, or that I should accuse any falsely! This man is always ready for any company, and for any talk: . . . he talks of prayer, of repentance, of faith; but he knows only to talk of them. . . ."

"Yes," said Faithful, "I see that saying and doing are two things: and hereafter I shall better observe this distinction."

"This Talkative is not aware of; he thinks that hearing and saying will make a good Christian, and thus he deceives his own soul. Hearing is but the sowing of the seed, and talking alone does not prove that fruit is indeed in the heart and life: and let us assure ourselves, that at the last day men shall be judged according to their fruits.

"It will not be said then, 'Did you believe?' but, 'Were you doers or talkers only?' and accordingly shall they be judged. The end of the world is compared to our harvest; and you know men at harvest care about nothing but fruit. . . . And I will add another thing: Paul called some men, yes, and those great talkers, too, 'sounding brass and tinkling cymbals.' . . .

"Yes, if a man has all knowledge he may still be nothing, and no child of God. When Christ said, 'Do ye know all these things?' and the disciples answered, 'Yes,' he added, 'Blessed are ye if ye do them.' He did not place the blessing in the knowing but in the doing. Indeed, to know is a thing that pleases talkers and boasters; but to do is that which pleases God."

JOHN BUNYAN (1628–1688)
English preacher and writer

It is better for a man to be silent and be a Christian, than to talk and not to be one. The kingdom of God is not in words, but in power. It is good to teach, if he who speaks also acts. For he who shall both "do and teach, the same shall be great in the kingdom." Our Lord and God, Jesus Christ, the Son of the living God, first did and then taught, as Luke testifies, "whose praise is in the Gospel through all the Churches."

Let us therefore do all things as those who have Him dwelling in us, that we may be His temples, and He may be in us as God. Let Christ speak in us, even as He did in Paul. Let the Holy Spirit teach us to speak the things of Christ in like manner as He did.

IGNATIUS (30–107)
Saint and bishop of Antioch

The greatest necessity of all is to control and curb our tongue. The mover of the tongue is the heart: what fills the heart is poured out through the tongue, and when feeling is poured out through the tongue it becomes strengthened and rooted in the heart. . . .

The feelings which seek expression in words are mostly egotistical, since they seek to express what flatters our self-love and can show us, we imagine, in the best light. Loquacity mostly comes from a certain vanity, which makes us think that we know a great deal and imagine our opinion on the subject of conversation to be the most satisfactory of all. So we experience an irresistible urge to speak out, and in a stream of words with many repetitions, to impress the same opinion in the hearts of others, thus foisting ourselves upon them as unbidden teachers and sometimes even dreaming of making pupils of others who understand the subject much better than the teacher.

This refers to cases where the subject is more or less worthy of attention, but in most cases loquacity is a synonym of empty talk, and there are no words to express the many evils which arise from this ugly habit. . . .

Empty talk is the door to criticism, and slander, the spreader of false rumors and opinions, the sower of discord and strife. It stifles the taste for mental work and practically always serves as a cover for the absence of sound knowledge. When wordy talk is over, and the fog of self-complacency lifts, it always leaves behind a sense of frustration and indolence. Is it not proof of the fact that, even involuntarily, the soul feels robbed?

UNSEEN WARFARE

"Therefore in all things be 'quick to listen and slow to speak' (James 1:19) lest the remark of Solomon be fulfilled in you: 'If you see a man too ready of speech know that a fool has more hope than he' (Prv. 29:20). And never dare to teach someone what you have not practiced yourself.

"Our Lord taught by His example that this was the procedure which we should follow. This is what is stated: 'Jesus began to do and to teach these things' (Acts 1:1). So have a care that you do not rush to teach something you have not done yourself. Otherwise, you will be counted among those in regard to whom Jesus had the following to say to His disciples: 'Do what they tell you and listen to what they say, but do not act as they do. They talk and do not act. They tie up heavy burdens and lay them on men's shoulders but they will not lift a finger to move them' (Mt. 5:19). Therefore 'he who breaks the least of the commandments and teaches men to do so shall be called least in the kingdom of heaven' (Mt. 5:19). . . .

"So be careful not to be caught doing as some others do. They give lessons. They manage to be articulate in discussion. And because they know how to talk elegantly and abundantly they seem to have spiritual knowledge, or so it appears to those who have not learned to recognize its true character. For it is one thing to be a skilled talker and a shining speaker. It is something else to enter into the very heart and core of heavenly utterances, to contemplate with heart's purest gaze the deep and hidden mysteries. This is not something to be possessed by humanistic lore and worldly erudition. It will be gained only by purity of heart and through the illumination of the Holy Spirit."

JOHN CASSIAN (360–after 435)
Monk and founder of monasteries near Marseilles

A religious saw one day two devils discoursing together and asking one another an account of what progress they had made against two monks whom they were employed to tempt.

"I find myself very well," says the one, "with him that I have to do with—I need only present a thought to him, and presently he takes hold of it, entertains himself with it, and immediately detecting himself in this thought, he goes over in his mind the whole series of those thoughts—he thinks how long he dwelled on it; whether it came by his fault; whether he resisted it, or consented to it; from where and how it came to him, whether he gave occasion to it, or did all he should to give none. As often as I like, I put him upon this rack."

"For my part," says the other, "I lose all the pains and measures I take with him whom I tempt, for as soon as I suggest a thought he has presently recourse to God, or to a pious meditation, or he turns to something else to hinder him from thinking of what I proposed to him, and thus I know not how to deal with him."

ALFONSO RODRIGUEZ (1526–1616)

Spanish Jesuit

Abba Stephen said, "When I was younger, I lived with Abba Gelasios. He did not tell me to do anything, but he himself set the table and said to me 'Brother, if you want to, come and eat.' I replied, 'I have come to learn, why do you never tell me to do anything?' But the old man gave me no reply whatever. So I went to tell the seniors. They came and said to him, 'Abba, the brother has come to your holiness in order to learn. Why do you never tell him to do anything?' The old man said to them, 'Am I an abba, that I should give orders? As far as I am concerned, I do not tell him anything, but if he wishes he can do what he sees me doing.' From that moment I took the initiative and did what the old man did. As for him, he did what he did in silence, so he taught me in silence."

DESERT FATHERS (fourth–sixth centuries)

A person inwardly turned to God attends to himself before all others, and one that can well attend to himself can easily be free of other men's deeds. You will never be a spiritual person and a devout follower of Christ unless you can keep yourself from meddling in other men's deeds and can closely attend to your own. If you attend wholly to God and to yourself, the faults that you see in others shall little move you.

Where are you when you are not present to yourself? When you have run about and been much troubled by the deeds of others, what does it profit you if you have forgotten yourself?

THOMAS À KEMPIS (1380–1471)
Dutch ecclesiastic and ascetical writer

It is the proper business of the Mind and Body too, of Thoughts and Actions, too to be quiet. And yet, alas, how many break their sleep in the night about things that disquiet them in the day too, and trouble themselves in the day about things that disquiet them all night too? We disquiet ourselves too much in being overtender, oversensible of imaginary injuries.

They that are too inquisitive about what other men say of them, they disquiet themselves; for that which others would but whisper, they publish.

We must not too jealously suspect, not too bitterly condemn, not too peremptorily conclude, that what ever is not done as we would have done it, or as we have seen it done in former times, is not well done.

JOHN DONNE (1572–1631)
English poet and dean of St. Paul's Cathedral, London

There is a fever called quotidian, that is, daily fever, which occurs when the heart is snared by manifold attachments. Persons so afflicted want to know and to talk about everything, to criticize and pass judgment on everything, and they often forget about themselves. They are burdened with many cares about things which do not concern them, and must often hear what they do not wish to hear. The most trivial matter is enough to disturb them. Their thoughts range everywhere, just like the wind. First this way, then that; first here, then there.

This is a daily fever for it causes these persons to be disturbed and anxious about many things from morning till evening and sometimes even during the night, whether they are asleep or lying awake. Although this condition may coexist with the state of grace and the absence of mortal sin, it is nevertheless an obstacle to the practice of fervent interior exercises and to the acquisition of a taste for God and for all the virtues, and this does lasting harm. . . . [It] prevents a person from understanding interior truth and destroys the foundation and the practice of all interior fervor.

JAN VAN RUUSBROEC (1293–1381)
Flemish mystic and theologian

Surge et illuminare, Jerusalem . . .
Rise up, Jerusalem and shine forth! . . . (Is. 60:1)

God desires and needs only one thing in all the world; and that He desires so ardently that He sets His whole heart upon it. It is this: to find the lofty ground with which He had endowed man's spirit empty and prepared so that He may accomplish His eternal work within it. God, Who is all-powerful in Heaven and on Earth, asks for man's consent to bring this about. What, then, ought we to do so that God may shine forth in this very sweet ground of the soul and perform His work there? We should rise, "*surge.*" The text says, "arise," which implies an active consent. Man must do his part and rise from everything that is not God, away from himself and all created things. And as he rises, the depth of his soul is seized by a powerful longing to be denuded and freed from everything that separates it from God. And the more he leaves behind all that is finite, the stronger his longing grows, it transcends itself, and when this denuded ground is touched, the desire often overflows into flesh and blood and bone. . . .

Ah, how glorious such men are! They are raised to a supernatural, a divine level, and none of their work is ever done without God. And if one may dare to utter it, they themselves no longer work, but God works in them. How blessed they are! They are the lofty pillars of the universe, on whom rests the weight of the whole world. To find oneself in such a state—what a glorious and joyful thing that would be. . . .

A man can never reach perfection unless he wishes to arise, lift up his spirit to God, and free his innermost ground. . . . He should do this with profound awe and with inward recollection, so that he may fully know what God wishes him to do. . . . For where God truly takes possession of the soul, all external activity ceases, but the interior perception of God mightily increases. Once a man has attained such a height to which God's grace and his own ardor have brought him, he must deny himself utterly. . . .

Even if he reaches the very highest peak he is to say and mean: "*Fiat voluntas tua*"—"Lord, thy will be done." Let him keep guard over himself lest he have any hidden attachments, so that God should find in his innermost ground an obstacle that would prevent Him from this work He performs so loftily and without means. May our loving God help us to "rise up," so that He may accomplish His work within us.

JOHANNES TAULER (1300–1361)

German Dominican contemplative

A man should accustom himself to seeking and wanting nothing for himself in anything, and to finding and accepting God in everything. For God does not give, he has never given, any gift so that we might have it and then rest upon it; but all the gifts he ever gave in heaven and on earth he gave so that he might give us the one gift that is himself. With all these other gifts he wants to prepare us for the gift that he himself is. All the works God has ever performed in heaven and in earth he performed for the sake of one work, so that he might perform that, and it is to be himself blessed, so that he may make us blessed.

Therefore I say: In every gift, in every work, we ought to learn to look toward God, and we should not allow ourselves to be satisfied or be detained by any thing. Whatever our way of life may be, we must not cease to progress; this has been true for everyone, however far he may have advanced. Above all else, we should always be preparing ourselves, always renewing ourselves to receive God's gifts.

MEISTER ECKHART (1260–1327)
German Dominican mystic and theologian

A brother once sorrowfully asked Sisoes the Great: "Father, what can I do? I have fallen into sin." The Staretz answered him: "Rise again." The brother said: "I rose up and fell." The Staretz answered: "Rise again." The brother answered: "How often must I fall and rise up?" The Staretz said: "Until your death."

IGNATIUS BYRANCHANINOV (1807–1867)
Russian bishop

Each of us ought in our own ways to imitate [Christ]. . . .

Christ fasted for forty days. Imitate him by considering what you are sure that you are most inclined and ready to do; apply yourself to this and observe yourself closely. It is often more profitable for you to refrain from these things than go without any food. Similarly, it is sometimes harder for you to suppress one word than to keep completely silent. So it is harder at times for a man to endure one little word of contempt, which really is insignificant, when it would be easy for him to suffer a heavy blow to which he had steeled himself, and it is much harder for him to be alone in a crowd than in the desert, and it is often harder for him to abandon some little thing than a big one, harder for him to carry out a trifling enterprise than one that people would think much more important. Thus a man in his weakness can very well imitate our Lord, and he need never consider himself far off from him.

MEISTER ECKHART (1260–1327)
German Dominican mystic and theologian

If you would see a short description of the happiness of a life rightly employed, wholly devoted to God, you must look at the man in the parable to whom his Lord had given five talents. "Lord," says he, "thou deliveredst unto me five talents; behold, I have gained beside them five talents more." His Lord said unto him, "Well done, thou good and faithful servant; thou hast been faithful over a few things, I will make thee ruler over many things: enter thou into the joy of thy Lord."

Here you see a life that is wholly intent upon the improvement of the talents, that is devoted wholly unto God, is a state of happiness, prosperous labors, and glorious success. Here are not any uneasy passions, murmurings, vain fears, and fruitless labors. The man is not toiling and digging in the earth for no end or advantage; but his pious labors prosper in his hands, his happiness increases upon him. . . .

We may for a while amuse ourselves with names and sounds, and shadows of happiness; we may talk of this or that greatness and dignity; but if we desire real happiness, we have no other possible way to it but by improving our talents, by so holily and piously using the powers and faculties of men in this present state, that we may be happy and glorious in the powers and faculties of Angels in the world to come.

How ignorant, therefore, are they of the nature of religion, of the nature of man, and the nature of God, who think a life of strict piety and devotion to God to be a dull uncomfortable state; when it is so plain and certain that there is neither comfort nor joy to be found in anything else!

WILLIAM LAW (1686–1761)
English contemplative and cleric

Every gift of God to man, his divine image and perfection itself, is a *temptation*—and above all the gift to man of his *I*, the miracle of his absolutely unique, eternal, unrepeatable and indivisible *personality*, which renders each man "like a king of creation." Temptation is *inherent* to the personality because out of all creation only man is called by God to love himself, that is, to be conscious of his divine gift and the miracle of his *I*.

The human personality is love for oneself and *thus* love for God, love for God and *thus* love for oneself, the apprehension of oneself as a bearer of the divine gift of knowledge and ascent into the fullness of life. And here it is innate to convert this *love for himself* that is implicit in man into *love of oneself,* into self-love, which constitutes the essence of *pride.* No, man is not enticed by "evil" but by himself, by his own divine image, by the divine miracle of his *I.* He heard the serpent's whisper "you will be like gods" not from outside, but from within, in the blessed fullness of paradise, and wanted to have life in himself and for himself. . . .

PAUL EVDOKIMOV (1901–1970)

Russian Orthodox theologian

At the same moment it seems as if you are capable of everything—and a selfish thought will sneak in as if it were *you* who are capable—at the same moment all can be lost for you; and at the same moment the selfish thought surrenders, you can have everything again. But God is not seen, and therefore, as God uses this instrument into which a human being has made himself in self-denial, it seems as if it were the instrument that is able to do everything, and this tempts the instrument itself to understand it in that way—until he is again able to do nothing. It is hard enough to work with a human being, but to work together with the Omnipotent One! Well, in a certain sense it is quite easy, since what is he not capable of, so I can simply let him do it. The difficulty, therefore, is just that I am to work together with Him, if not in any other way, then through the continual understanding that I am able to do nothing at all, something that is not understood once and for all. And it is difficult to understand this—to understand it not at the moment when one actually is unable to do anything, when one is sick, in low spirits, but to understand it at the moment when one seemingly is capable of doing everything.

SØREN KIERKEGAARD (1813–1855)

Danish theologian

So long as we continue to behave as sheep, we are victorious. Even if ten thousand wolves surround us, we conquer and are victorious. But the moment we become wolves, we are conquered, for we lose the help of the shepherd. He is the shepherd of sheep, not of wolves. If he leaves you and goes away, it is because you do not allow him to show his power.

These are his words: Do not be troubled that I send you out in the midst of wolves and tell you to be like sheep and like doves. I could have done just the opposite, and not have allowed you to suffer any hurt. I could have prevented you being the victims of wolves and made you fiercer than lions. But I chose a better way. My way makes you more glorious and proclaims my power. These were his words to Paul: "My grace is sufficient for you, for my power is made perfect in weakness." That is the way I made you. When he says: "I send you out as sheep," he implies: "Do not despair, for I know very well that in this way you will be invincible against all your enemies."

Next he wants them too to make some contribution of their own, so that everything will not seem to come from grace. He does not want it thought that their crown was not earned, and so he says: "So be as wise as serpents and innocent as doves." What power, he asks, does our wisdom have in such perils? How can we have wisdom at all when we are deluged by such billows? However wise the sheep may be when in the midst of wolves, and the wolves are as numerous as they are, what more will wisdom be able to achieve? However innocent the dove may be, what advantage will its innocence be when it is beset by so many hawks? So long as you are talking about irrational beasts, of course, the answer is none, but when you are dealing with men like you, the answer is, the greatest possible advantage.

JOHN CHRYSOSTOM (345–407)
Father of the Eastern church, saint, and bishop of Constantinople

Tegel, January 10, 1945

Dear Heart: First I must tell you that quite evidently the last twenty-four hours of one's life are no different from any others. I had always imagined that it would come as a shock to say to one-self: "Now the sun is setting for the last time for you, now the hour hand will make only two more revolutions before twelve, now you are going to bed for the last time."

Nothing of the sort. Perhaps I am a little cracked. For I cannot deny that I am in really high spirits. I only pray to God in heaven to sustain me in this mood, for surely it is easier for the flesh to die in this state. How merciful the Lord has been to me! Even at the risk of sounding hysterical—I am so full of thanks that there is actually no room for anything else. He has guided me so firmly and clearly during these two days. The whole court-room might have roared, like Herr Freisler [president of the People's Court] himself, and all the walls might have rocked—it would have made no difference to me. It was just as is written in

Isaiah 43:2: "When thou passest through the waters, I will be with thee; and through the rivers, they shall not overflow thee: when thou walkest through the fire, thou shalt not be burned; neither shall the flame kindle upon thee." That is to say, upon your soul.

When I was called up for my last words, I was in such a frame of mind that I nearly said, "I have only one thing to add to my defense. Take my goods, my honor, my child and wife; the body they may kill; God's truth abideth still, his kingdom is for ever." But that would only have made it harder for the others; therefore I said only, "I do not intend to say anything, Herr President."

Therefore I can say only one thing, dear heart. May God be as merciful to you as to me—then even the death of a husband matters not at all. For he can demonstrate his omnipotence even when you are making pancakes for the boys, or when you have to take Puschti out of the room (although I hope that isn't necessary any more).

I should be saying farewell to you—I can't do it. I should be mourning and regretting the drabness of your everyday life—I can't do it. I should indeed be thinking of the burdens that will now fall upon you—I can't do it. I can say only one thing to you: if you attain to a feeling of supreme security—if the Lord gives you that which, had it not been for this period in our lives and its conclusion, you would never have had, then I am leaving you a treasure that cannot be confiscated, a treasure compared to which even my life is of small account.

HELMUTH VON MOLTKE (1907–1945)
German jurist and statesman

The scriptures we are commanded to search. . . . They can make us wise unto salvation. If we be ignorant, they will instruct us; if out of the way, they will bring us home; if out of order, they will reform us; if in heaviness, comfort us; if dull, quicken us; if cold, inflame us. . . .

Take up and read, take up and read the scriptures, it was said unto Saint Augustine by a supernatural voice. "Whatsoever is in the scriptures, believe me, is high and divine"; said the same Saint Augustine, "there is truth, and a doctrine most fit for the refreshing and renewing of men's minds, and truly so tempered, that everyone may draw from them that which is sufficient for him." Thus Saint Augustine and Saint Jerome, "Love the scriptures, and wisdom will love thee."

"THE TRANSLATORS TO THE READER"
First edition of the 1611 Authorized Version of the Bible

If anyone should point out a footprint made by the foot of Christ, how we Christians would bow in reverence; how we should adore. But why do we not venerate His living, breathing image in the Gospels? If anyone were to place on exhibition Christ's cloak, where would we not travel on earth to be permitted to see it? But suppose you present all His goods, there will be nothing which represents Christ more clearly and truly than the Gospels. For the love of Christ we decorate a wood and stone statue with gems and gold. What else does an image express but the shape of the body, if indeed it does express anything.

But the Gospels bring to you the living image of that sacrosanct mind, Christ Himself, speaking, healing, dying, rising. In a word, they make Him so present that you would see less were He before your eyes.

DESIDERIUS ERASMUS (1466–1536)
Dutch theologian, scholar, and humanist

"The word of God is living and active, sharper than any two-edged sword. . . . " This word of God is living: the Father granted it to have life in himself, as he has life in himself. Therefore it is not only living, but is also life, as it says to itself, "I am the way, the truth, and the life. . . . "

It is active in the creation of things, active in the control of the world, active in the redemption of the world. What is more active or more powerful? "Who shall speak of his powers, or voice all his praises?" It is active in its working, active when preached. It does not return empty, but prospers in all things to which it is sent.

It is active and more piercing than any two-edged sword, when it is believed and loved. What is impossible to the believer or difficult to the lover? When this word speaks, its words pierce the heart, like the sharp arrows of a man of might, like nails driven in deep, and they go so far as to penetrate the inmost being. For this word is more penetrating than any two-edged sword, being more powerfully incisive than any other strength or power, and more subtle than any sharpness of the human mind, keener than any refinement of human wisdom or learned speech.

BALDWIN (d. 1190)
English archbishop of Canterbury

This is perhaps that final flame, which will fill the whole world and consume it: the appearance of God's Word in every creature, when nothing but the spiritual Light will shine any more for both the good and the bad.

This is the Light which already fills all things secretly, but then it will fill all things openly. This is, I think, the flame that says of itself: "I am a consuming fire." For he will consume all things when he shall be all in all and alone appear in all things.

JOHN THE SCOT ERIUGENA (810–877)

Irish theologian and scholar

Jesus said, "Let him who seeks continue seeking until he finds. When he finds, he will become troubled. When he becomes troubled, he will be astonished, and he will rule over the All."

Jesus said, "If those who lead you say to you, 'See, the Kingdom is in the sky,' then the birds of the sky will precede you. If they say to you, 'It is in the sea,' then the fish will precede you. Rather, the Kingdom is inside of you, and it is outside of you. When you come to know yourselves, then you will become known, and you will realize that it is you who are the sons of the living Father. But if you will not know yourselves, you dwell in poverty and it is you who are that poverty." . . .

Jesus said, "Recognize what is in your sight, and that which is hidden from you will become plain to you. For there is nothing hidden which will not become manifest."

GOSPEL OF THOMAS (first century)

THE STREAM
OF PROVIDENCE

Enlarging on Cycle Four, the emphasis here is on what takes us away from the present moment, and on the graces that can flow to us only when we inhabit it. It places the work of the Christian firmly in the here and now, time and eternity together, a work "to be by the help of eternity entirely contemporary with himself."

First of all, faith is not an emotion, not a feeling. It is not a blind subconscious urge toward something vaguely supernatural. It is not simply an elemental need in man's spirit. It is not a feeling that God exists. It is not a conviction that one is somehow saved or "justified" for no special reason except that one happens to feel that way. It is not something entirely interior and subjective, with no reference to any external motive. It is not just "soul force." It is not something that bubbles up out of the recesses of your soul and fills you with an indefinable "sense" that everything is all right. It is not something so purely yours that its content is incommunicable. It is not some personal myth of your own that you cannot share with anyone else, and the objective validity of which does not matter either to you or God or anybody else.

But also it is not an opinion. It is not a conviction based on rational analysis. It is not the fruit of scientific evidence. You can only believe what you do not know. As soon as you know it, you no longer believe it, at least not in the same way as you know it.

Faith is first of all an intellectual assent. It perfects the mind, it does not destroy it. It puts the intellect in possession of Truth which reason cannot grasp by itself.

Faith does not simply account for the unknown, tag it with a theological tag and file it away in a safe place where we do not have to worry about it. On the contrary, faith incorporates the unknown into our everyday life in a living, dynamic and actual manner. The unknown remains unknown. It is still a mystery, for it cannot cease to be one. The function of faith is not to reduce mystery to rational clarity, but to integrate the unknown and the known together in a living whole, in which we are more and more able to transcend the limitations of our external self.

Faith is primarily an intellectual assent. But if it were only that and nothing more, if it were only the "argument of what does not appear," it would not be complete. It has to be something more than an assent of the mind. It is also a grasp, a contact, a communion of wills, "the substance of things to be hoped for." By faith one not only assents to propositions revealed by God, one not only attains to truth in a way that intelligence and reason alone cannot do, but one assents to God Himself. One *receives* God. One says "yes" not merely to a statement *about* God, but to the Invisible, Infinite God Himself. One fully accepts the statement not only for its own content, but for the sake of Him Who made it.

Too often our notion of faith is falsified by our emphasis on the statements *about* God which faith believes, and by our forgetfulness of the fact that faith is a communion with God's own light and truth. Actually, the statements, the propositions which faith accepts on the divine authority are simply media through which one passes in order to reach the divine Truth. Faith terminates not in a statement, not in a formula of words, but *in God.*

If instead of resting in God by faith, we rest simply in the proposition or the formula, it is small wonder that faith does not lead to contemplation. On the contrary, it leads to anxious hairsplitting arguments, to controversy, to perplexity and ultimately to hatred and division.

In this superconscious realm of mystery is hidden not only the summit of man's spiritual being (which remains a pure mystery to his reason) but also the presence of God, Who dwells at this hidden summit, according to traditional metaphor. Faith then brings man into contact with man's own inmost spiritual depths and with God, Who is "present" within those same depths.

THOMAS MERTON (1915–1968)
American Cistercian monk

"I am a doubting Thomas," say the skeptics. And the orthodox look at them scornfully—or rather, through them, at St. Thomas himself. Both would do well to take another look. Judas betrayed, Peter denied, Thomas doubted—how easy it is to say this!

Thomas—one of the twelve whom Christ himself chose and appointed, and who remained close to him even after the "hard sayings" of Capernaum; who followed his Master everywhere, shared his trials, was present at his miracles. He was there when Jesus went into the house of Jairus, whose daughter had just died, and he took her by the hand and bade her rise; when the son of the widow of Nain sat up in his coffin and began to speak; he was there when Lazarus arose from his sepulcher at his Lord's command. He needed no conviction of Jesus' divinity. He believed in it, not with a sanctimonious and bigoted belief but with all the force of an inner certainty which was to lead him, in spite of taunts and threats, even to the Mount of Olives. After the "It is finished," he was still there, one of the eleven who remained united in their faith.

What did he still need to see? What new proof was necessary for this believer? What was the nature of the doubt that arose in him? He was an apostle. He had fully accepted his mission. He felt himself pledged, "committed," as we would say today. And this is precisely why he doubted—not Christ, certainly, nor the others, but himself. What was in question for him was not so much Mary Magdalen's testimony, nor that of the other ten; it was his own belief.

There was something that he had not yet been able to understand. Why was it that Jesus, the son of God, needed once more to assume the human condition? Son of David, are you never to be delivered? Has not everything then been fulfilled? And yet, to deny the resurrection would be to deny the divine utterance, to deny the Word.

Thus Thomas awoke to himself and knew that he was two. His soul had not ceased to believe, but it had left his body in the shadows. And inasmuch as his flesh hesitated, as his senses did not know or refused, he trembled before his destiny as an apostle; he felt helpless to bear witness in full. So evidently it was his body that he had to convince before he could go any further. "Except I shall see in his hands the print of the nails, and put my finger into the print of the nails, and thrust my hand into his side, *I will not believe.*"

Thomas, the Didymus, twin of Jesus, as the Gnostics were to call him—did he not feel Christ in himself as his divine brother? In order to realize this presence fully, he needed to experience this mystery in himself, to know for himself the return of Jesus of Nazareth into his body, allowing his faith to become incarnate through the communion of sense and spirit. And at this instant, the apostle Thomas was reborn. "My Lord and my God." He was transfigured by the overflowing joy of a new encounter; for at that moment, he *met* Christ, both in his spirit and in his body.

HENRI TRACOL (1909–1997)
French journalist and sculptor

We all live by the same bread, each of us receiving his own share . . . In this gift which I have received I possess the whole of Christ and Christ possesses the whole of me, just as the limb which is possessed by the body in its turn possesses the whole body. Therefore that portion of faith which has been distributed to you is the fragment put in your mouth; but unless you reflect, often and devoutly, on what you believe, unless you will as it were break it up into pieces with your teeth, that is, with your spiritual senses, chewing it and turning it over in your mouth, it will stick in your throat, that is, it will not go down into your understanding. . . . Faith offers to us things which we cannot see, and there must be great intellectual labor before such things are passed down into the mind. Unless this dry bread be moistened by the saliva of wisdom coming down "from the Father of light," you will labor in vain, for what you have gathered up by thinking does not penetrate to your understanding. . . . Therefore your faith will be idle, unless by often thinking about it "you earn your bread by the labor of your hands." And yet you cannot think about all you believe, or understand at once all that you think, but only by degrees, and as it were in fragments; and so your food can be properly prepared only by great labor.

GUIGO II (12th century)

French Carthusian monk and prior at the Grande Chartreuse monastery

We live in an age when the worth and meaning of everything are tested. We do not care how old a theory is, or how sacred it was in the middle ages; we ask at once, is it true? Does it meet our need, does it speak to our condition? Now the message of Quakerism declares that we were meant for God and that we can never be our true selves until God possesses us. That our darkness is made, like that of the earth, because we live in our own shadow. Wheel about and the light fronts you, and has been shining all the time. You made your own darkness. . . . Life truly begins with the creation of a new being within a person, and there is no substitute for this. . . .

This is a religion which not only makes us sure of heaven ultimately, but free in the truth *now*, conscious of His forgiveness and immediate presence *now*, able to withstand temptation *now*, victorious over sin *now*, possessed of peace and secure from fears *now*, triumphant in the power of the living spirit and in present possession of an earnest of eternal life.

We are not called to the other worldly but this worldly. Here is our sphere, here is our arena. We are not to stand gazing up into heaven. We are rather to build in our layer in the walls of a new Jerusalem here on the earth.

RUFUS M. JONES (1863–1948)

American Quaker

Those who have realized how dangerous and evil is the life they lead, the devil succeeds in keeping in his power mainly by the following simple but all-powerful suggestion: "Later, later; tomorrow, tomorrow." And the poor sinner, deluded by the appearance of good intention accompanying this suggestion, decides: "Indeed, tomorrow; today I shall finish what I have to do, and then, free of all care, will put myself in the hands of Divine grace and will follow unswervingly the path of spiritual life. Today I shall do this and that; tomorrow I shall repent." . . .

Nothing but negligence and blindness can explain why, when the whole of our salvation and all the glory of God are at stake, we fail to use immediately the most easy and simple and yet the most effective weapon, namely: to say to ourselves resolutely and ener- getically: "This moment! I shall start spiritual life at this moment and not later, *I shall repent now, instead of tomorrow. Now, this moment is in my hands, tomorrow and after is in the hands of God.* Even if God will grant me tomorrow and after, can I be sure that I shall have tomorrow the same good thought urging me to mend my ways? . . . Moreover how senseless it is when, for example, a sure remedy is offered for curing one's ills, to say: "Wait, let me be sick a little longer!"

UNSEEN WARFARE

Simple said, I see no danger; Sloth said, Yet a little more sleep: and Presumption said, Every vat must stand upon his own bottom. And so they lay down to sleep again, and Christian went on his way.

JOHN BUNYAN (1628–1688)
English preacher and writer

We complain that within thirty or forty years, a little more, or a great deal less, we shall descend again into the bowels of our mother, and that our life is too short for any great employment; and yet we throw away five and thirty years of our forty, and the remaining five we divide between art and nature, civility and customs, necessity and convenience, prudent counsels and religion: but the portion of the last is little and contemptible, and yet that little is all that we can prudently account of our lives. We bring that fate and that death near us, of whose approach we are so sadly apprehensive.

In taking the accounts of your life, do not reckon by great distances, and by the periods of pleasure, or the satisfaction of your hopes, or the sating of your desires; but let every intermedial day and hour pass with observation. He that reckons he hath lived but so many harvests, thinks they come not often enough, and that they go away too soon: some lose the day with longing for the night, and the night in waiting for the day. Hope and fantastic expectations spend much of our lives: and while with passion we look for a coronation, or the death of an enemy, or a day of joy, passing from fancy to possession without any intermedial notices, we throw away a precious year, and use it but as the burden of our time, fit to be pared off and thrown away, that we may come at those little pleasures which first steal our hearts, and then steal our life.

JEREMY TAYLOR (1613–1667)

English bishop and writer

How many of ours and our fathers' years have flowed away through Thy "today," and from it received the measure and the mould of such being as they had; and still others shall flow away, and so receive the mould of their degree of being.

But Thou are still the same, and all things of tomorrow, and all beyond, and all of yesterday, and all behind it, Thou wilt do in this Today, Thou hast done in this Today.

AUGUSTINE OF HIPPO (354–430)

Carthaginian saint, philosopher, and doctor of the church

Why take anxious thought for the things of tomorrow? Suppose you think ever so much, will it make your case any better? Can you change tomorrow? Can you render inoperative the law of cause and effect? Can you by solicitous forethought throw light into the shadow? It is an impossible thing.

You are master of yourself today; but God gives you supremacy for only one day at a time. Tomorrow is not your kingdom. Of tomorrow you have no scepter till tomorrow is today. No man owns anything until it has been converted into today. As fast as time is ours it is brought to us, and then we administer over it.

I never saw a person that could not get through a single day. That is a space that almost anybody can stride over. Almost everybody says, "I could get through today if I had reason to believe that tomorrow—"

Oh! Tomorrow does not exist to you. If you can bear your burden today, if you can endure your pain today, if you can suffer the shame of today, if you can put down the fear of today, if you can find contentment today, you will get along well enough.

Take what comes to you today.

HENRY WARD BEECHER (1813–1887)
American Congregational minister

Anxiety arises from an unregulated desire to be delivered from any pressing evil, or to obtain some hoped-for good. Nevertheless nothing tends so greatly to enhance the one or retard the other as overeagerness and anxiety. Birds that are captured in nets and snares become inextricably entangled therein, because they flutter and struggle so much. Therefore, whenever you urgently desire to be delivered from any evil, or to attain some good thing, strive above all else to keep a calm, restful spirit, steady your judgment and will, and then go quietly and easily after your object, taking all fitting means to attain it. By easily I do not mean carelessly, but without eagerness, disquietude, or anxiety; otherwise, so far from bringing about what you wish, you will hinder it, and add more and more to your perplexities. . . .

Do not allow any wishes to disturb your mind under the pretext of their being trifling and unimportant; for if they gain the day, greater and weightier matters will find your heart more accessible to disturbance. When you are conscious that you are growing anxious, commend yourself to God, and resolve

steadfastly not to take any steps whatever to obtain the result you
desire, until your disturbed state of mind is altogether quieted;
unless indeed it should be necessary to do something without
delay, in which case you must restrain the rush of inclination,
moderating it, as far as possible, so as to act rather from reason
than impulse.

FRANCIS OF SALES (1567–1622)
Saint, bishop of Geneva, and doctor of the church

They have care for the morrow who do not trust in the Divine
[Being] but in themselves; and who only look to worldly and ter-
restrial things, and not to heavenly. There universally prevails with
them a solicitude about things to come, a longing to possess all
things, and to rule over all. . . .

They grieve if they do not obtain the objects of their desire,
and are in anguish when they suffer the loss of them. Nor is there
any consolation for them; for they become angry against the
Divine, reject it together with all faith, and curse themselves.

Such are they with whom there is care for the morrow. It is
entirely different with those who trust in the Divine [Being]. They
are of tranquil mind whether they obtain the objects of their desire
or not; nor do they grieve at their loss. If they become rich they
do not set their heart upon riches; if exalted to honors, they do
not regard themselves more worthy than others. If they become
poor they are not made sad; if in humble condition they are not
dejected. . . .

It should be known that the Divine Providence is universal, in
the very least particulars of all things; and that they who are in the

stream of Providence are continually borne along to happinesses, however the means may appear; and that they are in the stream of Providence who put their trust in the Divine [Being] and ascribe all things to Him. . . .

It should be known also, that insofar as any one is in the stream of Providence he is in a state of peace; and insofar as one is in a state of peace from the good of faith, or trust, he is within the Divine Providence.

EMANUEL SWEDENBORG (1688–1772)
Swedish scientist and mystical thinker

Behold the birds of the air: for they sow not, neither do they reap, nor gather into barns, yet your heavenly Father feeds them (Mt. 6:26)

So then, be like the bird, get rid of the next day, and thus you are without the anxiety of self-torment; and this must be practicable, precisely for the reason that the next day is derived from the self. On the other hand, if we let today disappear almost entirely in comparison to the next day's worry, we are in deepest self-torment. The whole difference is that of only one day—and yet what an immense difference! It is easy enough for the bird to *be* free of the next—but to *become* free of it! Oh, of all the enemies that assail a human being by might or by cunning, none perhaps is so obstinately intrusive as this next day, which is always the same next day. It is said that to conquer one's spirit is greater than to take a city; but if one is to conquer his spirit, he must begin by *becoming* free of the next day. The next day—it is like a goblin which is able to assume every

form, it looks so exceedingly different, but for all that it is . . .
the next day.

The Christian has not this anxiety.

The Christian assumes exactly the opposite position to the self-
tormentors; for these forget today entirely by reason of their anxiety and preoccupation with the next day. The believer is present,
and at the same time is, as this word also denotes in Latin, mighty.
The self-tormentor is an absentee, and an enfeebled person. The
wish is often heard in the world to be contemporary with one
or another great event or great man, with the notion that contem-
poraneousness might develop a man and make him something
great. Perhaps! But might it not be worth more than a wish to be
contemporary with oneself? For how rare it is for a man to be contemporary with himself. Most persons, in feeling, in imagination,
in purpose, in resolution, in wish, in longing, are a hundred thousand miles in advance of themselves, or several human generations
in advance of themselves. But the believer (being present) is in the
highest sense contemporary with himself. And to be by the help of
eternity entirely contemporary with oneself is at the same time the
thing that most educates and develops, it is the great gain of
eternity.

Hence when the Christian works, or when he prays, he talks
only of today. He prays for daily bread "today," for a blessing
upon his work "today," that he may come nearer to God's kingdom "today." For if a person who had become acquainted with
this terror were to pray thus in the passion of his soul, "Save
me, O God, from myself and from the next day," he would not
be praying Christianly, and the next day would already have

acquired too much power over him. For the Christian prays, "Save me today from the evil." This is the surest salvation from the next day, with the understanding that one will pray thus every day; if for one day this is forgotten, the next day comes at once into view.

SØREN KIERKEGAARD (1813–1855)
Danish theologian

We will never possess peace as long as we fear to lose it. You who find in the present every motive of consolation, will you seek fears in futurity? Is repose a burden to you? "Why?" you ask. While each day is sufficient for its own evil, you collect in a moment what is spread throughout a lifetime. You unite by your anticipations, temptations which God only wanted you to subdue singly. This is the most dangerous of all temptations. It is very difficult not to yield to it; it is tempting God. It is drawing on yourself enemies to whom He does not wish you to expose yourself at present.

AMBROISE DE LOMBEZ (date of treatise: 1750)
French Capuchin theologian

The Christian can, of course, like other people, foresee events which will probably or certainly befall him, such as pain, bereavement and death, but he knows, as others do not, that the person to whom they will happen will not be the person he is at the moment, his present self. God gives us grace at the moment we need it. The person to whom those hard events will occur will be one who has been prepared by Him for their happening and full of the present grace of the Lord which is at that moment being given to him (but not at an earlier moment) expressly to deal with that happening.

It is the present moment which is being given to us, and that moment is the nearest we can get here to experiencing eternity. In it alone we move with a measure of freedom since each moment brings the opportunity for obedience, for gratitude and for doing something for God. And each moment brings the grace of God for the doing of what has to be done and the enduring of what must be endured.

PATRICK HANKEY (1886–?)
Dean of Ely Cathedral, England

What water flowing by is, so is our life and everything happening in it. . . . I was a baby and this passed by. I was an adolescent and this passed by. I was a youth and this left me. I was a mature and strong man, and I am no more. Now my hair is white and I am weary with old age but this is also passing by. I approach my end and I will go the way of all flesh. I was born in order to die. I die in order to live. "Remember me, O Lord, in your kingdom!"

What happened to me happens to everybody. I was in good health and ill, again in health and again ill. All that passed by. I was happy and unhappy. Time passed by and with it everything disappeared. I was honored; the time came when honor left me. People honored and revered me. Time passed and I see this no more. I was sometimes gay and sometimes sad. I was joyful and I wept. The same happens to me also now. Days go by and with them sadness and gaiety, joy and weeping. People praised and glorified me, then they blamed and abused me. Those who praised me, the same damned me and those who abused me also praised me. Time passed by and all that disappeared. Praise and abuse, glory and dishonor, all that passed by. . . .

TIKHON OF ZADONSK (1792–1866)
Russian bishop and spiritual writer

Time is precious, but its value is unknown to us. We shall attain this knowledge when we can no longer profit by it. Our friends require it of us as though it was nothing; and we give it to them in the same manner. It is often a burden to us; we know not what to do with it. The day will come when a quarter of an hour will appear of more value, and more desirable, than all the riches of the universe. . . .

It is true we cannot every moment perform great actions, but we may do such as are in accordance with our state. When we are not called to any outward employment, to be silent or to pray is to offer much to God. A disappointment, a contradiction, a complaint, a vexation, or unjust accusation received and suffered in the sight of God is as valuable as time spent in prayer.

FRANÇOIS FÉNELON (1651–1715)
French Roman Catholic archbishop of Cambrai

We have neither memory of death, nor attention on ourselves, we do not question ourselves about how we spend our time, but live heedlessly.

ABBA DOROTHEUS (sixth century)
Saint, ascetical writer, and founder of a Palestinian monastery

Never delay in undertaking any work you have to do, for the first brief delay will lead to a second, more prolonged one, and the second to a third, still longer, and so on. Thus work begins too late and is not done in its proper time, or else is abandoned altogether, as something too burdensome. Having once tasted the pleasure of inaction, you begin to like and prefer it to action. In satisfying this desire, you will little by little form a habit of inaction and laziness, in which the passion for doing nothing will possess you to such an extent that you will cease even to see how incongruous and criminal it is; except perhaps when you weary of this laziness, and are again eager to take up your work. Then you will see with shame how negligent you have been and how many necessary works you have neglected, for the sake of the empty and useless "doing what you like."

Scarcely perceptible at first, this negligence permeates everything and not only poisons the will, planting in it aversion to all kind of effort and all forms of spiritual doing and obedience, but also blinds the mind, and prevents it from seeing all the folly and falsehood of the arguments which support this disposition of will; for it hinders the mind from presenting to the consciousness the sound reasonings, which would have the power of moving the slothful will to perform the necessary work as quickly and diligently as possible, without putting it off till another time. For it is not enough to perform the work quickly; each thing has to be done in its proper time, as required by its nature, and needs to be performed with full attention and care, to make it as perfect as possible.

UNSEEN WARFARE

There is absolutely no need to run after time to catch it. Whether you are intent on the next minute coming your way, or whether you are completely unaware of it, it will come your way. We can simply wait for it to be there, and we can perfectly well be completely stable and yet move in time, because it is time that moves.

The mistake we often make with our inner life is to imagine that if we hurry we will be in our future sooner—when we continually try to live an inch ahead of ourselves we do not feel the absurdity of it. Yet that is what prevents us from being completely in the present moment.

What can we do? This is the first exercise. It can be done at moments when nothing pulls you backward or forward and when you can use five minutes, three minutes, or half an hour for leisure and for doing nothing. You sit down and say, "I am seated, I am doing nothing. I will do nothing for five minutes," and then relax, and continually throughout this time (one or two minutes is the most you will be able to endure to begin with) realize, "I am here in the presence of God, in my own presence and in the presence of all that is around me, just still, moving nowhere."

You must further decide that within these minutes, you will not be pulled out of it by the telephone, or by a sudden upsurge of energy that prompts you to do at once what you have left undone for the past ten years.

ANTHONY BLOOM (1914–)
Russian Orthodox monk and metropolitan of Sourozh

Therefore be attentive to time and the way you spend it. Nothing is more precious. This is evident when you recall that in one tiny moment heaven may be gained or lost. God, the master of time, never gives the future. He gives only the present, moment by moment, for this is the law of the created order, and God will not contradict himself in his creation. Time is for man, not man for time. God, Lord of nature, will never anticipate man's choices which follow one after another in time. Man will not be able to excuse himself at the last judgment, saying to God: "You overwhelmed me with the future when I was only capable of living in the present."

UNKNOWN ENGLISH MYSTIC (14th century)
The Cloud of Unknowing

The earthly man already lives in eternity. The true state of affairs is not that this fleeting, temporal existence with all its decisions is pure here-and-now, followed by the reward or punishment of an eternal beyond as a second existence. Rather, the two are one; one is the reverse side of the other: time is concealed eternity, and eternity is revealed time. The transfigured paradisiacal world is none other than the one in which we presently live, only contemplated with different eyes.

HANS URS VON BALTHASAR (1905–1998)
Swiss Roman Catholic theologian

The Now in which God created the first human being and the Now in which the last human being will disappear and the Now in which I am speaking—are all the same in God, and there is only one Now.

MEISTER ECKHART (1260–1327)
German Dominican mystic and theologian

CYCLE SEVEN

THE HEART
OF STRUGGLE

There is unanimity among Christian teachers that we must consciously accept sacrifice, and that what we must sacrifice chiefly is our own self-will. This cycle tracks the path from pride to humility, and to the point where "infinite loss is infinite gain."

People say: "O Lord, how much I wish that I stood as well with God, that I had as much devotion and peace in God as others have, I wish that it were so with me!" Or, "I should like to be poor," or else, "Things will never go right for me till I am in this place or that, or till I act one way or another. I must go and live in a strange land, or in a hermitage, or in a cloister."

In fact, this is all about yourself, and nothing else at all. This is just self-will, only you do not know it or it does not seem so to you. There is never any trouble that starts in you that does not come from your own will, whether people see this or not. We can think what we like, that a man ought to shun one thing or pursue another—places and people and ways of life and environments and undertakings—that is not the trouble, such ways of life or such matters are not what impedes you. It is what you are in these things that causes the trouble, because in them you do not govern yourself as you should.

Therefore, make a start with yourself, and abandon yourself. Truly, if you do not begin by getting away from yourself, wherever you run to, you will find obstacles and trouble wherever it may be. People who seek peace in external things—be it in places or ways of life or people or activities or solitude or poverty or degradation—however great such a thing may be or whatever it may be, still it is all nothing and gives no peace. People who seek in that way are doing it all wrong; the further they wander, the less will they find what they are seeking. They go around like someone who has lost his way; the further he goes, the more lost he is. Then what ought he to do? He ought to begin by forsaking himself, because then he has forsaken everything. Truly, if a man renounced a kingdom or the whole world but held on to himself, he would not have renounced anything.

MEISTER ECKHART (1260–1327)
German Dominican mystic and theologian

While we are shut up in ourselves, we are exposed to the contradictions of men; our passions clash with those of our neighbors; the sensibility of our passions, and the jealousy of our pride, render us open to attacks from all sides; there is not peace or hope in ourselves while we are at the mercy of a troop of covetous and insatiable desires, and while we know not how to content this *me*, that is so jealous, so delicate, and so suspicious of everything that touches it.

Hence it comes to pass that in our relations with our neighbor we are like a sick man who has languished a long time in bed: there is no part of his body that is not sore to the touch: diseased self-love is so softened by itself it cannot bear to be touched without crying out. To this delicacy add the rudeness of a neighbor, so full of imperfections, that he does not even know them himself, and likewise the reproaches of that neighbor against our imperfections which are as great as his. Thus do the sons of Adam punish each other: behold in all nations, all towns, all communities, all families, and even between two friends, the martyrdom of self-love.

The remedy by which peace is to be found is to come out of self. We must renounce it, and sacrifice all self-interest, that we may no longer have anything more to love, to fear, or to be solicitous about. It is then we taste the true peace reserved for *men of a good will;* that is to say, for such as have no other will but that of God, which becomes theirs.

FRANÇOIS FÉNELON (1651–1715)
French Roman Catholic archbishop of Cambrai

The intellectual and physical parts are in and of themselves sinless, and natural to us; but the man who has been shaped by the intellectual, or even worse, by the carnal, is not sinless. He is guilty of granting supremacy within himself to something that was not meant for supremacy, and that is supposed to be in a subordinate position. It turns out that although the intellectual is natural, for a man to be intellectual is unnatural; in the same way carnality is natural, but for a man to be carnal is unnatural. The error here is in the exclusive predominance of that which is supposed to be subordinate.

When the spiritual reigns supreme in someone, then although this is his exclusive character and attitude, he does not err. This is because, in the first place, spirituality is the *norm* of human life, and so as a result, being spiritual, he is a real person, whereas the intellectual or carnal man is not a real person.

Secondly, no matter how spiritual someone is, he cannot help but give the intellectual and carnal their rightful place; he maintains just a little of them, in subordination to the spirit. Let intellectuality be not too broad within him (in scientific knowledge, arts and other subjects), and let carnality be firmly restrained—then he is a real, whole person. But the man of intellect (the expert, the connoisseur, the shrewd man)—and even more so the carnal man—is not a real person, no matter how appealing he seems outwardly. He is foolish. Hence the simple man who fears God is superior to the man who is diverse and elegant, but who does not have among his goals and yearnings the pleasing of God. . . .

From this you see that according to natural purpose, man must live in the spirit, subordinate everything to the spirit, be penetrated by the spirit in all that is of the soul, and even more so in all that is physical—and beyond these, in the outward things too, that is, family and social life. This is the norm!

THEOPHAN THE RECLUSE (1815–1894)
Russian Orthodox monk and saint

There is nothing we can offer to God more precious than our good will. But what is good will? To have good will is to experience concern for someone else's adversities as if they were your own; to give thanks for our neighbour's prosperity as for our own; to believe that another person's loss is our own, and also that another's gain is ours; to love a friend in God, and to bear with an enemy out of love; to do to no one what we do not want to suffer ourselves, and to refuse to no one what we rightly want for ourselves; to choose to help a neighbour who is in need, not only to the whole extent of our ability, but even beyond our means. What offering is richer, what offering is more substantial than this one? What we are offering to God on the altar of our hearts is the sacrifice of ourselves!

GREGORY THE GREAT (d. 604)
Pope Gregory I, doctor of the church and saint

Far too often the Cross is presented for our adoration, not so much as a sublime end to be attained by our transcending ourselves, but as a symbol of sadness, of limitation and repression. . . . This ends by conveying the impression that the kingdom of God can only be established in mourning, and by thwarting and going against the current of man's aspirations and energies.

In its highest and most general sense, the doctrine of the Cross is that to which all men adhere who believe that the vast movement and agitations of human life opens on to a road which leads somewhere, and that that road climbs upward. Life has a term: therefore it imposes a particular direction, orientated, in fact, towards the highest possible spiritualisation by means of the greatest possible effort. To admit that group of fundamental principles is already to range oneself among the disciples—distant perhaps, and implicit, but nevertheless real—of Christ crucified.

PIERRE TEILHARD DE CHARDIN (1881–1955)
French paleontologist and Jesuit priest

We must be continually sacrificing our own wills, as opportunity serves, to the will of others; bearing, without notice, sights and sounds that annoy us; setting about this or that task, when we had far rather be doing something very different; persevering in it, often, when we are thoroughly tired of it; keeping company for duty's sake, when it would be a great joy to us to be by ourselves; besides all the trifling untoward accidents of life; bodily pain and weakness long continued, and perplexing us often when it does not amount to illness; losing what we value, missing what we desire; disappointments in other persons, willfulness, unkindness, ingratitude, folly, in cases where we least expect it.

JOHN KEBLE (1792–1866)

English priest

Do not condemn or think hardly of those who cannot see just as you see, or who judge it their duty to contradict you, whether in a great thing or a small. I fear some of us have thought hardly of others merely because they contradicted what we affirmed. All this tends to division; and, by every thing of this kind, we are teaching them an evil lesson against ourselves.

O, beware of touchiness, of testiness, not bearing to be spoken to; starting at the least word; and flying from those who do not implicitly receive mine or another's sayings!

Expect contradiction and opposition together with crosses of various kinds. Consider the words of Saint Paul: "To you it is given, in the behalf of Christ [for his sake, as a fruit of his death and intercession for you,] not only to believe but also to suffer for his sake."

It is given! God gives you this opposition or reproach; it is a fresh token of his love. And will you disown the Giver; or spurn his gift, and count it a misfortune? Will you not rather say, "Father, the hour is come that thou shouldst be glorified: now thou gives thy child to suffer something for thee: do with me according to thy will?" Know that these things, far from being hindrances to the work of God, or to your soul, unless by your own fault, are not only unavoidable in the course of providence, but profitable, yea, necessary for you. Therefore receive them from God—not from chance—with willingness, with thankfulness. Receive them from men with humility, meekness, yieldingness, gentleness, sweetness. Why should not even your outward appearance and manner be soft?

JOHN WESLEY (1703–1791)
English founder of the Methodist Movement

Many people feel unaware of any guidance, unable to discern or understand the signals of God; not because the signals are not given, but because the mind is too troubled, clouded, and hurried to receive them. "He who is in a hurry," said St. Vincent de Paul, "delays the things of God." But when those who are at least attempting to live the life of the spirit, and have consequently become more or less sensitive to its movements, are confronted by perplexing choices, and seem to themselves to have no clear light, they will often become aware, if they will wait in quietness, of a subtle yet insistent pressure in favor of the path they should take. The early friends were accustomed to trust implicitly in indications of this kind, and were usually justified. Where there is no such pressure, then our conduct should be decided by charity and common sense, qualities given to us by God in order that they may be used.

Next, we are obliged to face the question as to how the demand of modern psychology for complete self-expression, as the condition of a full and healthy personal life, can be reconciled with the discipline, choice, and sacrifice that are essential to a spiritual life; and with this the allegation made by many psychologists that the special experiences of such a spiritual life may be dismissed as disguised wish-fulfillments. In the first place, the complete expression of everything of which we are capable—the whole psychological zoo living within us, as well as the embryonic beginnings of artist, statesman or saint—means chaos, not character. We must select in order to achieve; we can only develop some faculties at the expense of others.

This is just as true for the person of action or of science as it is for the person of religion. But where this discipline is consciously accepted for a purpose greater than ourselves, it will result in a far greater strength and harmony, a far more real personality, than the policy of so-called self-expression. As to the attempt to discredit the spiritual life as a form of wish-fulfillment, this has to meet the plain fact that the real life of the spirit has little to do with emotional enjoyments, even of the loftiest kind. Indeed, it offers few attractions to the natural man; nor does it set out to satisfy his personal desires. The career to which it calls him is one that he would seldom have chosen for himself. It proceeds by way of much discipline and renunciation, often of many sufferings, to a total abandonment to God's purpose that leaves no opening even for the most subtle expressions of self-love.

EVELYN UNDERHILL (1875–1941)

English writer on mysticism

Devotion is neither private nor public prayer; but prayers, whether private or public, are particular parts or instances of devotion. Devotion signifies a life given, or devoted, to God.

He, therefore, is the devout man, who lives no longer to his own will, or the way and spirit of the world, but to the sole will of God, who considers God in everything, who serves God in everything, who makes all the parts of his common life parts of piety, by doing everything in the Name of God, and under such rules as are conformable to His glory.

WILLIAM LAW (1686–1761)
English contemplative and cleric

XXVII. *How we are to take Christ's words when he bade us to forsake all things; and wherein the union with the Divine Will lies.*

Now, according to what has been said, you must observe that when we say, as Christ also says, that we ought to resign and forsake all things, this is not to be taken in the sense that we are neither to do nor to plan anything; for a man must always have something to do and to work at as long as he lives. But we are to understand by it that the union with God lies not in any person's powers, in his working or abstaining, perceiving or knowing, nor in that of all the creatures taken together.

Now what is this union? It is that we should be of a truth purely, simply, and wholly at one with the One Eternal Will of God, or, altogether without will, so that the created will should flow out into the Eternal Will, and be swallowed up and lost within, so that the Eternal Will alone should do, and leave undone, in us.

Now mark what may help or further us towards this end. Behold, neither exercises, nor words, nor works, nor any creature nor creature's work, can do this. Because of this, we must not imagine or suppose that any words, works, or exercises, any skill or cunning or any created thing can help or serve us here. Therefore we must suffer those things to be what they are, and enter into the union with God. Yet outward things must be, and we must do and refrain so far as is necessary, especially we must sleep and wake, walk and stand still, speak and be silent, and much more of the like. These must go on so long as we live.

XXVIII. *How after a union with the Divine Will, the inward man stands immovable, while the outer man is moved hither and thither.*

Now, when this union truly comes to pass and becomes established, the inward man stands henceforward immovable in this union; and God suffers the outward man to be moved hither and thither, from this to that, among things necessary and right. So that the outward man says in sincerity, "I have no will to be or not to be, to live or die, to know or not to know, to do or to leave undone and the like; but I am ready for all that is to be, or ought to be, and obedient to whatever I have to do or to suffer."

And thus the outward man has no motive or purpose, but only to do his part to further the Eternal Will. For it is perceived truly that the inward man shall stand immovable, and that it is necessary for the outward man to be moved. And if the inward man have any motive in the actions of the outward man, he says only that such things must be and ought to be, as are ordained by the Eternal Will. And where God Himself dwells in a person, it is this way, as we plainly see in Christ.

Moreover, where there is this union, which is the offspring of a Divine Light and dwells in its beams, there is no spiritual pride or irreverent spirit, but boundless humility, and a lowly broken heart; also an honest blameless walk, justice, peace, content, and all that is of virtue. Where they are not, there is no right union, as we have said. For just as neither this thing nor that can bring about or further this union, so there is nothing which has power to frustrate or hinder it, save the person himself with his self-will, that does him this great wrong. Of this be well assured.

UNKNOWN GERMAN MYSTIC (14th century)

Theologica Germanica

The reason why things are not rightly discerned by us is that at their first appearance we attach to them either love or hatred. Because of this the understanding is darkened, and cannot rightly judge what they are. . . .

When any object happens to be set before you, look at it with the understanding and consider it maturely before you are moved by hatred, if it is something contrary to your natural inclinations, or by love, if it brings you delight, either to desire it or to reject it.

That this error may not be found in you, take care as much as possible always to keep your will purified and free from inordinate attachment of any kind.

For then the understanding, not being encumbered with passions, is free and clear, and is able to know the truth, and to perceive the evil which may lie hidden under false pleasing, and to the good which may be covered by the appearance of evil.

LORENZO SCUPOLI (1530–1610)

Italian Roman Catholic priest

Our greatest protection is self-knowledge, and to avoid the delusion that we are seeing ourselves when we are in reality looking at something else. This is what happens to those who do not scrutinize themselves. What they see is strength, beauty, reputation, political power, abundant wealth, pomp, self-importance, bodily stature, a certain grace of form or the like, and they think that this is what they are.

Such persons make very poor guardians of themselves: because of their absorption in something else they overlook what is their own and leave it unguarded. How can a person protect what he does not know? The most secure protection for our treasure is to know ourselves: each one must know himself as he is, and distinguish himself from all that he is not, that he may not unconsciously be protecting something else instead of himself.

GREGORY OF NYSSA (330–395)
Saint, bishop of Nyssa, and Cappadocian father of the church

None Can Harm Him Who Does Not Injure Himself.

It is the common assumption of mankind, which in the course of centuries has taken deep root in the minds of the multitude, that "all things have been turned upside down," that the human race is full of much confusion and many are they who every day are being wronged, insulted, subjected to violence and injury, the weak by the strong, the poor by the rich: and as it is impossible to number the waves of the sea, so is it impossible to reckon the multitude of those who are the victims of intrigue, insult, and suffering; and neither the correction of law, nor the fear of being brought to trial, nor anything else can arrest this pestilence and disorder, but the evil is increasing every day, and the groans, and lamentations, and weeping of the sufferers are universal; and the judges who are appointed to reform such evils, themselves intensify the tempest, and inflame the disorder, and hence many of the more senseless and despicable kind, seized with a new kind of frenzy, accuse the providence of God, and when they see the forbearing man often violently seized, racked, and oppressed, and the audacious, impetuous, low and low-born man waxing rich, and invested with authority, and becoming formidable to many, and inflicting countless troubles upon the more moderate, and this perpetrated both in town and country, and desert, on sea and land.

This discourse of ours directly opposes these allegations, asserting a contention which is new, as I said at the beginning, and contrary to opinion, yet useful and true, and profitable to those who will give heed to it and be persuaded by it. What I undertake is to prove (only make no commotion) that no one of those who are wronged is wronged by another, but experiences this injury at his own hands.

JOHN CHRYSOSTOM (345–407)
Father of the Eastern church, saint, and bishop of Constantinople

Perhaps this text in the Psalm strikes one of you, "He who loves wickedness hates his own soul." But I say he hates his body too. . . . this hatred of body and soul is not so much found in the form of a feeling; rather it is revealed by its effects. Thus the madman hates his body when he lays hands on himself when his powers of rational thought are asleep. . . . In the same way we have lacerated ourselves and given ourselves ulcers on our unhappy souls by our own hands—except that in a spiritual creature it is more serious because its nature is finer and so more difficult to mend. We have not done it in a spirit of enmity, but in a stupor of inner insensibility. The absent mind does not notice the internal damage, for it is not looking inward, but perhaps concentrating on its stomach—or beneath the stomach. The minds of some men are on their plates, of others in their pockets. "Where your treasure is," he says, "there is your heart" (Mt 6:21). Is it surprising if a soul does not feel its wound when it is not noticing what is happening to it, and is somewhere else, far away? The time will come when it will return to itself and realize how cruelly it has eviscerated itself.

BERNARD OF CLAIRVAUX (1091–1153)
Cistercian abbot, saint, and theologian

The reason for all disturbance is that no one blames himself.

Let us see, my brothers, why it is that sometimes when a person hears words that hurt him he can let them pass by without any bother as if he had not heard them, whilst at other times, as soon as he hears them he is troubled and upset. My question is—what is the cause of this difference? Is there one reason for this or are there many? I think there are several, but there is one in particular which is the source of all the others, as the saying goes: it results from the state of mind the person is in at that particular time.

For example, when someone is caught as he comes from prayer or contemplation, he is then in the best of dispositions and is able to put up with his brother and remain undisturbed. It may be that he has great affection for the other and so, out of love, puts up patiently with everything. . . .

The brother who insults us may upset us either because we are not at that moment in the right mood or because we dislike him intensely. There are many other reasons as well which are described in different ways. But, if we examine the matter closely, we can say that the reason for all disturbance is that no one blames himself.

This is the reason for every taking of offense and upset. This is why at times it is impossible to find peace of soul. Nor should we be surprised at this, since it is the teaching of spiritual men that there is no other way of peace for us. And yet we hope for peace but do not follow their teaching. Or, we believe that we are on the right path while we are irritated by everything and cannot bear to take any blame upon ourselves.

That is the way things are. A man may indeed accomplish innumerable good deeds, but if he does not master this he will never attain peace. Instead, he will always oppress himself and oppress others and his labors will go for nothing.

Whenever some sort of inconvenience or penalty or dishonor or trouble of any kind happens to one who is ready to find fault with himself, he bears it with a smile, considers that he deserves it and so is not in the least put out by it. Who could be more peaceful than such a person?

Perhaps someone will object, "But what if a brother should vex me and after examining myself I find that I have given him no cause, how then can I blame myself?"

But surely if a person were to examine himself carefully in the light of the fear of God he will never find that he is blameless. He will see that he has provided an occasion by some action or word or attitude. Even if such a one finds himself guiltless in all these ways at the present time, it is quite likely that at some other time he has vexed his brother by the very same deed or by some other. Or he may have upset another brother. Hence he deservedly suffers for that offense or for many other offenses that he has committed elsewhere.

Another may ask why he should accuse himself when he has been sitting in peace and quiet and a brother has come up and upset him with some hurtful or insulting word. Since he is not going to put up with that, he feels that it is reasonable for him to be annoyed and upset. For, if the other had not intruded and spoken and made trouble he would not have sinned. This is indeed ridiculous and it is bad logic. Surely that brother did not inject the passion of anger into him by saying what he did? Rather he revealed the passion already within him, so that if he so wishes he may repent of it. This brother is like early wheat, outwardly bright and shining and when it is crushed its rottenness appears.

So this man who sits in peace and quiet, as he thinks, has within him a passion he does not see. One hurtful word spoken by another who happens by and immediately all the poison and rottenness within gushes out. If he wishes to gain mercy let him repent and purify himself and make serious efforts to do better and he will see that instead of insults he should give thanks to that brother as one responsible for bringing him such a benefit.

ABBA DOROTHEUS (sixth century)
Saint, ascetical writer, and founder of a Palestinian monastery

There are some persons who are very subtle in their use of words and skillful in elucidating lofty matters and yet have not attained an enlightened state or a generous love toward all. In order that such persons might come to know themselves as they are and might also be recognized by others, I wish to make three points. Through the first they can come to know themselves and through the other two any intelligent person will be able to recognize them.

The first point is this: Whereas an enlightened person, by reason of a divine light, is simple, stable, and free of curious reflections, these persons are complex, unstable, and full of subtle reasonings. They have no taste for interior unity or for that rest which comes from being devoid of images. Through these signs they can come to know themselves.

The second point is this: Whereas an enlightened person has a wisdom infused into him by God, whereby he knows the truth distinctly and effortlessly, this other kind of person has subtle insights to which he cleverly turns his imagination and his powers of reflection and reason. But there is neither depth nor liberality in the way he presents his teaching, which instead is complicated, esoteric, and abstruse, so as to trouble, hinder, and lead astray those who are interiorly fervent. This teaching neither leads nor directs a person to unity but only shows him how to make clever observations in diversity. People who teach in this way hold stubbornly to their doctrine and opinions, as though no other opinion were as good as their own. They are unpracticed in all the virtues and careless of them, and they are spiritually proud in all they are and do. This is the second point.

The third point is this: Whereas an enlightened, loving person flows forth with a charity that is common to everyone whether in heaven or on earth, as you have already heard, this other kind of person sets himself apart in all things. He thinks he is the wisest and best person alive and wants others to think highly of himself and of his teaching. He thinks that all those whom he does not himself teach or counsel, as well as all who do not follow his way or look to him as their master, are certain to go astray. He is tolerant and even lax when it comes to fulfilling his own needs and thinks little of minor faults. He is neither righteous nor humble nor generous; he does not serve the poor and is not fervent or zealous; he does not feel any affection for the things of God and knows neither God nor himself in the way of true virtue. This is the third point.

You should note and reflect on these things and avoid them both in yourself and in all those persons in whom you recognize them.

JAN VAN RUUSBROEC (1293–1381)
Flemish mystic and theologian

What arrogance is greater, what pride is more dangerous than to think that you alone know what is right in one's situation, when human frailty is completely deceived either through blind love or latent ambition or some other diabolical deception of this type?

Such illusions lie in ambush in a thousand ways and place innumerable traps before the feet of the one who walks. They are conquered only by humility.

But humility in the soul is twofold: there being one in the will, another in the intellect or reason. Each type is difficult to obtain, but according to my judgment there are more problems with humility in the intellect. Nothing lies in wait more deceitfully nor flatters more falsely nor enters by stealth more imperceptibly nor is put to flight with more difficulty than the conviction that one is able to pass judgment on one's own situation. People think that no one else is able to see the individual concerns that they think they alone can consider, also in terms of experience. Each says to himself, "No one knows what belongs to a person except the spirit of the person which is within" (I Cor. 2:11).

JEAN GERSON (1363–1429)
French Roman Catholic churchman and spiritual writer

Excerpts from St. Bernard's response in a letter when asked to write about the steps of humility:

The first step of pride is curiosity. You see a monk of whom you had thought well up to now. Wherever he stands, walks, sits, his eyes begin to wander. His head is lifted. His ears are alert. . . . These unusual movements show that his soul has fallen sick. He has grown careless about his own behavior. He wastes his curiosity on other people. . . . truly, O man, if you concentrate hard on the state you are in it will be surprising if you have time for anything else. . . .

Rightly is curiosity considered the first step of pride. Unless it is checked at once it leads swiftly to the second step: levity. . . .

For the monk who instead of concentrating on himself looks curiously at others, trying to judge who is his superior and who is his inferior, will see things to envy in others and things to mock. Thus it is that the light-minded follow their roving eyes and, no longer pinned down by proper responsibility, are now swept up to the heights by pride, now cast down into the depths by envy. In one mood he is wicked, in the other vain. In both he shows himself to be proud, because he makes it a matter for self-congratulation both when he grieves to be outdone and when he is pleased to outdo others. . . . Now his words are few and grudging; now numerous and trivial; now he is laughing; now he is depressed; but there is never any reason for his mood. . . . But now let us come, not descending but teaching to the third step, foolish merriment. . . .

The monk who has come down these two steps of pride in arriving at light-mindedness by way of pride will find that the joy he is always seeking is often disturbed by sadness. . . . Anyone who thus continues to juggle joy and sorrow can enjoy only an empty happiness. This is the third step. Note the signs, which you can recognize in yourself or in anyone else.

He makes scurrilous gestures. He giggles. He preens himself. He is always joking and ready to laugh at the slightest thing. If anything has happened which would bring contempt on him or cast him down, he wipes it from his memory. And if he notes any good things in himself, he will add them up and parade them before his mind's eye. He thinks only of what he wants and he does not ask himself whether he ought to want it. At times he is seized by fits of laughter; he is unable to suppress his foolish mirth. He is like a blown-up bladder which has been punctured and squeezed. As it goes down it squeaks, and the air does not come out everywhere but whistles through the little hole in a series of shrieks. So, the monk who fills his heart with vain and scurrilous thoughts cannot let them out all at once because of the rule of silence, so they burst out at odd moments in giggles. Often he hides his face for shame, purses his lips, clenches his teeth. He still cannot stop laughing and giggling. When he puts his hand in front of his mouth the giggles can still be heard popping out through his nose.

When vanity has begun to swell the bladder and enlarge it, it makes a bigger hole for the wind to escape. Otherwise it would burst. So the monk, when he cannot express his empty merriment by laughter or gesture . . . [comes to the fourth step: boasting]. Speak or burst! . . . He hungers and thirsts for listeners to whom he can make empty boasts, to whom he can pour out all he feels, and whom he can tell what he is and how great he is. . . .

He butts in before he is asked. He does not answer other people's questions. He asks the questions himself and he answers them, and he cuts off anyone who tries to speak. If the subject is religion . . . he discusses patience, humility, and all the other virtues at great length, but in utter emptiness. . . . If the talk turns to lighter things, he is discovered to be even more talkative, because this is something he really knows about. . . . Here you have the fourth step described and named. Avoid the thing but remember the name. The same warning is appropriate to the fifth step, which I call singularity. . . .

It is not enough for him to keep the common rule of the monastery and obey his superiors. But he is more interested in seeming to be better than others than in being so. . . . He prides himself more on fasting for one day when the others are feasting than on fasting for seven days with the others. One special little prayer seems to him finer than a night spent in singing psalms. During a meal he often looks up and down the table to see if anyone is eating less than he, and then he grieves at being outdone and begins cruelly to deprive himself even of what he used to think it necessary to eat, for he fears a blow to his reputation more than the pangs of hunger. . . . He is very anxious to perform his own special exercises and lazy about performing the common ones everyone does. He lies awake in his bed and sleeps when he is in choir. . . . When the others are resting in the cloister he stays behind by himself to pray in the chapel. . . .

. . . [At the sixth step, arrogance,] he believes the praises he hears. . . . He does not give a thought to his intentions. He puts that from his mind when he accepts what others think of him. He believes that he knows more than everybody about everything else, but when they praise him he believes them rather than his own conscience. As a result he now not only shows off his piety in what he does and says, but in his own heart warmly believes that he is holier than others. . . .

He who thinks himself superior to others, how can he not presume more for himself than others? . . . [And so he arrives at the seventh step, presumption.] At meetings he must sit in the most important place. In discussions he speaks first. He comes without being invited. He interferes without being asked. He changes the rules and alters things which have been settled. What he himself has not done or ordained he considers not to have been done right, or to be arranged displeasingly. He judges the judges, and prejudges every case. If he is not promoted to be prior he thinks his abbot is jealous of him, or else deceived. If obedience imposes some humble task on him he is indignant. He disdains to do it, thinking that he ought not to be bothered with trivial things. For he feels himself to be fitted for great tasks. . . .

If you see someone answering back when he is reprimanded you will know that he has fallen to the eighth step of pride, which is self-justification. . . .

There are many ways of making excuses for sin. One person will say, "I did not do it." Another will say, "I did it, but it was the right thing to do." Another will admit that it was wrong but say, "It was not very wrong." Another will concede that it was very wrong, but he will say, "I meant well." If he is forced to admit that he did not mean well, he will say as happened in the case of Adam and Eve that someone else persuaded him to do it. . . . [And thus to the ninth step: insincere confession.] . . . some, when they defend their obvious sins, knowing that they will not be believed if they do so, make up a more subtle defense in the form of pretended self-accusation. . . . His face is downcast; his body is bowed down to the ground; people of this sort wring tears out of themselves if they can. . . . These men prefer you to think they are untruthful rather than to believe that they lack humility. . . . If the sin is so obvious that there is no way it can be hidden, they will make great play of penitence, hoping that others will admire their frank confession so much that they forget their sin; nevertheless, their penitence is in the voice not in the heart, and so they do not purge their sins. . . .

The divine mercy may look on such a man and inspire him to do what is very difficult for him, to submit without a word to the judgment of the community. But if his response is to frown and be insolent, by his rebellion he falls lower and to a more desperate state, to the tenth step, and he who before secretly despised his brothers in his arrogance now openly shows by his disobedience that he despises his superiors. . . .

When a monk spurns the agreement of his brothers and the opinion of his superior, how can he remain in the monastery without being a stumbling-block? And so after the tenth step, which is called rebellion, the monk is expelled from his monastery, or leaves it, and at once he is at the eleventh stage . . . [freedom to sin]. When he stands there, the monk who recognizes and fears no superior and who has no brothers whom he may respect enjoys doing what he wants the more safely as he does it the more freely. . . . But even if he does not now fear his brothers or the abbot, he is not yet entirely without awe of judgment. Reason, still murmuring faintly, puts this awe in front of him and he still hesitates a little before committing certain sins. Like someone entering a river, he does not plunge, but goes step by step into the torrent of vices.

And after he finds that his first sins go unpunished by the terrible judgment of God, he freely seeks to enjoy again the pleasures he has experienced. Habit binds him as desire revives, and conscience slumbers. . . . [At the twelfth step, habitual sin,] he cannot tell good from evil now. Nothing holds him back, in mind, hand, or foot, from wrong thoughts, plans, or action. Whatever is in his heart comes to his mouth or his hand. He conceives an idea. He chatters about it. He carries it out. . . .

Those in the middle of the climb or the descent are weary and constrained, now struck by fear of the pain of hell, now held back by the force of old habits. Only those at the top or the bottom run unimpeded and without strain. . . . Truth gives one of them a sense of security, the other gets it from blindness. The twelfth step, then, can be called habitual sin, because the fear of God is lost and replaced by contempt. . . .

You are perhaps saying, brother Geoffrey, that I have done something different from what you asked and I promised, and instead of writing about the steps of humility I have written about the steps of pride. I reply, "I can teach only what I have learned. I did not think I could fittingly describe the steps up when I know more about going down than going up." . . . But if you look carefully, you will find there the way up. If on your way to Rome you meet a man coming from there and ask him the way, how can he do better than show you the way he has come? . . . Similarly, in these steps of our descent you will perhaps find steps up. As you climb you will read them better in your heart than in this book.

BERNARD OF CLAIRVAUX (1091–1153)

Cistercian abbot, saint, and theologian

Living in religion (as I can speak from experience) if one is not in a right course of prayer and other exercises between God and our soul, one's nature grows much worse than ever it would have been if one had lived in the world.

For pride and self-love find means to strengthen themselves exceedingly in religion if the soul is not in a course that may teach

her and procure her true humility. For by the corrections and contradictions of the will (which cannot be avoided by any living in a
religious community) I find my heart grown, as I may say, as hard
as a stone; and nothing would have been able to soften it but by
being put into a course of prayer, by which the soul tends toward
God and learns of Him the lesson of truly humbling herself.

DAME GERTRUDE MORE (1606–1633)
English Benedictine nun and spiritual writer

Humility is just as much the opposite of self-abasement as it is of
self-exaltation. To be humble is *not to make comparisons*. Secure in its
reality, the self is neither better nor worse, bigger nor smaller, than
anything else in the universe. It *is*—is nothing, yet at the same time
one with everything. It is in this sense that humility is absolute self-
effacement.

To be nothing in the self-effacement of humility, yet, for the
sake of the task, to embody *its* whole weight and importance in
your bearing, as the one who has been called to undertake it. To
give to people, works, poetry, art, what the self can contribute, and
to take, simply and freely, what belongs to it by reason of its identity. Praise and blame, the winds of success and adversity, blow over
such a life without leaving a trace or upsetting its balance.

Towards this, so help me, God—

DAG HAMMARSKJÖLD (1905–1961)
Swedish statesman and secretary-general of the United Nations

Let us then humbly and pragmatically put into practice the advice
Saint Bernard rightly gives in his sermon on the Canticle, "I do not

want you to compare yourself to those greater or lesser than you, to a particular few, not even to a single person, etc." For we do not even know for sure what state we are in or what shall become of us tomorrow—much less can we know the truth about others. We are all created by one Creator, who establishes the members of the Body of Christ not according to our judgments but according to his own knowledge.

GUIGO DE PONTE (d. 1297)
Carthusian monk and spiritual writer

The message of Christ to Man was simple: "Be thyself." That is the secret of Christ . . . and so he who would lead a Christian life is he who is perfectly and absolutely himself. He may be a great poet, or a great man of science, or a young student at a university, or one who watches sheep upon a moor; or a maker of dramas, like Shakespeare, or a thinker about God, like Spinoza; or a child who plays in a garden, or a fisherman who throws his net into the sea.

It does not matter what he is, as long as he realizes the perfection of the soul that is within him. All imitation in morals and in life is wrong. Father Damien was Christlike when he went out to live with the lepers because in such service he realized fully what was best in him. But he was not more Christlike than Wagner when he realized his soul in music; or than Shelley, when he realized his soul in song. There is no one type for man. And while to the claim of charity a man may yield and yet be free, to the claims of conformity no man may yield and remain free at all.

OSCAR WILDE (1854–1900)
English playwright

... The most ruinous evasion of all is to be hidden in the crowd in an attempt to escape God's supervision of him as an individual, in an attempt to get away from hearing God's voice as an individual. Long ago, Adam attempted this same thing when his evil conscience led him to imagine that he could hide himself among the trees. It may even be easier and more convenient, and more cowardly to hide oneself among the crowd in the hope that God should not be able to recognize one from the other. But in eternity each shall render account as an individual. That is, eternity will demand of him that he shall have lived as an individual. Eternity will draw out before his consciousness, all that he has done as an individual, he who had forgotten himself in noisy self-conceit. In eternity, he shall be brought to account strictly as an individual, he who intended to be in the crowd where there should be no such strict reckoning. Each one shall render account to God as an individual. The King shall render account as an individual; and the most wretched beggar, as an individual. No one may pride himself at being more than an individual, and no one despondently think that he is not an individual. ...

SØREN KIERKEGAARD (1813–1855)
Danish theologian

Be sensible of your wants, that you may be sensible of your treasures.
He is most like God that is sensible of everything. Did you not from all Eternity want some one to give you a Being? Did you not want one to give you a Glorious Being? Did you not from all Eternity want some one to give you infinite Treasures? And some one to give you Spectators, Companions, Enjoyers? Did you not want

a Deity to make them sweet and honorable by His infinite Wisdom? What you wanted from all Eternity, be aware of to all Eternity. Let your wants be present from everlasting.

Is not this a strange life to which I call you? Asking you to be present with things that were before the world was made? And at once present even like God with infinite wants and infinite Treasures: Be present with your want of a Deity, and you shall be present with the Deity. You shall adore and admire Him, enjoy and prize Him; believe in Him, and Delight in Him, see Him to be the Fountain of all your joys, and the Head of all your Treasures.

THOMAS TRAHERNE (1637–1674)

English cleric and poet

And so the new year is coming. A year like all the rest. A year of trouble and disappointment with myself and others. . . . We lament and become melancholy if in the prospect of a new year we think we can see nothing but the demolition of the house of our life, which in reality is being quietly built up for eternity behind this scaffolding that is put up and taken down again. No, the coming year is not a year of disappointments or a year of pleasing illusions. It is God's year. The year in which decisive hours are approaching me quietly and unobtrusively, and the fullness of my time is coming to enter my life. Shall I notice those hours? Or will they remain empty? Because to me they will seem too small, too humble and commonplace? Outwardly, of course, they will not look any different from anyone's everyday moments of good works and proper omissions. Consequently I may overlook them—the slight patience which makes life slightly more tolerable for those around me; the omission of an excuse; taking the risk of building on the good faith of those whom I would be inclined to mistrust because I think I have had unfortunate experiences with them before; genuine acceptance of there being good grounds for someone else's criticism of me (how hard this is when something is at stake which involves my self-esteem); to allow an injury done to me to die away in myself, without prolonging it by complaints, rancour, bitterness, and revenge; fidelity in prayer which is not rewarded with "consolations" or "religious experience"; the attempt to love those who get on my nerves (through their fault, of course), and not merely to put up with them by swallowing one's rage out of calculated egoism; the attempt to see in someone else's "stupidity" a different kind of intelligence which is not mine but need not necessarily be stupid on that account; the tolerance which does not pay back another's intolerance in kind; the endeavor not to trade on one's virtues as a charter for one's faults; a prompt will to improve oneself when we see sins in others and would dearly like to reform them; the firm conviction, firmly maintained against oneself, that we very willingly and very easily delude ourselves and leave a number of faults and pettinesses undisclosed which would strike us as patently obvious in anyone else; the suppressed complaint and the self-praise omitted and many other things which would only be really good if one practised them constantly, though it is true that it is better to do something than not to do anything at all, for one cannot manage everything at once.

We only need seriously to try to do such commonplace everyday things. Then they become terrible. . . . one has the impression of paying out more than one gets back. It brings in no returns, neither in the world, nor by a good conscience or inner recognition for so much self-made virtue; for even that loses its attraction. And then in all these trifles that go with a decent attitude (which fundamentally is very Christian, at least without realizing it), the point comes where morality actually becomes really moral and religious, the point where it becomes the gate to the infinite and eternal. Where one is rewarded by nothing more, that is, by nothing specific, whether outside or within, then in truth God is present as that "nothing," and infinite loss is infinite gain. . . .

One pays for it in life with oneself. God is not to be had for less. We ought to learn this mysticism of everyday life. Only then does fulfillment of the law out of respect for the prescriptions of the supreme government of the universe (which can never be fully achieved and which simply irritates and makes one resentful like an overworked laborer) become voluntary striving in the spirit of the children of God. Such mysticism of everyday life is grace. Wholly and entirely grace.

But that of course does not mean that there is nothing to do but impiously to wait until God's grace compels one against one's will. It "compels" in fact by bestowing the good will, and the good will thus given by God, viewed from below, is the great and honest endeavor of the human being himself. And this has to be carried out properly, by learning to form a taste for eternity in time by practice in the mysticism of daily life.

KARL RAHNER (1904–1984)

German Jesuit theologian

CYCLE EIGHT

A RECOLLECTED SPIRIT

Here we enter the realm of activity and of work, and, inevitably, come into the realm of conscience as well. John Chrysostom urges us to review our actions with an "informed conscience": Are we sensitive to the current of impulses within, or are we blind to what is motivating us? Are we aware, or are we asleep? And how can our "doing" support our "being"?

How is it that we have so many complaints, each one saying that his occupation is a hindrance to him? Dear children, know that it is not your work which gives you this disquiet. No: it is your want of order in fulfilling your work. If you performed your work in the right method, with a sole aim to God, and not to yourselves, nor sought your own gain or pleasure, but only God's glory in your work, it would be impossible that it should grieve your conscience.

JOHANNES TAULER (1300–1361)
German Dominican contemplative

In order then, my brethren, that he who loves quiet and bestows it may rest in you, make a point, as the Apostle advises, of being quiet. How will this come about? "I tell you," he says, "to attend to your own business and work with your hands." Work is a load by which our ships are given weight so hearts are given quiet and gravity, and in it the outward man finds a firm foundation and a settled condition.

To achieve the wisdom of continuing in wisdom, it is important, I think, not readily to allow restlessness or any kind of slight provocation to keep you away from any of the exercises of wisdom: the divine office, private prayer, *lectio divina*, the appointed daily labor, or the practice of silence.

Do not then be too sparing of your feet, brothers, in the ways of obedience and in the comings and goings which work demands.

GUERRIC OF IGNY (12th century)

French Cistercian abbot

A brother came to visit Abba Sylvanus at Mount Sinai. When he saw the brothers working hard, he said to the old man: "Do not work for the food that perishes. For Mary has chosen the good part."

Then the old man called his disciple: "Zachary, give this brother a book and put him in an empty cell." Now when it was three o'clock, the brother kept looking out the door to see whether someone would come to call him for the meal. But nobody called him, so he got up, went to see the old man, and asked, "Abba, didn't the brothers eat today?" The old man said, "Of course we did." Then he said, "Why didn't you call me?" The old man replied, "You are a spiritual person and do not need that kind of food, but since we are earthy, we want to eat, and that's why we work. Indeed, you have chosen the good part, reading all day long, and not wanting to eat earthy food."

When the brother heard this he repented and said, "Forgive me, Abba." Then the old man said to him, "Mary certainly needed Martha, and it is really by Martha's help that Mary is praised."

DESERT FATHERS (fourth–sixth centuries)

Some believe that leading a spiritual life means that they must reject worldly things such as riches and honors, and that they must walk continually in pious meditation about God, salvation, and eternal life, and must spend their life in prayers, and in reading the Word and pious books. This they conceive to be renouncing the world, and living after the spirit and not after the flesh. But it has been given me to know by much experience, and from conversation with the angels, that the fact is quite otherwise. No, that they who renounce the world and live after the spirit in this manner acquire a sorrowful life, which is not receptive of heavenly joy (for with every one his own life remains forever).

In order that a man may receive the life of heaven it is altogether necessary that he live in the world, and engage in its duties and occupations; and then by moral and civil life he may receive spiritual life. And in no other way can spiritual life be formed in a man, or his spirit be prepared for heaven; for to live an internal life and not at the same time an external is like dwelling in a house that has no foundation, which gradually sinks, or cracks and yawns with crevices, or totters till it falls.

EMANUEL SWEDENBORG (1688–1772)
Swedish scientist and mystical thinker

If I were able to husband all my time so thriftily as not only not to wound my soul in any minute by actual sin, but not to rob and cozen her by giving any part to pleasure or business, but bestow it all upon her in meditation, yet even in that I should wound her more, and contract another guiltiness: as the eagle were very unnatural if because she is able to do it, she should perch a whole day upon a tree, staring in contemplation of the majesty and glory of the sun, and let her young eaglets starve in the nest.

JOHN DONNE (1572–1631)
English poet and dean of St. Paul's Cathedral, London

It is not only prayer that gives God glory but work. Smiting on an anvil, sawing a beam, whitewashing a wall, driving horses, sweeping, scouring, everything gives God some glory if being in his grace you do it as your duty. To go to communion worthily gives God great glory, but a man with a dungfork in his hand, a woman with a slop-pail, give him glory too. He is so great that all things give him glory if you mean they should.

So then, my brethren, live.

GERARD MANLEY HOPKINS (1844–1889)
English Jesuit priest and poet

An old man said, "The reason why we do not make progress is because we do not know our own measure, and we do not persevere in the work we undertake, and we want to acquire virtue without labor."

DESERT FATHERS (fourth–sixth centuries)

In the midst of our work can we fulfill the duty of prayer, giving thanks to Him who has granted strength to our hands for performing our tasks, and cleverness to our minds for acquiring knowledge, and for having provided the materials, both that which is in the instruments we use and that which forms the matter of the arts in which we may be engaged, praying that the work of our hands may be directed toward its goal, the good pleasure of God.

Thus we acquire a recollected spirit—when in every action we beg from God the success of our labors and satisfy our debt of gratitude to Him who gave us the power to do the work, and when, as has been said, we keep before our minds the aim of pleasing Him. If this is not the case, how can there be consistency in the words of the Apostle bidding us to "pray without ceasing," and in those others, "we worked night and day."

BASIL THE GREAT (330–379)
Doctor of the church, saint, and bishop of Caesarea

God grant us the desire to be useful—to look upon ourselves not simply as centers of pleasure and good, but rather as instruments in Thy hands for helping and cheering and doing. We would not forget, O God, that great and wonderful as this Thy world is, it holds but dross and disappointment for them that seek simply to enjoy it. Only to those who seek life in the happiness of human souls, and in the service of those whom Thou has builded in Thine own image—only then and to them are the secret treasures of the world revealed. This is the lesson of life. May we learn it. Amen.

W. E. B. DU BOIS (1868–1963)
American scientist, scholar, and human rights advocate

Since everything holds together in a world which is on the way to unification, the spiritual success of the universe is bound up with the correct functioning of every zone of that universe and particularly with the release of every possible energy in it. Because your undertaking—which I take to be perfectly legitimate—is going well, a little more health is being spread in the human mass, and in consequence a little more liberty to act, to think, and to love. Whatever we do, we can and must do it with the strengthening and broadening consciousness of working, individually, to achieve a result which (even as a tangible reality) is required, at least indirectly, by the body of Christ. As you say yourself, to the value of the work done is added the value of the actual doing, which by its fidelity creates in us the personality expected of us by Christ.

Our own soul—in itself and in its being at the heart of the universe—is the first of the tasks calling for our efforts. Because you are doing the best you can (even though you may sometimes fail), you are forming your own self within the world, and you are helping the world to form itself around you. How, then, could you fail from time to time to feel overcome by the boundless joy of creation?

PIERRE TEILHARD DE CHARDIN (1881–1955)
French paleontologist and Jesuit priest

I must continue on the path I have taken now. If I don't do anything, if I don't study, if I don't go on seeking any longer, I am lost. Then woe is me. That is how I look at it: to continue, to continue, that is what is necessary.

But you will ask, What is your definite aim?

That aim becomes more definite, will stand out slowly and surely, as the rough draft becomes a sketch, and the sketch becomes a picture—little by little, by working seriously on it, by pondering over the idea, vague at first, over the thought that was fleeting and passing, till it gets fixed. . . .

During your visit last summer, when we walked together . . . [you said], "You have changed so much, you are not the same any longer."

Well, that is not quite true. What has changed is that my life then was less difficult and my future seemed less dark; but the inner state, my way of looking at things and my way of thinking, has not changed. If there has been any change at all, it is that I think and believe and love more seriously now what I already thought and believed and loved then.

You must not think that I disavow things—I am rather faithful in my unfaithfulness and, though changed, I am the same; my only anxiety is, How can I be of use in the world? Can't I serve some purpose and be of any good? How can I learn more and study certain subjects profoundly? You see, that is what preoccupies me constantly; and then I feel imprisoned by poverty, excluded from participating in certain work, and certain necessities are beyond my reach. That is one reason for being somewhat melancholy. And then one feels an emptiness where there might be friendship and strong and serious affections, and one feels a terrible discouragement gnawing at one's very moral energy, and fate seems to put a barrier to the instincts of affection, and a choking flood of disgust envelops one. And one exclaims, "How long, my God!"

Well, what shall I say? Do our inner thoughts ever show outwardly? There may be a great fire in our soul, yet no one ever comes to warm himself at it, and the passers-by see only a wisp of smoke coming through the chimney, and go along their way. Look here, now, what must be done? Must one tend that inner fire, have salt in oneself, wait patiently yet with how much impatience for the hour when somebody will come and sit down near it—maybe to stay? Let him who believes in God wait for the hour that will come, sooner or later.

VINCENT VAN GOGH (1853–1890)
Dutch painter

Bear with all, even as the Lord does with you. Support all in love. Give yourself to prayer without ceasing.

Bear the infirmities of all, as being a perfect athlete [in the Christian life]: where the labor is great, the gain is all the more.

IGNATIUS (30–107)
Saint and bishop of Antioch

In no case was work [among the Shakers] to be done in a hurry or under pressure, or indeed under any form of spiritual compulsion. The competitive spirit was banned because of its occult relationship with lust and violence. Overworking was frowned upon. The workers were encouraged to engage in a variety of tasks, to escape obsession and attachment. At all times their work had to be carried on at a steady, peaceful rhythm, for, as one of the Elders said: "We are not called to labor to excel, or to be like the world; but to excel them in order, union, peace and in good works—works that are truly virtuous and useful to man in this life."

Sometimes the simple Shaker maxims remind one of William Blake. This one, for instance: "Order is the creation of beauty. It is heaven's first law, and the protection of souls." Or especially this other: *"Every force evolves a form."*

THOMAS MERTON (1915–1968)

American Cistercian monk

People ought never to think too much about what they could do, but they ought to think about what they could be. If people and their way of life were only good, what they did might be a shining example. If you are just, then your works too are just. . . .

We ought not to think of building holiness upon action; we ought to build it upon a way of being, for it is not what we do that makes us holy, but we ought to make holy what we do. However holy the works may be, they do not, as works, make us at all holy; but, as we are holy and have being, to that extent we make all our works holy, be it eating, sleeping, keeping vigil or whatever it may be. It does not matter what men may do whose being is mean; nothing will come of it. Take good heed: We ought to do everything we can to be good; it does not matter so much what we may do, or what kinds of works ours may be. What matters is the ground on which the works are built.

MEISTER ECKHART (1260–1327)

German Dominican mystic and theologian

Let each of us, with an informed conscience, enter into a review of our actions, and bring our whole life before our minds for assessment and try to discern whether we are deserving of correction or punishment. When we are indignant that somebody whom we reckon guilty of various crimes escapes with impunity, let us first reflect upon our own faults, and perhaps our indignation will cease. Crimes appear great because they usually involve great or notorious matters; but once we inquire into our own actions, we will perhaps find numerous other matters for concern.

For example, to steal or to defraud a person is the same thing: the gravity of the offence is not lessened by whether it is gold or silver that is at stake. In either case it is the attitude of mind that is the root cause. A person who steals a small object will not baulk at the chance of stealing something bigger. If he does not steal, it is probably because he lacks the opportunity. A poor man who robs a poorer person would not hesitate to rob the rich given half the chance. His forebearance issues simply from weakness, not from choice. You say to me: "That ruler is robbing his subjects." But tell me now, do you not steal from others yourselves? It is no use you objecting that he is stealing vast sums of money whereas you are taking only a little.

God sees the intentions of the heart and is not interested in quantity. Just as the widow who offered two coppers was considered equal to the greatest benefactor, thanks to her good intention, so you who steal even two coppers are as guilty as thieves who rob on a bigger scale.

JOHN CHRYSOSTOM (345–407)
Father of the Eastern church, saint, and bishop of Constantinople

... The praise is not in the deed done, but in the manner of its doing. If a man visits his sick friend, and watches at his pillow for charity's sake, and because of his old affection, we approve it: but if he does it in hope of legacy, he is a vulture, and only watches for the carcase. The same things are honest and dishonest: the manner of doing them, and the end of the design, makes the separation.

Holy intention is to the actions of a man that which the soul is to the body, or form to its matter, or the root to the tree, or the sun to the world, or the fountain to a river, or the base to a pillar: for without these the body is a dead trunk, the matter is sluggish, the tree is a block, the world is darkness, the river is quickly dry, the pillar rushes into flatness and a ruin; and the action is sinful, or unprofitable and vain.

The poor farmer that gave a dish of cold water to Artaxerxes was rewarded with a golden goblet; and he that gives the same to a disciple in the name of a disciple, shall have a crown: but if he gives water in despite when the disciple needs wine or a cordial, his reward shall be to want that water to cool his tongue.

JEREMY TAYLOR (1613–1667)
English bishop and writer

There appears to be a conscience in mankind which severely punishes the man who does not somehow and at some time, at whatever cost to his pride, cease to defend and assert himself, and instead confess himself fallible and human. Until he can do this, an impenetrable wall shuts him out from the living experience of feeling himself a man among men.

Conscience, and particularly bad conscience, can be a gift from heaven; a genuine grace if used as a superior self-criticism. Self-criticism, as an introspective, discriminating activity, is indispensable to any attempt to understand one's own psychology. If you have done something which puzzles you and you ask yourself what has prompted you to such an action, you need the motive of a bad conscience and its corresponding discriminating faculty in order to discover the real motive of your behavior. It is only then that you are able to see what motives are ruling your deeds. The sting of bad conscience even spurs you on to discover things which were unconscious before and in this way you might cross the threshold of the unconscious mind and become aware of those impersonal forces that make you the unconscious instrument of the wholesale murderer in man.

C. G. JUNG (1875–1961)
Swiss psychiatrist and philosopher

I told you once that I couldn't *really* regret the past. But now I do regret it, very much. It's as if absolution and communion and prayer let us through into a place where we get a horribly clear view—a new view—so that we see all the waste, and the cost of it, and how its roots struck deep down into the earth, poisoning the springs of our own loves and other people's. Such waste, such cost in human and spiritual values. The priest says, "Go in peace, the Lord has put away sin." But of course one doesn't go in peace, and in one sense He can't put it away, it has done its work. You can't undo what's done. . . .

Perhaps I shall mind more and more, all my life. Is this what absolution and communion do to one? I see now why belief in God fades away and has to go, while one is leading a life one knows to be wrong. The two can't live together.

ROSE MACAULAY (1881–1958)
English novelist and essayist

How is it with you? Are you conscious that you have put doing right under all circumstances higher than everything else? Is that life which you are living . . . a life which has come to this point of prompt obedience to duty?

Are you conscious that at the moment you perceive the right, you perform it? Have you come to this settled conclusion: "I will never fail to follow that which is revealed to me as right, whether in little things or in great things, whether in words or deeds; whatever I see to be right, no matter what company I may be in, no matter what interest I may sacrifice, no matter what risks I may run, I will follow"? . . .

Is there this determination in you: "I will follow my moral convictions in my interests, in my pleasures, in my sympathies, in the customs of society; I will follow, not the thing which my business will allow, but what seems to me right; if I fail to do this, I shall be guilty in the sight of my own conscience and before God"?

HENRY WARD BEECHER (1813–1887)
American Congregational minister

The greatest part of mankind—nay, of Christians—may be said to be asleep, and that particular way of life which takes up each man's mind, thoughts, and actions may be very well called his particular dream. This degree of vanity is equally visible in every form and order of life. The learned and the ignorant, the rich and the poor, are all in the same state of slumber, only passing away a short life in a different kind of dream.

But why so? It is because man has an eternity within him, is born into this world, not for the sake of living here, not for anything this world can give him, but only to have time and place to become either an eternal partaker of a divine life with God or to have an hellish eternity among fallen angels. And therefore, every man who has not his eye, his heart, and his hands continually governed by this twofold eternity may be justly said to be fast asleep—to have no awakened sensibility of himself.

And a life devoted to the interests and enjoyments of this world, spent and wasted in the slavery of earthly desires, may be truly called a dream, as having all the shortness, vanity, and delusion of a dream; only with this great difference, that when a dream is over nothing is lost but fictions and fancies; but when the dream of life is ended only by death, all that eternity is lost, for which we were brought into being. Now, there is no misery in this world, nothing that makes either the life or death of man to be full of calamity, but this blindness and insensibility of his state, into which he so willingly—nay, obstinately—plunges himself.

WILLIAM LAW (1686–1761)
English contemplative and cleric

What man is he that lives, and shall not see death?

We are all conceived in close prison; in our mother's wombs, we are close prisoners all. When we are born, we are born but to the liberty of the house; prisoners still, though within larger walls; and then all our life is but a going out to the place of execution, to death.

Now, was there ever any man seen to sleep in the cart, between Newgate and Tyburn? Between the prison and the place of execution, does any man sleep?

And we sleep all the way; from the womb to the grave we are never thoroughly awake; but pass on with such dreams, and imaginations as these: I may live as well as another, and why should I die, rather than another? But awake, and tell me, says this text, who is that other you speak of? What man is he that lives, and shall not see death?

JOHN DONNE (1572–1631)
English poet and dean of St. Paul's Cathedral, London

Holy thoughts of God must be assiduously watered by prayer, earthed up by meditation, and defended by watchfulness; and yet all this is sometimes too little to preserve them alive in our souls. Alas! the heart is a soil that agrees not with them; they are tender things, and a small matter will nip and kill them. To this purpose is the complaint of the divine poet [George Herbert]:

Who would have thought a joy
    so coy?
To be offended so,
    and go
So suddenly away?
Hereafter I had need
    take heed,
Joys among other things
    have wings
And watch their opportunities of flight,
Converting in a moment day to night.

But vain thoughts and unholy suggestions, these spread themselves, and root deep in the heart, they naturally agree with the soil; so that it is almost impossible at any time to be rid of them. It is hard to forget what it is our sin to remember.

JOHN FLAVEL (1630–1691)
English writer and preacher

If to do were as easy as to know what were good to do, chapels had been churches and poor men's cottages princes' palaces. It is a good divine that follows his own instructions: I can easier teach twenty what were good to be done, than be one of the twenty to follow mine own teaching. The brain may devise laws for the blood, but a hot temper leaps o'er a cold decree. . . .

WILLIAM SHAKESPEARE (1564–1616)
England's bard

When I lived in a monastic community I could keep my tongue from idle chatter and devote my mind almost continually to the discipline of prayer. However, since assuming the burden of pastoral care, I find it difficult to keep steadily recollected because my mind is distracted by many responsibilities. I am forced to consider matters affecting churches and monasteries, and often I must judge the lives and actions of individuals. One moment I am required to participate in civil life, and the next moment to worry over the incursions of barbarians. . . .

At another time I have to exercise political responsibility in order to give support to those who uphold the rule of law; at one moment I have to cope with the wickedness of criminals, and the next moment I am asked to confront them, but in all charity.

My mind is in chaos, fragmented by the many and serious matters I am required to give attention to. When I try to concentrate and focus my intellectual resources for preaching, how can I do justice to the sacred ministry of the Word? I am often compelled by virtue of my office to socialize with people of the world and sometimes I have to relax the discipline of my speech. I realize that if I were to maintain the inflexible pattern of conversation that my conscience dictates, certain weaker individuals would simply shun my company, with the result that I would never be able to attract them to the goal I desire for them. So inevitably, I find myself listening to their mindless chatter. And because I am weak myself, I find myself gradually being sucked into their idle talk and saying the very things that I recoiled from listening to before. I enjoy lying back where beforehand I was conscious lest I fall myself.

Who am I? What kind of watchman am I? I do not stand on the pinnacle of achievement; I languish in the pit of my frailty. And yet although I am unworthy, the creator and redeemer of us all has given me the grace to see life whole and an ability to speak effectively of it. It is for the love of God that I do not spare myself in preaching him.

GREGORY THE GREAT (d. 604)
Pope Gregory I, doctor of the church, and saint

Be always ready to own any fault you have been in. If you have at any time thought, spoke, or acted wrong, be not backward to acknowledge it. Never dream that this will hurt the cause of God; no, it will further it. Be ever open and frank, when you are taxed with anything.

Do not seek either to evade or disguise it. But let it appear just as it is, and will thereby not hinder, but adorn the Gospel.

JOHN WESLEY (1703–1791)
English founder of the Methodist Movement

The reason why we live starving in the coldness and deadness of a formal, historical, hearsay religion is this: we are strangers to our own inward misery and wants, we keep all things quiet within us, partly by outward forms and modes of religion and morality, and partly by the comforts, cares, and delights of this world. . . .

WILLIAM LAW (1686–1761)
English contemplative and cleric

There are some people who have lived forty or fifty years in the world, and have had scarcely one hour's discourse with their own hearts. It is a hard thing to bring a man and himself together on such business; but saints know those soliloquies to be very salutary.

Though bankrupts care not to look into their accounts, yet upright hearts will know whether they go backward or forward. "I commune with mine own heart," says David. The heart can never be kept until its case be examined and understood. . . .

It is the hardest work. Heart-work is hard work indeed. To shuffle over religious duties with a loose and heedless spirit, will cost no great pains; but to set yourself before the Lord, and tie up your loose and vain thoughts to a constant and serious attendance upon him; this will cost thee something.

To repress the outward acts of sin, and compose the external part of thy life in a laudable manner, is no great matter; even carnal persons, by the force of common principles, can do this: but to kill the root of corruption within, to set and keep up an holy government over your thought, to have all things lie straight and orderly in the heart, this is not easy. . . .

It is a constant work. The keeping of the heart is a work that is never done till life is ended. There is no time or condition in the life of a Christian which will suffer an intermission of this work. . . .

He that performs duty without the heart, that is, heedlessly, is no more accepted with God than he that performs it with a double heart, that is, hypocritically. A neglected heart is so confused and dark, that the little grace which is in it is not ordinarily discernible: the most accurate and laborious Christians sometimes find it difficult to discover the pure and genuine workings of the Spirit in their hearts. How then shall the Christian, who is comparatively negligent about heart-work, be ever able to discover grace? Sincerity, which is the thing sought, lies in the heart like a small piece of gold on the bottom of a river; he that would find it must stay till the water is clear, and then he will see it sparkling at the bottom. That the heart may be clear and settled, how much pains and watching, care and diligence, are required! The improvement of our graces depends on the keeping of our hearts. . . .

You must exercise the utmost vigilance to discover and check the first symptoms of departure from God, the least decline of spirituality, or the least indisposition to meditation by yourself, and holy conversation and fellowship with others. These things you must undertake, in the strength of Christ, with invincible resolution in the outset. And if you thus engage in this great work, be assured you shall not spend your strength for naught; comforts which you never felt or thought of will flow in upon you from every side.

Awake then, this moment.

JOHN FLAVEL (1630–1691)
English writer and preacher

First you should return to yourself, enter into your heart, and learn to assess your spirit. Analyze what you are, have been, ought to be, are able to be; what you are by nature, what you are now by sin, what you ought to be by effort, what you yet could be by grace.

Abundant riches grow from this practice, knowledge is multiplied, wisdom expands, the eye of the heart is purified, abilities are honed, and understanding broadens. He who knows not himself cannot properly assess anything. She who does not weigh the worthiness of her own condition does not realize that all worldly glory should lie beneath her feet. He who does not think about his own spirit first knows not at all what to think of the angelic or divine spirit. If you are unfit to enter into yourself, how shall you ever be fit to explore the things that are above you? . . . If you wish to fly away to the second or third heaven, you must go the way of the first.

RICHARD OF ST. VICTOR (d. 1173)
Scottish theologian and mystic

The Servant: Lord, I should like to hear about the union of Pure Reason with the Holy Trinity when, in the true reflection of the eternal birth of the Word, and in the regeneration of her own

Spirit, Reason is ravished from herself and stands face to face with God.

Eternal Wisdom: Let not him ask about what is highest in doctrine, who still stands on what is lowest in a good life. I will teach you what will profit you more.

The Servant: Lord, what will you teach me?

Eternal Wisdom: I will teach you to die and will teach you to live. I will teach you to receive Me lovingly, and will teach you to praise Me lovingly. Behold, this is what properly belongs to you.

The Servant: Eternal Wisdom, if I had the power to fulfill my wishes, I would wish nothing else but to know how to die to myself and all the world, how to live wholly for you. But Lord, do you mean a spiritual dying or a bodily dying?

Eternal Wisdom: I mean both one and the other.

The Servant: What need have I, Lord, of being taught how to die bodily? Surely it teaches itself when it comes.

Eternal Wisdom: He who puts his teaching off till then, will find it too late.

HENRY SUSO (1300–1366)

German contemplative

Father Zossima: If you do not attain happiness, always remember that you are on the right road, and try not to leave it. Above all, avoid falsehood, every kind of falsehood, especially falseness to yourself. Watch over your own deceitfulness and look into it every hour, every minute. Avoid being scornful, both to others and to yourself. What seems to you bad within you will grow purer from the very fact of your observing it in yourself. Avoid fear, too, though fear is only the result of falsehood. Never be frightened even at your evil actions. I am sorry I can say nothing more consoling to you, for love in action is a harsh and dreadful thing compared with love in dreams. Love in dreams is greedy for immediate action, rapidly performed and in sight of all. Men will even give their lives if only the ordeal does not last long but is soon over, with all looking on and applauding as though on the stage. But active love is labor and fortitude, and for some people too, perhaps, a complete science. But I predict that just when you see with horror that in spite of all your efforts you are getting further from your goal instead of nearer to it—at that very moment I predict that you will reach it.

FYODOR DOSTOYEVSKY (1821–1881)

Russian novelist

CYCLE NINE

HOLY FIRE

"Your Being does not let go of my being," says Nicholas of Cusa. To experience this reality requires silence and solitude, and the cultivation of prayer. This cycle both affirms the indwelling of the divine, and exposes all that clouds and obstructs the experience of union.

Excerpts from a letter written in response to a request from Pope Paul VI for "a message of contemplatives to the world":

God seeks Himself in us, and the aridity and sorrow of our heart is the sorrow of God who is not known to us, who cannot yet find Himself in us because we do not dare to believe or trust the incredible truth that He could live in us, and live there out of choice, out of preference. But indeed we exist solely for this, to be the place He has chosen for His presence, His manifestation in the world, His epiphany. But we make all this dark and inglorious because we fail to believe it, we refuse to believe it. It is not that we hate God, rather that we hate ourselves, despair of ourselves. If we once began to recognize, humbly but truly, the real value of our own self, we would see that this value was the sign of God in our being, the signature of God upon our being.

The contemplative is not the man who has fiery visions of the cherubim carrying God on their imagined chariot, but simply he who has risked his mind in the desert beyond language and beyond ideas where God is encountered in the nakedness of pure trust, that is to say in the surrender of our own poverty and incompleteness in order no longer to clench our minds in a cramp upon themselves, as if thinking made us exist. The message of hope the contemplative offers you, then, is not that you need to find your way through the jungle of language and problems that today surround God; but that whether you understand or not, God loves you, is present to you, lives in you, dwells in you, calls you, saves you, and offers you an understanding and light which are like nothing you ever found in books or heard in sermons. The contemplative has nothing to tell you except to reassure you and say that if you dare to penetrate your own silence and dare to advance without fear into the solitude of your own heart, and risk sharing that solitude with the lonely other who seeks God through you and with you, then you will truly recover the light and the capacity to understand what is beyond words and beyond explanations because it is too close to be explained: it is the intimate union in the depths of your own heart, of God's spirit and your own secret inmost self, so that you and He are in all truth One Spirit. I love you, in Christ.

THOMAS MERTON (1915–1968)
American Cistercian monk

The first thing I would like to say, and really, the only thing I have to say, is that I don't know what prayer is.

Here and now, that is what matters.

On an existential level, I am quite incapable of saying, after a time of prayer, whether or not I have really prayed. I just can't determine the dividing line between prayer and what is simply a rambling mind, or dreaming, or an emptiness which is only a completely natural rest or peace.

But that doesn't really worry me. When you are actually praying, and you seem to be touching on real prayer, you think: this is it . . . or something quite different. Prayer itself is something you can't take hold of. Introspection can only touch on the psychological side of it.

One thing is sure: you can't possess prayer; it's something interior. What is prayer? Is it a gazing upon? . . . I'm not completely happy with that expression. I would prefer a word that evokes a mutual gaze, God looking at me, and me looking at God.

I prefer "presence," or "abandonment" (but that doesn't say enough). I go to the oratory to pray. I don't know what I am going to do. Afterwards, I don't know what I am coming from. That's how it is at the moment.

PETER (contemporary)

Carthusian novice

You, Lord, the Absolute Being of all, are as entirely present to each of us as though there were no other. . . . I cannot imagine that You love anything else more than me, for Your gaze never leaves me, me only.

And just as Your gaze beholds me so attentively that it never turns aside, even so it is with Your love. Hence You are ever with me, Lord, You take most diligent care of me. Your Being does not let go of my being. . . .

You are ever ready to show Your face to all that seek You, for never do You close Your eyes, never do You turn them away. If You do not behold me with the eye of grace the fault is mine, who has cut me off from You by turning aside to some other thing which I prefer before You.

Yet even so, You do not turn utterly away, but Your mercy follows me, so that if at any time I turn to You again, I may be capable of grace.

NICHOLAS OF CUSA (1401?–1464)
German cardinal, theologian, and mathematician

We were created by love, for love, and so that we should love. "Before I formed you in the womb, I knew you," is what God said to Jeremiah. These are words that apply to each of us. We were planned for from all eternity. None of us is a mere divine afterthought. None of us is an accident. *Before the foundation of the world* God chose us to be his children in Jesus Christ. . . .

There is nothing you can do that will make God love you less. There is nothing you can do to make God love you more. God's love for you is infinite, perfect, and eternal.

DESMOND TUTU (1931–)
Archbishop, Anglican South African Council of Churches

True prayer is a direct raising of the mind and heart to God, without intermediary. This and nothing else is the essence of prayer.

This loving ascent to God, in profound longing and humble surrender, that one is true prayer. . . . Nevertheless, no external prayer is as devout and as deserving of our love as is the sacred Our Father. The greatest of all the masters taught it to us and said it

Himself. More than any other, it leads to essential prayer; indeed it is a heavenly prayer. This true prayer is said and contemplated in Heaven without ceasing: It is a genuine ascent to God, a lifting of the spirit upward so that God may in reality enter the purest, most inward, noble part of the soul—its deepest ground—where alone there is undifferentiated unity.

JOHANNES TAULER (1300–1361)
German Dominican contemplative

It would be well for us to consider that our Lord has taught this prayer to each one of us, individually, and that He still teaches it to us at this very moment. The Master is never so distant that His disciple need raise his voice to be heard. On the contrary, He is very near. To enable you to recite the Pater Noster well, I should like to see you perfectly convinced of this truth, namely, that you must remain close to the Master who teaches it to you. . . . You must devote yourself with attention, and not finish the prayer amidst distracting thought.

TERESA OF ÁVILA (1515–1582)
Spanish Carmelite saint and mystic

Last night, going to bed alone, I suddenly found myself (I was taking off my waistcoat) reciting the Lord's Prayer in a loud, emphatic voice—a thing I had not done for many years—with deep urgency and profound disturbed emotion.

While I went on I grew more composed; as if it had been empty and craving and were being replenished, my soul grew still;

every word had a strange fullness of meaning which astonished and delighted me. It was late; I had sat up reading; I was sleepy; but as I stood in the middle of the floor half-undressed, saying the prayer over and over, meaning after meaning sprang from it, overcoming me again with joyful surprise; and I realized that this simple petition was always universal and always inexhaustible, and day by day sanctified human life.

EDWIN MUIR (1887–1959)
English novelist and poet

Thou seest, hearest, and feelest nothing of God because thou seekest for him abroad with thy outward eyes, thou seekest for him in books, in controversies, in the Church and outward exercises, but there thou wilt not find him till thou hast first found him in thy heart. Seek for him in thy heart, and thou wilt never seek in vain, for there he dwells, there is the seat of his light and Holy Spirit. For this turning to the light and Spirit of God within thee is thy only true turning unto God. There is no other way of finding him, but in that place where he dwelleth in thee. For though God be everywhere present, yet he is only present to thee in the deepest and most central part of thy soul. . . .

This holy spark of the divine nature within . . . came forth from God, it came out of God, it partaketh of the divine nature and therefore it is always in a state of tendency and return to God.

And all this is called the breathing, the moving, the quickening of the Holy Spirit within us, which are so many operations of this spark of life tending towards God.

WILLIAM LAW (1686–1761)
English contemplative and cleric

No one can come to me unless the Father draws him.

You must not imagine that you are being drawn against your will, for the mind can also be drawn by love. . . .

Show me a lover and he will understand what I am saying. Show me someone who wants something, someone hungry, someone wandering in this wilderness, thirsting and longing for the fountains of his eternal home, show me such a one and he will know what I mean. But if I am talking to someone without any feeling, he will not know what I am talking about.

Offer a handful of grass to a sheep and you draw it after you. Show a boy nuts and he is enticed. He is drawn by the things he is running to take, drawn because he desires, drawn without any physical pressures, drawn simply by the pull on his appetite. If, then, the things that lovers see as the delights and pleasures of earth can draw them, because it is true that "everyone is drawn by his delight," then does not Christ draw when he is revealed to us by the Father?

AUGUSTINE OF HIPPO (354–430)
Carthaginian saint, philosopher, and doctor of the church

We must strive for a quiet mind. The eye cannot appreciate an object set before it if it is perpetually restless, glancing here, there and everywhere. No more can our mind's eye apprehend the truth with any clarity if it is distracted by a thousand worldly concerns. . . .

For just as it is impossible to write upon a wax tablet without first having erased the marks on it, so it is impossible to receive the impress of divine doctrine without unlearning our inherited preconceptions and habitual prejudices. Solitude offers an excellent opportunity in this process because it calms our passions, and creates space for our reason to remove their influence. . . .

Tranquillity is indeed the first step in the process of our sanctification, for through it our conversation is purged of idle gossip; our eyes are enabled to concentrate without searching for beautiful bodies to ogle at; our ears are not forever assaulted by invasive noise or worse still, by superficial chatter or revelry. With our senses thus reoriented, our attention is no longer dissipated and our mind is thrown back upon itself. . . .

BASIL THE GREAT (330–379)
Doctor of the church, saint, and bishop of Caesarea

So fit and useful is morning devotion, it ought not to be omitted without necessity. If our circumstances will allow the privilege, it is a bad sign when no part of the morning is spent in prayer. If God find no place in our minds at that early and peaceful hour, He will hardly recur to us in the tumults of life. If the benefits of the morning do not soften us, we can hardly expect the heart to melt with gratitude through the day. If the world then rush in and take possession of us, when we are at some distance and have had a respite from its cares, how can we hope to shake it off when we shall be in the midst of it, pressed and agitated by it on every side?

Let a part of the morning, if possible, be set apart to devotion; and to this end we should fix the hour of rising, so that we may have an early hour at our own disposal. Our piety is suspicious if we can renounce, as too many do, the pleasures and benefits of early prayer, rather than forego the senseless indulgence of unnecessary sleep.

WILLIAM ELLERY CHANNING (1780–1842)
American Unitarian pastor

I find that meditation, morning and evening, every day, is the best and most direct method of getting in touch with reality. In meditation, I try to let go of everything of the outer world of the senses, of the inner world of thoughts, and listen to the inner voice, the voice of the Word, which comes in the silence, in the stillness when all activity of body and mind cease. Then, in the silence, I become aware of the presence of God, and I try to keep that awareness during the day. . . .

Meditation is naturally followed by prayer—*oratio.* Our understanding of the deeper meaning of the text depends on our spiritual insight and this comes from prayer. Prayer is opening the heart and mind to God. . . . This demands devotion—that is, self-surrender. As long as we remain on the level of the rational mind we are governed by our ego, our independent rational self. We can make use of all kinds of assistance, of commentaries and spiritual guides, but as long as the individual self remains in command, we are imprisoned in the rational mind with its concepts and judgments. Only when we surrender the ego, the separate self, and turn to God, the supreme spirit, can we receive the light which we need to understand the deeper meaning of the scriptures. This is passing from *ratio* to *intellectus,* from discursive thought to intuitive insight.

BEDE GRIFFITHS (1906–1993)
English Benedictine monk

If we really want prayer, we'll have to give it time. We must slow down to a human tempo and we'll begin to have time to listen. And as soon as we listen to what's going on, things will begin to take shape by themselves. . . . The whole thing boils down to giving ourselves in prayer a chance to realize that we have what we seek. We don't have to rush after it. It is there all the time, and if we give it time it will make itself known to us.

In prayer we discover what we already have. You start where you are, you deepen what you already have, and you realize that you are already there. We already have everything, but we don't know it, and we don't experience it. Everything has been given to us in Christ. All we need is to experience what we already possess.

THOMAS MERTON (1915–1968)
American Cistercian monk

I take it for granted that every Christian that is in health is up early in the morning; for it is much more reasonable to suppose a person up early because he is a Christian than because he is a laborer or a tradesman or a servant or has business that wants him. We naturally conceive some abhorrence of a man that is in bed when he should be at his labor or in his shop. We cannot tell how to think any good thing of him who is such a slave to drowsiness as to neglect his business for it. . . .

If he is to be blamed as a slothful drone that rather chooses the lazy indulgence of sleep than to perform his proper share of worldly business, how much is he to be reproved that had rather lie folded up in a bed than be raising up his heart to God in acts of praise and adoration? Prayer is the noblest exercise of the soul, the most exalted use of our best faculties, and the highest imitation of the blessed inhabitants of heaven.

WILLIAM LAW (1686–1761)
English contemplative and cleric

Do not believe your flesh when it threatens you with weakness during prayer; it lies. As soon as you begin to pray you will find that the flesh will become your obedient slave. Your prayer will vivify it also.

Always remember that the flesh is lying.

FATHER JOHN SERGIEFF (ST. JOHN OF KRONSTADT) (1829–1909)

Russian monk

It is no small pity, and should cause us no little shame, that, through our own fault, we do not understand ourselves, or know who we are. Would it not be a sign of great ignorance, my daughters, if a person were asked who he was, and could not say, and had no idea who his father or his mother was, or from what country he came? Though that is great stupidity, our own is incomparably greater if we make no attempt to discover what we are, and only know that we are living in these bodies, and have a vague idea, because we have heard it and because our Faith tells us so, that we possess souls. . . .

As to what good qualities there may be in our souls, or Who dwells within them, or how precious they are—those are things which we seldom consider and so we trouble little about carefully preserving the soul's beauty. All our interest is centered in the rough setting of the diamond, and in the outer wall of the castle, that is to say, in these bodies of ours. . . .

Now let us return to our beautiful and delightful castle and see how we can enter it. I seem rather to be talking nonsense, for, if this castle is the soul, there can clearly be no question of our entering it. For we ourselves are the castle: and it would be absurd to tell someone to enter a room when he was in it already! But you must understand that there are many ways of "being" in a place. Many souls remain in the outer court of the castle, which is the place occupied by the guards; they are not interested in entering it, and have no idea what there is in that wonderful place, or who dwells in it, or even how many rooms it has. You will have read certain books on prayer which advise the soul to enter within itself: and that is exactly what this means.

A short time ago I was told by a very learned man that souls without prayer are like people whose bodies or limbs are paralyzed: they possess feet and hands but they cannot control them. In the same way, there are souls so infirm and so accustomed to busying themselves with outside affairs that nothing can be done for them, and it seems as though they are incapable of entering within themselves at all. . . .

Let us rather think of certain souls who do eventually enter the castle. These are very much absorbed in worldly affairs; but their desires are good; sometimes, though infrequently, they commend themselves to Our Lord; and they think about the state of their souls, though not very carefully. Full of a thousand preoccupations as they are, they pray only a few times a month, and as a rule they are thinking all the time of their preoccupations, for they are very much attached to them, and, where their treasure is, there is their heart also. From time to time, however, they shake their minds free of them and it is a great thing that they should know themselves well enough to realize that they are not going the right way to reach the castle door. . . .

Eventually they enter the first rooms on the lowest floor, but so many reptiles get in with them that they are unable to appreciate the beauty of the castle or to find any peace within it. Still, they have done a good deal by entering at all.

TERESA OF ÁVILA (1515–1582)
Spanish Carmelite saint and mystic

From a letter to a Russian nun:
In the beginning, when someone turns to the Lord, prayer is the first exercise. He starts to go to church and to pray at home either with a prayerbook or without one. But his thoughts wander all the time. It is impossible to control them. But with exercise in prayer his thoughts begin to settle down and prayer becomes purer.

Nevertheless, the atmosphere of the soul remains unpurified until a spiritual flame appears in his heart. This little flame is the work of divine grace which is common to all and is nothing special. This flame appears as the result of a certain measure of purity in the moral life of the person who is making progress. When this little flame appears or when a continuous warmth is formed in the heart, then the whirling of thoughts stops. . . .

In this state prayer becomes more or less unceasing. The prayer of Jesus serves as an intermediary. This is the limit which prayer practiced by man can attain without special grace. I believe that all this is clear to you. Later on in that state infused prayer which is not the work of man comes as a gift. A prayerful spirit comes and summons one down into the heart, just as one person might take another by the hand and draw him forcibly from one room into another. The soul is bound by an external force and remains willingly within while the prayerful spirit is with it.

THEOPHAN THE RECLUSE (1815–1894)
Russian Orthodox monk and saint

Those that meditate by snatches and uncertain fits, when only all other employments forsake them, or when good motions are thrust upon them by necessity, let them never hope to reach to any perfection: for these feeble beginnings of lukewarm grace, which are wrought in them by one fit of serious meditation, are soon extinguished by intermission; and, by miswonting, perish.

This day's meal, though large and liberal, strengthens thee not for tomorrow: the body languisheth, if there be not a daily supply of repast. Thus feed thy soul by meditation. Set thine hours, and keep them; and yield not to an easy distraction.

There is no hardness in this practice but in the beginning: use shall give it, not ease only, but delight.

JOSEPH HALL (1574–1656)
English Puritan bishop

How to attain real and steadfast progress in holiness.

The first means, which while it seems the most ordinary, is in truth the hardest—it is the will to attain it. The will must be sincere, effectual, and persevering; and such a will is no common thing. We deceive ourselves into thinking we have it, while really we have only vague wishes and desires, which are very different from a firm resolute will. . . .

Many people lose heart as soon as any effort is required, when faults must be overcome, or when natural inclinations or imperfections resisted. There may be a fervent beginning, but such persons soon grow slack, they give up what was scarcely begun, and shut their eyes to the fact that everything depends on perseverance. Ask God daily to confirm and strengthen your will and each day's perseverance will help forward the morrow.

The second means for attaining a steadfast progress in holiness is to have a daily rule, and to observe it punctually. But it is not well to overload one's self with observances at first—it is better to increase spiritual exercises gradually. . . .

The third means is the continual recollection of God's Presence; and to this end you must firmly believe that God dwells within our hearts, and that He is to be found there by those who seek Him. We often call conscience that which is in truth God's own Voice; warning, rebuking, enlightening, directing the soul;—our part is to be attentive in listening, and steadfast in obeying this Voice.

Dissipation and excitement hinder us from hearing it; it is when we are calm and still—our passions and imagination at rest—that the Voice of God fills the heart; and there is no step towards perfection so great as when we learn the habit of always watching for it. But for this we require a tranquil heart, avoiding whatever disturbs, engrosses, or distracts it;—and all this is the work of time, together with diligent self-examination and resolute efforts.

The fourth means is to give a fixed daily time to God, during which His Presence is our sole occupation, and in which we listen to Him and talk with Him, not with the lips, but in the heart. . . . At first a quarter of an hour morning and evening is enough, but you should acquire, if possible, the habit of at least half an hour's morning meditation. When you learn to take delight in it, and can dispense with the help of books, it is well at times merely to lie passive before your Lord, asking Him to work His own good pleasure in your soul: it is a great mistake to fancy such time to be lost, whether you are conscious of His Grace operating within you or not.

JEAN NICHOLAS GROU (1731–1803)
French Jesuit

When we listen to someone, we think we are silent because we do not speak; but our minds continue to work, our emotions react, our will responds for or against what we hear, we may even go further than this, with thoughts and feelings buzzing in our heads which are quite unrelated to what is being said.

The real silence towards which we must aim as a startingpoint is a complete repose of mind and heart and will, the complete silence of all there is in us, including our body, so that we may be completely aware of the word we are receiving, completely alert and yet in complete repose.

The silence I am speaking of is the silence of the sentry on duty at a critical moment; alert, immobile, poised and yet alive to every sound, every movement. This living silence is what discipleship requires first of all, and this is not achieved without effort. It requires from us a training of our attention, a training of our body, a training of our mind and our emotions so that they are kept in check, completely and perfectly. . . .

In our struggle for prayer the emotions are almost irrelevant; we must remember that the fruits of prayer are not this or that emotional state, but a deep change in the whole of our personality. What we aim at is to be made able to stand before God and to concentrate on his presence, all our needs being directed Godwards, and to be given power, strength, anything we need that the will of God may be fulfilled in us. That the will of God should be fulfilled in us is the only aim of prayer, and it is also the criterion of right prayer. It is not the mystical feeling we may have, or our emotions that make good praying.

ANTHONY BLOOM (1914–)
Russian Orthodox monk and metropolitan of Sourozh

When you begin your prayer, direct your intention quite briefly to God as purely as you can, and then begin and do your best. And though your original intention seems entirely frustrated, do not be too much upset, nor too angry with yourself, nor impatient against God, because He does not give you that sensible devotion and spiritual sweetness that you think He gives to others. . . .

Play your part, and let our Lord do what He will, and do not try to instruct Him. And even though you seem to yourself to be careless and negligent and much to blame for this inability to pray, nevertheless for this, lift up your heart to God, acknowledging your wretchedness, and beg for mercy with confidence. And do not struggle with yourself, dwelling on your weakness, as though by your own effort you could avoid feeling it. Leave your prayer and go to some other good work, spiritual or corporal, and resolve to do better another time. But though you fall in just the same way another time, yes, and a hundred or a thousand times, do as I have said, and all shall be well. And a soul that never does find rest of heart in prayer, but all her life is striving with distractions and troubled by them, if she keep herself in humility and charity, shall have great reward for her efforts.

WALTER HILTON (1343–1396)
English contemplative writer

I throw my self down in my chamber, and I call in, and invite God, and his angels thither, and when they are there, I neglect God and his angels, for the noise of a fly, for the rattling of a coach, for the whining of a door.

I talk on, in the same posture of praying; eyes lifted up; knees bowed down; as though I prayed to God; and, if God, or his angels should ask me, when I last thought of God in that prayer, I cannot tell. Sometimes I find that I had forgot what I was about, but when I began to forget it, I cannot tell. A memory of yesterday's pleasures, a fear of tomorrow's dangers, a straw under my knee, a noise in my ear, a light in my eye, an any thing, a nothing, a fancy, a chimera in my brain, troubles me in my prayer.

JOHN DONNE (1572–1631)

English poet and dean of St. Paul's Cathedral, London

We must, no doubt, as far as it depends on us, employ all the attention of our mind in prayer, in meditation and every pious exercise which requires interior application, but without fear of the distractions which may come to us, without uneasiness when they come, and without alarm when they are past. It is nearly the same thing with respect to attention as intention; they subsist in the same action until they are revoked voluntarily. Whatever the wanderings of the mind, we are always attentive unless our distractions have been willful and with reflection.

Let us apply ourselves without expectation of being settled; the instability of our mind is incapable of it, but on the contrary, becomes irritated and often wandering in proportion to the efforts made to restrain it. It will sometimes remain quietly enough with us; but only the effort to keep it, is sure to drive it away. Let us neither think of it or its distractions, and then we will be attentive. The straining of our imagination will only be a useless fatigue to the brain, destruction of the health to no purpose, and certain interruption of the peace of the soul. It is aiming at impossibility, and a folly to expect to rule it by force; it would be as easy to shut the air in our hand by closing it, as to fix the imagination by constraining it; for should we succeed to drive away every other object for a moment, it would then be occupied by the constraint itself.

AMBROISE DE LOMBEZ (date of treatise: 1756)

French Capuchin theologian

Daydreaming during prayer is worse than distraction. Distraction makes prayer sterile while daydreaming engenders false fruits, self-delusion and what the Holy Fathers call devilish illusion. . . .

Reject seemingly good thoughts and seemingly bright revelations which come to you in time of prayer and take you away from prayer. They come from the province of false reason. They, like horsemen, sit astride vanity. Their dark faces are hidden in order that he who prays may not recognize in them his foes. . . .

The fruit of true prayer is a holy peace of soul united with a quiet, silent joy, free of daydreaming, self-esteem, and disordered inclinations and movements. . . . Be wise in your prayer. Do not ask in it anything corruptible and vain. Remember the command of the Savior: "Seek first of all the Kingdom of God and its truth and all that is needed for temporal like will be given to you."

IGNATIUS BYRANCHANINOV (1807–1867)

Russian bishop

The most difficult and the most decisive part of prayer is acquiring the ability to listen. To listen, according to the dictionary, is "attentively to exercise the sense of hearing." It is not a passive affair, a space when we don't happen to be doing or saying anything and are, therefore, automatically able to listen. It is a conscious, willed action, requiring alertness and vigilance, by which our whole attention is focused and controlled. So it is difficult, and it is decisive because it is the beginning of our entry into a personal relationship with God in which we gradually learn to let go of ourselves, and allow the word of God to speak within us.

MOTHER MARY CLARE (1907–)
English nun

Letter to the Reverend Mother N.:
Hold yourself before God as a poor mute, unable to talk, or as a paralytic at the door of a rich man. Busy yourself with keeping your mind in the presence of the Lord. If it strays and withdraws sometimes, do not worry about it. Worrying only serves to distract the mind rather than to call it back to God. The will must recall it gently. If you persevere in this way, God will have mercy on you.

One way to call your mind easily back to God during your fixed prayer times and to hold it more steady, is not to let it take much flight during the day. You must keep it strictly in the presence of God. As you become used to doing that over and over, it will be easy to *remain* at peace during your prayer times, or at least to recall your mind from its wanderings.

BROTHER LAWRENCE (17th century)
Lay brother among Carmelites in Paris

Take care that nothing remains for your mind's activity but the simple extension of your will, reaching out to God, not dressed up in any particular thought concerning God as he is in himself, or as revealed in any of his works; simply that he is as he is. Let him be just so, I pray you; do not make anything else of him. Do not seek to penetrate any deeper into him by subtle reasoning; let faith be your foundation.

This simple extension, freely established and grounded in true faith, must be nothing else, as regards your thinking and your feeling, except a simple thought and blind feeling of your own existence; as if you were to speak to God inwardly, with this for your meaning: "What I am, Lord, I offer to you, without looking to any quality of your being, but only that you are what you are and nothing else." This humble darkness is to be the reflection of yourself and your entire mind. Think no further on yourself than I bid you do on your God, so as to be one with him in spirit, and this without dividing or dissipating your awareness. . . .

See to it that your thought is single and undefiled, that you yourself, unencumbered, just as you are, may be touched by grace and secretly fed in your feeling with him alone, be just as he is; remembering that this union shall be blind and incomplete, as it can only be here in this life, so that your longing desire may always be active.

Look up, then, with joy and say to your Lord, either aloud or in your heart: "What I am, Lord, I offer to you; for you are what I am." And think single-mindedly, plainly, and vigorously that you are as you are without racking your brains at all. To think in this way requires little expertise, even of the most illiterate man or woman alive, with the minimum of natural intelligence; or so it seems to me. . . .

For I would consider him too illiterate and uncultured by far who could not think and be conscious of himself—that he is. Not what he is, but that he is. For clearly it is an attribute of the most ignorant cow or the most irrational animal to be aware of its own individual being. Much more then is it an attribute of man, who alone above all the other animals is endowed with reason, to think and to be conscious of his own individual being.

UNKNOWN ENGLISH MYSTIC (14th century)

A Letter of Private Direction

Our Lord is greatly cheered by our prayer. He looks for it, and he wants it. By his grace he aims to make us as like himself in heart as we are already in our human nature. This is his blessed will. So he says, "Pray inwardly, even if you do not enjoy it. It does good, though you feel nothing, see nothing. Yes, even though you think you are doing nothing. For when you are dry, empty, sick, or weak, at such a time is your prayer most pleasing to me though you find little enough to enjoy in it." This is true of all believing prayer.

JULIAN OF NORWICH (14th century)

English contemplative and anchoress

This [inward prayer] is a silent prayer, and much more powerful than any other, and it is the prayer which God does always hear. The soul having presented herself before God, he instructs her in the way of his commandments: for God takes delight in instructing the soul as soon as the soul is attentive.

Even this I desire of you, that your prayers may be simple, so that God, who pours out his Spirit upon the simple, may himself be your prayer—simple in thoughts, abandoning and not entertaining them, simple in understanding, depending wholly on God.

✦

That we may be constant in prayer so must we be faithful to do all our business the whole day through with such a steadiness that nothing may make us wavering.

This prayer, which is performed in outward business, is a fruit of the inward prayer or Prayer of Silence. It is like the heat of a stove, which holds long though you put no more wood in; it is the anointing of prayer, . . . it is an impression of the Love and Presence of God in the heart itself which is continued in the performing of our business, and which serves to call a man back to his inward business when he has been scattered outwardly. And instead of suffering the mind to rove, when we rise up from inward prayer which is performed at set times, we should rather take care to preserve what we have therein received as a precious powerful water which we must be careful not to let evaporate.

JOHANNES KELPIUS (1673–1708)
German recluse, mystic, and teacher

In many cases, a man suffers because of the difference between what his prayer is and what he knows it should be. He suffers from the contrast between his willingness to pray, often and every day, and his apparent incapability. His heart seems to be paralyzed, and he fears he may be labeled a hypocrite through pretending to do something which in reality is beyond his power.

He thinks that in sincerity towards himself and towards God, he must wait until the fountains in the depths of his heart spring up again, to provide the healing waters of grace, of spontaneous emotion and of vital spiritual experience, thus making true prayer possible in a sincere outpouring of the heart. This difficulty tempts many a responsible and good person to pray infrequently. These are persons whose everyday life becomes void of prayer, not because they have succumbed to the superficiality of mundane routine, but because they are conscientious and honest. They refuse to pray unless their prayer comes from the heart.

They do not believe that it needs only the will of man to make his prayer the voice of the heart.

KARL RAHNER (1904–1984)
German Jesuit theologian

The soul has such satisfaction in God that although the other two faculties may be distracted, yet, since the will is in union with God for as long as the recollection lasts, its quiet and repose are not lost, but the will gradually brings the understanding and memory back to a state of recollection again. For although the will is not yet completely absorbed it is so well occupied, without knowing how, that, whatever the efforts made by the understanding and memory, they cannot deprive it of its contentment and rejoicing: indeed, without any labor on its part, it helps to prevent this little spark of love from being quenched.

TERESA OF ÁVILA (1515–1582)
Spanish Carmelite saint and mystic

My ignorance has gained more light from interior prayer than from anything else, and that I have not reached by myself, it has been granted me by the mercy of God and the teaching of my *starets*. And that can be done by anyone. It costs nothing but the effort to sink down in silence into the depths of one's heart and call more and more upon the radiant Name of Jesus. Everyone who does that feels at once the inward light, everything becomes understandable to him, he even catches sight in this light of some of the mysteries of the Kingdom of God. And what depth and light there is in the mystery of a man coming to know that he has this power to plumb the depths of his own being, to see himself from within. . . .

The trouble is that we live far from ourselves and have but little wish to get any nearer to ourselves. Indeed we are running away all the time to avoid coming face to face with our real selves, and we barter the truth for trifles. We think, "I would very gladly take an interest in spiritual things, and in prayer, but I have no time, the fuss and cares of life give no chance for such a thing." Yet which is really important and necessary, salvation and the eternal life of the soul, or the fleeting life of the body on which we spend so much labor?

ANONYMOUS RUSSIAN PILGRIM (c. 1850)

The path of light is contrary to all the ways of the world. . . . Whenever the world perceives this holy fire of love in God's children, it concludes immediately that they are turned fools, and are beside themselves. But to the children of God, that which is despised of the world is the greatest treasure; yea, so great a treasure it is, as no life can express, nor tongue so much as name what this enflaming, all-conquering love of God is.

It is brighter than the sun; it is sweeter than anything that is called sweet; it is stronger than all strength; it is more nutrimental than food; more cheering to the heart than wine, and more pleasant than all the joy and pleasantness of this world. Whosoever obtains it is richer than any monarch on earth; and he who gets it is nobler than any emperor can be, and more potent and absolute than all power and authority.

JACOB BOEHME (1575–1624)
German Lutheran theosophist

Father in Heaven! What is a man without Thee! What is all that he knows, vast accumulation though it be, but a chipped fragment if he does not know Thee! What is all his striving, could it even encompass the world, but a half-finished work if he does not know Thee: Thee the One, who art one thing and who art all! So may Thou give to the intellect, wisdom to comprehend that one thing; to the heart, sincerity to receive this understanding; to the will, purity that wills only one thing. In prosperity may Thou grant perseverance to will one thing; amid distractions, collectedness to will one thing; in suffering, patience to will one thing. Oh, Thou that giveth both the beginning and the completion, may Thou early, at the dawn of day, give to the young man the resolution to will one thing. As the day wanes, may Thou give to the old man a renewed remembrance of his first resolution, that the first may be like the last, the last like the first, in possession of a life that has willed only one thing.

SØREN KIERKEGAARD (1813–1855)
Danish theologian

God made Sun and Moon to distinguish seasons, and day, and night, and we cannot have the fruits of the earth but in their seasons. But God hath made no decree to distinguish the seasons of his mercies. In paradise, the fruits were ripe the first minute, and in heaven it is always Autumn: his mercies are ever in their maturity. . . .

He brought light out of darkness, not out of a lesser light; he can bring thy Summer out of Winter, though thou have no Spring. Though in the ways of fortune, or understanding, or conscience, thou have been benighted till now, wintered, and frozen, clouded and eclipsed, damped and benumbed, smothered and stupefied till now, now God comes to thee, not as in the dawning of the day, not as in the bud of the spring, but as the Sun at noon to illustrate all shadows, as the sheaves in harvest, to fill all penuries. All occasions invite his mercies, and all times are his seasons.

JOHN DONNE (1572–1631)

English poet and dean of St. Paul's Cathedral, London

CYCLE TEN

HAVING NOTHING, POSSESSING ALL THINGS

We end with witnesses to the fruits of grace, to the joy and peace of contemplation, to the ecstasy of longing and love. It is on this way that heaven is found "even in that very place where you stand and walk . . . for heaven stands in the innermost moving everywhere."

A beautiful breathing instrument of music the Lord made humankind, after His own image. And He Himself also, surely, who is the supramundane Wisdom, the celestial Word, is the all-harmonious, melodious, holy instrument of God. What, then, does this instrument—the Word of God, the Lord, the New Song—desire? To open the eyes of the blind, and unstop the ears of the deaf, and to lead the lame or the erring to righteousness.

The instrument of God loves humankind. The Lord pities, instructs, exhorts, admonishes, saves, shields, and of His bounty promises us the kingdom of heaven. . . . You have, then, God's promise; you have His love: become partaker of His grace. And do not suppose the song of salvation to be new, as a vessel or a house is new. For "before the morning star it was."

For human beings have been constituted by nature, so as to have fellowship with God. As, then, we do not compel the horse to plough, or the bull to hunt, but set each animal to that for which it is by nature fitted; so, placing our finger on what is the peculiar and distinguishing characteristic of human beings above other creatures, it is that we are invited, born, as we are for the contemplation of heaven, and being a truly heavenly plant—to the knowledge of God.

Practise husbandry, we say, if you are a husbandman; but while you till your fields, know God. Sail the sea, you who are devoted to navigation, yet call the meanwhile on the heavenly Pilot.

No hindrance stands in the way of those who are bent on the knowledge of God. Neither childlessness, nor poverty, nor obscurity, nor want, can hinder those who eagerly strive after the knowledge of God.

CLEMENT OF ALEXANDRIA (150–220)
Greek theologian and church father

Contemplation is the goal of all life. It is knowledge by love. St. Paul often prays for his disciples that they may have knowledge (*gnosis*) and understanding (*epignosis*) in the mystery of Christ. The mystery of Christ is the ultimate truth, the reality towards which all human life aspires. And this mystery is known by love. Love is going out of oneself, surrendering the self, letting the reality, the truth take over. It is not limited to any earthly object or person. It reaches out to the infinite and the eternal. This is contemplation. It is not something which we achieve for ourselves; it is something that comes when we let go. We have to abandon everything, all words, thoughts, hopes, fears, all attachment to ourselves or to any earthly thing, and let the divine mystery take possession of our lives. It feels like death and is a sort of dying. It is encountering the darkness, the abyss, the void. It is facing nothingness or, as the English Benedictine mystic Augustine Baker said, it is the "union of the nothing with the Nothing."

BEDE GRIFFITHS (1906–1993)

English Benedictine monk

If one could silence the clamorous appetites of the flesh, and hush one's perceptions of earth, the waters and air; if one could silence the vault of heaven; and could one's very soul be silent to itself, and by ceasing to think of itself, mount above the awareness of self; if one could silence all dreams and images which the mind can imagine; if one could hush all tongues, and signs and symbols that pass: for all these say to any who listen, "we did not make ourselves, but he made us that abides for ever"; if after speaking thus, they were then to be silenced after drawing the mind's attention to him who made them, and he were now to speak alone not through them but by himself, so that we might hear his Word, not through human tongue, nor through the voice of an angel, not through a voice speaking out of a cloud, nor through any false appearance, but that we might hear instead without these things, himself in his very Being—himself whose presence we love in those things; . . . if this movement continued on, and all other visions were to pass away as totally unequal; and this one vision were to ravish the beholder, immerse him and draw him into these inner joys, so that life might be forever like that fleeting moment of awareness which we have longed for; would not this be "Enter into the joy of your Lord?"

AUGUSTINE OF HIPPO (354–430)
Carthaginian saint, philosopher, and doctor of the church

It is the character only of a good person to be able to deny and disown himself, and to make a full surrender of himself unto God; forgetting himself, and minding nothing but the will of his Creator; triumphing in nothing more than in his own nothingness, and in the allness of the Divinity.

But indeed this, his being nothing, is the only way to be all things; this, his having nothing, the truest way of possessing all things.

JOHN SMITH (1618–1652)
English Platonist

The way in which they are to conduct themselves in this night of sense is to devote themselves not at all to reasoning and pious thought, since this is not the time for it, but to allow the soul to remain in peace and quietness, although it may seem clear to them that they are doing nothing and are wasting their time, and although it may appear to them that it is because of their weakness that they have no desire in that state to think of anything.

The truth is that they will be doing quite sufficient if they have patience and persevere in prayer without making any effort. What they must do is merely to leave the soul free and disencumbered and at rest from all knowledge and thought, troubling not themselves, in that state, about what they shall think or meditate upon, but contenting themselves with merely a peaceful and loving attentiveness toward God, and in being without anxiety, without the ability and without desire to have experience of Him or to perceive Him. For all these yearnings disquiet and distract the soul from the peaceful quiet and sweet ease of contemplation.

JOHN OF THE CROSS (1542–1591)
Spanish saint and mystic

I want you (and others like you who may read this) to understand one thing very clearly. Although I have encouraged you to set out in the contemplative way with simplicity and boldness, nevertheless I am certain, without doubt or fear of error, that Almighty God himself, independently of all techniques, must always be the chief worker in contemplation. It is he who must always awaken this gift in you by his grace. And what you (and others like you) must do is make yourselves completely receptive, consenting and suffering his divine action in the depths of your spirit. Yet the passive consent and endurance you bring to this work is really a distinctively active attitude; for by the singleness of your desire ever reaching up to your Lord, you continually open yourself to his action. All this, however, you will learn for yourself through experience and the insight of spiritual wisdom.

UNKNOWN ENGLISH MYSTIC (14th century)
The Book of Privy Counseling

My friend Timothy, whenever you set yourself, by the stirring of grace, for the practical exercise of your dark contemplation, be intent on abandoning, with an intense, sagacious, and loving contrition, both your bodily senses of hearing, seeing, smelling, tasting, and touching, and your spiritual faculties also—those which are called your intellectual operations; all those things outside yourself which can be known by any of your five bodily senses; all those things within you which can be known by your spiritual faculties; all the things that now exist, or have existed in the past, though they now exist no longer; and all those things which do not exist now, yet which must exist in time to come, though they are not in existence now. And insofar as it is possible for me to speak of this and for you to understand, be intent on ascending with me in this grace, in a manner such as you could never understand [with your reason], to be made one with him who is above every substance and every kind of knowledge. For it is by passing beyond yourself and all other things, and so purifying yourself of all worldly, carnal, and natural love in your affection, and of everything that can be known according to its own proper form in your intellect; it is in this way, when all things are done away with, that you shall be carried up in your affection and above your understanding to the Substance beyond all substances, the radiance of the divine darkness.

DENIS (fifth century)
Syrian monk, mystic, and teacher

In order to have pleasure in everything
Desire to have pleasure in nothing.
In order to arrive at possessing everything
Desire to possess nothing.
In order to arrive at being everything

Desire to be nothing.
In order to arrive at knowing everything
Desire to know nothing.
In order to arrive at that wherein you have no pleasure
You must go by a way in which you have no pleasure.
In order to arrive at that in which you know not
You must go by a way in which you know not.
In order to arrive at that which you possess not
You must go by a way that you possess not.
In order to arrive at that which you are not
You must go through that which you are not.

JOHN OF THE CROSS (1542–1591)

Spanish saint and mystic

Shall I say it again? In order to arrive there,
To arrive where you are, to get from where you are not,
You must go by a way wherein there is no ecstasy.
In order to arrive at what you do not know
You must go by a way which is the way of ignorance.
In order to possess what you do not possess
You must go by the way of dispossession.
In order to arrive at what you are not
You must go through the way in which you are not.
And what you do not know is the only thing you know
And what you own is what you do not own
And where you are is where you are not.

T. S. ELIOT (1888–1965)

Anglo-American poet

Having Nothing, Possessing All Things

Blessed are the poor in spirit, for theirs is the kingdom of heaven.

In the first place we say that a poor person is someone who desires nothing. Some people do not understand this point correctly. I mean those who cling to their own egos in their penances and external devotions, which such people regard as being of great importance. God have mercy on them, for they know little of the divine truth! These people are called holy because of what they are seen to do, but inside they are asses, for they do not know the real meaning of divine truth.

Although such people are happy to say that a poor person is one who desires nothing, they interpret this as meaning that we must live in such a way that we never perform our own will in anything but that we should desire rather to carry out God's most precious will. These people are all right, for they mean well and that is why they deserve our praise. May God in his mercy grant them heaven! But I tell you by the divine truth that such people are not truly poor, nor are they like those who are poor. They are greatly esteemed by people who know no better. But I tell you that they are asses, who understand nothing of God's truth. May they attain heaven because of their good intent, but of that poverty, of which we now wish to speak, they know nothing.

If someone were now to ask me what it means to be a poor person who desires nothing, then I would say that as long as it is someone's will to carry out the most precious will of God, such a person does not have that poverty of which we wish to speak. For this person still has a will with which they wish to please God, and this is not true poverty. If we are to have true poverty, then we must be so free of our own created will as we were before we were created. I tell you by the eternal truth that as long as you have the will to perform God's will, and a desire for eternity and for God, you are not yet poor. They alone are poor who will nothing and desire nothing.

MEISTER ECKHART (1260–1327)
German Dominican mystic and theologian

Whatever God imparts of the vision and knowledge of God to the faithful here below, it is an enigmatic vision, as if in a mirror. . . . —except when God on occasion reveals his face to his chosen and beloved in a sort of intermittent light, just as a candle enclosed in someone's hands sheds light and conceals light according to the will of the person holding it. Permitted thus to glimpse the fleeting and passing light, the mind can then blaze with ardent longing for full possession of eternal light. Sometimes, to give one a sense of what he lacks, the lover's consciousness is, as it were, briefly seized by grace, snatched away from him, carried off to the light of reality, away from the tumult of affairs into silent joys. There, in a manner suited to his capacity, for a moment, for an instant, utter reality as it is in itself is revealed to him. For a time indeed he may be transformed, in his own way, into something like that ultimate reality. When he has thus learned the difference between clean and unclean, he is returned to himself and returned to the task of cleansing his heart for vision, to the task of fitting his mind for likeness, so that, should he be granted another glimpse, he might see in greater purity and enjoy it more steadily.

WILLIAM OF ST. THIERRY (1075–1148)
Belgian Benedictine monk and theologian

Now, as soon as some people discover and experience this rare comfort, they would like to immerse themselves and fall asleep in it, rest forever in its bliss, just as Saint Peter, tasting one drop of this joy, wished to build three tents and remain there forever. But this was not Our Lord's wish; for the goal to which he would guide and lead him was still far off. And as it was with Saint Peter, who exclaimed, "It is good for us to be here," so it is with us: As soon as we become aware of this bliss, we believe ourselves in possession of the entire sun, and we would like to bask in its radiance and stretch out under its warmth. Those who act thus will always remain in the same place; nothing will come of them, they have missed the point.

Others, again, fall into a different trap by wishing to find a false freedom in this sweetness. In this state of emotional joy, nature cleverly turns back upon itself and takes possession; and this is what human nature is most inclined to do, it likes to rely upon emotions. The effect is as bad as with some people who take too many medicines; as soon as nature grows accustomed to them, it becomes dependent, relents, turns lazy, and thinks that it has a good crutch there, and would not work as hard as it would otherwise. If, however, it is left without any assurance of such help, it becomes active again and helps itself. Just observe, Beloved, how sly and treacherous this nature of ours is, and how it invariably seeks its own comfort and convenience. And this is true to a much higher degree in spiritual matters. For, as soon as a person experiences this pleasure and feels this extraordinary well-being, he thinks he can rely upon it. He leans on it and does not work with the same zeal and fidelity as before.

JOHANNES TAULER (1300–1361)
German Dominican contemplative

Know that when you seek anything of your own, you will never find God because you do not seek God purely. You are seeking something along with God, and you are acting just as if you were to make a candle out of God in order to look for something with it. Once one finds the things one is looking for, one throws the candle away. This is what you are doing: Whatever else you are looking for in addition to God, it is nothing, no matter what it might be—whether it be something useful or reward or devotion or whatever it might be. You are seeking nothing, and so you also find nothing. The reason why you find nothing is that you are seeking nothing. All creatures are a pure nothing. I do not just say that they are insignificant or are only a little something: They are a pure nothing. Whatever has no being *is* not. Creatures have no being because their being depends on God's presence. If God were to turn away from creatures for an instant, they would turn to nothing. I once said (and it is true), if someone were to have the whole world and God, he would not have more than if he had God alone. All creatures have nothing more without God than a gnat has without God—(they are) just the same, neither less nor more.

MEISTER ECKHART (1260–1327)

German Dominican mystic and theologian

Reject the thought and experience of all created things, but most especially learn to forget yourself, for all your knowledge and experience depends upon the knowledge and feeling of yourself. All else is easily forgotten in comparison with one's own self. See if experience does not prove me right. Long after you have successfully forgotten every creature and its works, you will find that a naked knowing and feeling of your own being still remains between you and your God. And believe me, you will not be perfect in love until this, too, is destroyed.

Without God's special grace, freely given, and without perfect correspondence to his grace on your part, you can never hope to destroy the naked knowing and feeling of your being. Perfect correspondence to his grace consists in a strong, deep interior sorrow.

But it is most important to moderate this sorrow. You must be careful never to strain your body or spirit irreverently. Simply sit relaxed and quiet but plunged and immersed in sorrow. The sorrow I speak of is genuine and perfect, and blessed is the one who experiences it. Every one has plenty of cause for sorrow, but he alone understands the deep universal reason for sorrow who experiences *that he is.* Every other motive pales beside this one. He alone feels authentic sorrow who realizes not only *what he is* but *that he is.*

And yet, in all this, never does he desire not-to-be, for this is the devil's madness and blasphemy against God. In fact, he rejoices that he is and from the fullness of a grateful heart he gives thanks to God for the gift and goodness of his existence. At the same time, however, he desires unceasingly to be freed from the knowing and feeling of his being.

Everyone must sooner or later realize in some manner both this sorrow and this longing to be freed.

UNKNOWN ENGLISH MYSTIC (14th century)
The Cloud of Unknowing

Therefore, O spiritual soul, when you see your desire obscured, your affections arid and constrained, and your faculties bereft of their capacity for any interior exercise, be not afflicted by this, but rather consider it a great happiness, since God is freeing you from yourself and taking the work from your hands. For with those hands, howsoever well they may serve you, you would never labor so effectively, so perfectly and so securely (because of their clumsiness and uncleanness) as now, when God takes your hand and guides you in the darkness, as though you were blind, to an end and by a way which you know not nor could you ever hope to travel with the aid of your own eyes and feet, howsoever good you may be as a walker.

JOHN OF THE CROSS (1542–1591)
Spanish saint and mystic

Eternal rest is not idleness, since from idleness comes languor, torpor, dullness, and stupefaction of mind, and therefore of the whole body; and these are death and not life, and still less eternal life, in which the angels of heaven are. Eternal rest is therefore a rest which dispels these, and causes a man to live.

It is therefore some study and work by which the mind is excited, vivified, and delighted; and this effect is produced according to the use from which, in which, and for which it works. Hence it is that the universal heaven is regarded by the Lord as the containant of use; and every angel is an angel according to its use. The delight of use carries him along as a favorable current a ship, and causes him to be in eternal peace, and in the rest of peace. Eternal rest from labors is thus to be understood.

EMANUEL SWEDENBORG (1688–1772)
Swedish scientist and mystical thinker

If you fix your thoughts on heaven, and wish to conceive in your mind what it is and where it is and how it is, you need not cast your thoughts many thousand miles off, for that place, that heaven, is not your heaven.

And though indeed that is united with your heaven as one body, and so together is but the one body of God, yet you are not a creature in that very place which is far further than many hundred thousand miles off, but you are in the heaven of this world, which contains in it such a Deep as is not of any human numbering.

The true heaven is everywhere, even in that very place where you stand and walk; and so when your spirit presses through the astral and the fleshly, and apprehends the innermost moving of God, then it is clearly in heaven.

But that there is assuredly a pure glorious heaven in all the three movings far above the deep of this world, in which God's Being together with that of the holy angels springs up very purely, brightly, beauteously, and joyfully, is undeniable. And he is not born of God that denies it.

You must know that this world in its innermost unfolds its properties and powers in union with the heaven high above us; and so there is one Heart, one Being, one Will, one God, all in all.

The outermost moving of this world cannot comprehend the outermost moving of heaven high above this world, for they are one to the other as life and death, or as a man and a stone are one to the other.

There is a strong firmament dividing the outermost of this world from the outermost of the upper heaven; and that firmament is Death, which rules and reigns everywhere in the outermost in this world, and sets a great gulf between them.

The second moving of this world is in the life; it is the astral, out of which is generated the third and holy moving; and therein love and wrath strive one with the other. For the second moving stands in the seven fountain spirits of this world, and is in all places and in all the creatures as in man. But the Holy Ghost also rules and reigns in that second, and helps to generate the third, the holy moving.

This, the third, is the clear and holy heaven which unites with the Heart of God, distinct from and above all heavens, as one heart.

If man's eyes were but opened he should see God everywhere in his heaven; for heaven stands in the innermost moving everywhere.

JACOB BOEHME (1575–1624)
German Lutheran theosophist

Theologians call the divine sometimes an erotic force, sometimes love, sometimes that which is intensely longed for and loved. Consequently, as an erotic force and as love, the divine itself is subject to movement; and as that which is intensely longed for and loved it moves towards itself everything that is receptive of this force and love. To express this more clearly: the divine itself is subject to movement since it produces an inward state of intense longing and love in those receptive to them; and it moves others since by nature it attracts the desire of those who are drawn towards it. In other words, it moves others and itself moves since it thirsts to be thirsted for, longs to be longed for, and loves to be loved.

The divine erotic force also produces ecstasy, compelling those who love to belong not to themselves but to those whom they love. . . .

It was in consequence of this that St. Paul, possessed as he was by this divine erotic force and partaking of its ecstatic power, was inspired to say: "I no longer live, but Christ lives in me" (Gal. 2:20). He uttered these words as a true lover and, as he himself says, as one who has gone out from himself to God (cf. 2 Cor. 5:15), not living his own life but that of the beloved, because of his fervent love for Him. . . .

God is said to be the originator and begetter of love and the erotic force. For He externalized them from Himself, that is, He brought them forth into the world of created things. This is why Scripture says that "God is love" (I John 4:16), and elsewhere that He is "sweetness and desire" (cf. Song of Songs 5:16. LXX), which signifies the erotic force. For what is worthy of love and truly desirable is God Himself. Because loving desire is poured out from Him, He Himself, as its begetter, is said to be in movement, while because He is what is truly longed for, loved, desired, and chosen, He stirs into motion the things that turn towards Him, and which possess the power of desiring each in the degree appropriate to it.

You should understand that God stimulates and allures in order to bring about an erotic union in the Spirit; that is to say, He is the go-between in this union, the one who brings the parties together, in order that He may be desired and loved by His creatures. God stimulates in that He impels each being, in accordance with its own principle, to return to Him. Even though the word "allurement" signifies something impure to the profane, here it stands for the mediation which effects the union with God.

The erotic impulsion of the Good, that pre-exists in the Good, is simple and self-moving; it proceeds from the Good, and returns again to the Good, since it is without end or beginning. This is why we always desire the divine and union with the divine. For loving union with God surpasses and excels all other unions.

We should regard the erotic force, whether divine, angelic, noetic, psychic or physical, as a unifying and commingling power. It impels superior beings to care for those below them, beings of equal dignity to act with reciprocity, and, finally, inferior beings to return to those that are greater and more excellent than they.

MAXIMOS THE CONFESSOR (580–662)

Greek saint, theologian, and writer

What is this eternal coming of our Bridegroom? It is a new birth and a new illumination which are without interruption; for the source from which the brightness streams, and which is itself the brightness, is living and fertile; and so the manifestation of the eternal light is renewed without interruption, in the secret depths of the spirit. . . .

And the coming of the Bridegroom is so swift that He is always coming, and that He dwells within us with His unfathomable riches, and that He returns ever anew in person, with such new brightness that it seems as if He had never come before. For His coming is comprised beyond all limit of time, in an eternal Now; and He is ever received with new desires and a new delight.

Behold, the joys and the pleasures which this Bridegroom brings with Him at His coming are boundless and without limit, for they are Himself. And this is why the eyes of the spirit, by which the loving soul beholds its Bridegroom, are opened so wide that they will never shut again.

For the contemplation and the fixed gaze of the spirit are eternal in the secret manifestation of God. And the comprehension of the spirit is so widely opened, as it waits for the appearance of the Bridegroom, that the spirit itself becomes vast as that which it comprehends. And so is God beheld and understood by God, in whom all our blessedness is found.

JAN VAN RUUSBROEC (1293–1381)

Flemish mystic and theologian

Under this immense force she loses herself.
In this most dazzling light she becomes blind in herself.
And in this utter blindness she sees most clearly.
In this pure clarity she is both dead and living.

The longer she is dead, the more blissfully she lives.
The more blissfully she lives, the more she experiences.
The less she becomes, the more flows to her.
The more she fears . . .
The richer she becomes, the poorer she is.
The deeper she dwells, the more she expands.
. . . , the more forbearing she is.
The deeper her wounds become, the more violently
    she struggles.
The more loving God is to her, the higher she soars.
The more radiantly she shines in the reflected effulgence
    of the Godhead, the closer she approaches him.

The more she labors, the more contentedly she rests.

..., the more she grasps.

The more quiet her silence, the louder she calls.

..., the greater the marvels she works with his strength
in proportion to her power.

MECHTHILD OF MAGDEBURG (1210–1297)

German mystic

The eye in which I see God is the same eye in which God sees me.
My eye and God's eye are one eye and one seeing, one knowing and
one loving.

MEISTER ECKHART (1260–1327)

German Dominican mystic and theologian

ACKNOWLEDGMENTS AND SOURCES

To the staff of St. Mark's Library at the General Theological Seminary in New York City, I express my thanks for their unfailingly courteous and cheerful assistance, and for allowing me to roam their stacks at will—without a murmur, they watched me pile up dozens of books a day for reshelving; to the Paulist Press for their invaluable Classics of Western Spirituality Series, and for inviting me to quote freely from its volumes; to those publishers who have granted permission to publish excerpts from their works; and, finally, to Toinette Lippe, an editor's editor. L. K.

ADAMNAN (521–597)
Irish saint, abbot of Iona, and missionary.
   p. 4: *Life of St. Columba* by St. Adamnan, translated by Wentworth Huyshe, London: G. Routledge.

ANCHORESS'S RULE (c. 1220)
English.
   p. 65: From *Anchoritic Spirituality: Ancrene Wisse and Associated Works,* translated and introduced by Anne Savage and Nicholas Watson; preface by Benedicta Ward, New York: Paulist Press, 1991. Copyright © 1991 by Paulist Press.

ANKER-LARSEN, JOHANNES (1874–1957)

Danish novelist.

    p. 10: From *With the Door Open* by Johannes Anker-Larsen, translated by Erwin and Pleasaunce von Gaisberg, London and New York: Macmillan, 1931.

AUDEN, W. H. (1907-1973)

He is generally considered the greatest English poet of the 20th century, and his work has exerted a major influence on succeeding generations of poets in both England and the United States. Auden was also a noted playwright, librettist, editor, and essayist.

    p. 52: From *Forewords and Afterwords* by W. H. Auden. Copyright © 1973 by W. H. Auden. Reprinted by permission of Random House Inc.

AUGUSTINE OF HIPPO (354–430)

Carthaginian saint, philosopher, and doctor of the church. Immensely influential. City of God, Confessions, and On the Trinity are his major works.

    p. 26: Exposition of Psalm 121, verse 6. From *Spiritual Classics From the Early Church*, introduced and compiled by Robert Atwell, OSB, London: Church House Publishing, 1995. Reprinted by permission of the Society of the Salutation of Mary the Virgin Ltd.

    p. 76: From *The Confessions of St. Augustine*, translated by Rex Warner, New York: The New American Library, 1967.

    p. 126: From *The Confessions of St. Augustine*, Vol. I, translated by E. B. Pusey, Oxford: J. H. Parker, 1838.

    p. 195: From *The Homilies of St. Augustine* on *St. John's Gospel*, in The Divine Office, London: Collins, 1974. Copyright © 1974 by The Hierarchies of England and Wales, Ireland and Australia. Reprinted by permission of A. P. Watt Ltd. on behalf of The Hierarchies of England and Wales, Ireland and Australia.

    p. 218: Cited in *The Pursuit of Wisdom and Other Works, by the Author of The Cloud of Unknowing*, translated, edited, and annotated by James A. Walsh, SJ, preface by George A. Maloney, SJ, New York: Paulist Press, 1998. Copyright © by the British Province of the Society of Jesus. Reprinted by permission of Paulist Press.

BALDWIN (d. 1190)

Archbishop of Canterbury and author of sermons and theological works.

    p. 116: From Treatise 6, cited in *From the Fathers to the Churches,* edited by Brother Kenneth, CGA, London: Collins, 1983.

Acknowledgments and Sources

BALDWIN, JAMES (1924–1987)

The first of nine children of a clergyman and factory worker, Baldwin was born in Harlem and was himself a storefront preacher from age 14 to 17. Go Tell It on the Mountain, Giovanni's Room, *and* Tell Me How Long the Train's Been Gone *are among his major novels;* The Amen Corner *and* Blues for Mr. Charlie *are plays, and* Nobody Knows My Name *is his distinguished and best-selling essay collection.*

p. 80: From *Notes of a Native Son* by James Baldwin, Boston: Beacon Press, 1955.

BALTHASAR, HANS URS VON (1905–1988)

Swiss theologian and writer. Born in Lucerne and became a Jesuit in 1929. Nominated a cardinal, but died before admittance. Enormous literary output aimed at rescuing theology from an arid scholasticism by uniting knowledge and love in contemplation; his theology has been called a theology of "kneeling theologians."

p. 5: From *The Grain of Wheat: Aphorisms* by Hans Urs von Balthasar, translated by Erasmo Leiva-Merikakis, San Francisco: Ignatius Press, 1995.

p. 91: From *Prayer* by Hans Urs von Balthasar, translated by A. V. Littledale, London: G. Chapman, 1961.

p. 136: *The Grain of Wheat.*

BARCLAY, ROBERT (1648–1690)

Scottish Quaker apologist and theologian. His Apology for the True Christian Religion *is a classic exposition of Quaker principles.*

p. 94: From *Quaker Classics in Brief,* Wallingford, Pa.: Pendle Hill Publications, 1978.

BASIL THE GREAT (330–379)

Doctor of the church, saint, and bishop of Caesarea.

p. 29: From *Spiritual Classics From the Early Church,* introduced and compiled by Robert Atwell, OSB, London: Church House Publishing, 1995. Reprinted by permission of the Society of the Salutation of Mary the Virgin Ltd.

p. 83: Ibid.

p. 171: From *Ascetical Works: The Long Rules,* translated by M. Monica Wagner, Vol. 9, New York: Fathers of the Church, Inc., 1950.

p. 195: *Spiritual Classics.*

BEECHER, HENRY WARD (1813–1887)

American Congregational minister. One of the eight sons of Calvinist theologian Lyman Beecher who became ministers, and brother of Uncle Tom's Cabin author Harriet Beecher Stowe.

   pp. 49, 126, and 179: From *Morning and Evening Exercises, Selected From the Published and Unpublished Writings of the Rev. Henry Ward Beecher,* edited by Lyman Abbott, New York: Harper & Brothers, Publishers, 1891.

BERDYAEV, NICHOLAS (1874–1948)

Russian existentialist religious philosopher whose thought evolved from Marxism to Idealism to Orthodox mysticism. From 1922 an émigré in Paris. Major works include The Destiny of Man, Slavery and Freedom, *and* Freedom and the Spirit.

   p. 54: From *The Destiny of Man* by Nicholas Berdyaev, translated by Natalie Duddington, New York: Charles Scribner's Sons, 1937.

   p. 62: Reprinted with the permission of Scribner, a Division of Simon & Schuster, from *Slavery and Freedom* by Nicholas Berdyaev, translated from the French by R. M. French. Translation copyright © 1944 by Charles Scribner's Sons; copyright renewed 1972.

   p. 74: From *The Beginning and the End* by Nicholas Berdyaev, translated from the Russian by R. M. French, New York: Harper & Brothers, 1952.

BERNARD OF CLAIRVAUX (1091–1153)

Cistercian abbot, saint, and theologian. Founder and abbot of Clairvaux, which became one of the chief centers of the Cistercian Order, he founded or adopted 160 monasteries before his death. His best-known work is the series of sermons on the Song of Songs. An expressive writer of great humanity and insight.

   p. 95: From *Bernard of Clairvaux: Selected Works,* translation and foreword by G. R. Evans, introduction by Jean Leclercq, preface by Ewart H. Cousins, New York: Paulist Press, 1987. Copyright © 1987 by Paulist Press. Reprinted by permission of Paulist Press.

   p. 149: Ibid.

   p. 155: Ibid.

BLOOM, ANTHONY (1914–)

French Resistance fighter, army surgeon, Russian Orthodox monk, and metropolitan of Sourozh.

   p. 20: From *Living Prayer* by Anthony Bloom (Metropolitan Anthony of Sourozh), Springfield, Ill.: Templegate Publishers, copyright © 1966 and 1999 by Darton, Longman and Todd Ltd. Permission granted by Templegate Publishers and Darton, Longman and Todd Ltd.

p. 32: From *Beginning to Pray*, by Archbishop Anthony Bloom. A Deus Books Edition of Paulist Press, originally published under the title *School for Prayer* by Metropolitan Anthony Sourozh, published and copyright 1970 and 1999 by Darton, Longman & Todd, Ltd., London, and used by permission of the publishers.

p. 70: From *Courage to Pray* by Metropolitan Anthony of Sourozh and Georges Lefebvre, translated from the French by Dinah Livingstone, copyright © 1984 by Darton, Longman and Todd, London: Darton, Longman and Todd and Crestwood, N.Y.: St. Vladimir's Seminary Press, 1984. Used by permission of the publishers.

p. 78: *Living Prayer.*

p. 135: *Beginning to Pray.*

p. 204: *Living Prayer.*

BOEHME, JACOB (1575–1624)

German Lutheran theosophist. Boehme lived from childhood in a state of religious exaltation. He is an obscure and difficult writer, but he remains influential.

p. 213: From *The Signature of All Things With Other Writings by Jacob Boehme*, London: J. M. Dent, 1912.

p. 229: From *The Confessions of Jacob Boehme*, translated by Frederick D. Maurice; compiled and edited by W. Scott Palmer; introduction by Evelyn Underhill, London: Methuen and Company, Ltd., 1920.

BONHOEFFER, DIETRICH (1906–1945)

German Lutheran pastor, opposed to the Nazis from the first. He was forbidden to teach, banned from Berlin, and dismissed from his lectureship there. Worked at Union Theological Seminary in New York City and returned to Germany at the outbreak of the war. Bonhoeffer was arrested in 1943 and hanged by the Gestapo at Flossenburg in 1945.

p. 34 and 51: From *Life Together* by Dietrich Bonhoeffer. English translation copyright © 1954 by Harper & Brothers, copyright renewed 1982 by Helen S. Doberstein. Reprinted by permission of HarperCollins Publishers, Inc.

BOOK OF PRIVY COUNSELING.
See *THE CLOUD OF UNKNOWING.*

BUNYAN, JOHN (1628–1688)

The most popular religious writer in the English language. Son of a tinker, he became a preacher and led an irreproachable Christian life.

   pp. 99 and 125: From *The Pilgrim's Progress* by John Bunyan.

BYRANCHANINOV, IGNATIUS (1807–1867)

Russian bishop.

   pp. 108 and 207: From *Russian Mystics* by Sergius Bolshakoff; introduction by Thomas Merton, Kalamazoo, Mich.: Cistercian Publications, copyright © 1977 by the Abbey of Gethsemani, Inc. Reprinted by permission of Cistercian Publications.

CARTHUSIAN MONK (anonymous), CONTEMPORARY.

   pp. 11 and 73: From *They Speak by Silences* by a Carthusian, translated from the French by a monk of Parkminster, London: Longmans, Green, and Co., 1955.

CASSIAN, JOHN (360–435)

Saint. Born in the Roman province of Scythia Minor, went to Bethlehem, and soon after to Egypt to study monasticism. He founded two monasteries near Marseilles.

   p. 102: From *John Cassian: The Conferences,* translated and annotated by Boniface Ramsey, New York: Paulist Press, 1997. Copyright © 1997 by Paulist Press. Reprinted by permission of Paulist Press.

CATHERINE OF SIENA (1347–1380)

Italian Dominican mystic and saint. The only woman other than Teresa of Ávila to be granted the title of doctor of the Roman Catholic Church. The Dialogue was one of the first books to see print in Spain, Germany, Italy, and England.

   p. 39: From *Catherine of Siena—The Dialogue,* translated and with an introduction by Suzanne Noffke, OP, New York: Paulist Press, 1980. Copyright © 1980 by Paulist Press.

CHANNING, WILLIAM ELLERY (1780–1842)

American Unitarian pastor.

   p. 196: From the tract "Daily Prayer." Cited in *The Fellowship of the Saints: An Anthology of Christian Devotional Literature,* compiled by Thomas S. Kepler, New York: Abingdon-Cokesbury Press, 1948.

CHRYSOSTOM, JOHN (345–407)

Father of the Eastern church, saint, and bishop of Constantinople, he was a powerful preacher (Chrysostom means "golden-mouthed"), reformer, and expositor.

p. 67: From *The Nicene and Post-Nicene Fathers*, translated by W. R. W. Stephens, Grand Rapids, Mich.: Wm. B. Eerdmans Publishing Company, 1889.

p. 112: From *Chrysostom:* Homily 33.1.2 on *St. Matthew's Gospel*, in The Divine Office, London: Collins, 1974. Copyright ©1974 by The Hierarchies of England and Wales, Ireland and Australia. Reprinted by permission of A. P. Watt Ltd. on behalf of The Hierarchies of England and Wales, Ireland and Australia.

p. 148: *Nicene and Post-Nicene Fathers.*

p. 175: From *Spiritual Classics From the Early Church*, introduced and compiled by Robert Atwell, OSB, London: Church House Publishing, 1995. Reprinted by permission of the Society of the Salutation of Mary the Virgin Ltd.

CLEMENT OF ALEXANDRIA (150–220)

Greek theologian and church father, head of catachetical school in Alexandria famous for learning.

p. 17: From "Office of the Instructor" in *The Ante-Nicene Fathers*, the Rev. Alexander Roberts, DD, and James Donaldson, LLD, editors, Grand Rapids, Mich.: Wm. B. Eerdmans Publishing Company, 1887.

p. 216: Ibid.

CLIMACUS, JOHN (520–603)

Father of Eastern Church. Ascetic writer on the spiritual life. He arrived as a novice at Mt. Sinai at the age of 16 and later served as abbot of Sinai.

p. 64: From *The Ladder of Divine Ascent* by John Climacus, translated by Colm Luibheid and Norman Russell, New York: Paulist Press, 1982. Copyright © 1982 by Paulist Press. Reprinted by permission of Paulist Press.

CLOUD OF UNKNOWING, THE and THE BOOK OF PRIVY COUNSELING (also known as *The Letter of Private Direction* and *The Letter of Privy Counseling*) *Written by an unknown 14th-century English mystic.*

p. 73: From *The Cloud of Unknowing and The Book of Privy Counseling* by William Johnston, 1973. Copyright © 1973 by William Johnston. Used by permission of Doubleday, a division of Random House Inc.

p. 135: Ibid.

p. 208: From *The Pursuit of Wisdom and Other Works, by the Author of The Cloud of Unknowing*, translated, edited, and annotated by James A. Walsh, SJ; preface by George A. Maloney, SJ, New York: Paulist Press, 1998. Copyright © by the British Province of the Society of Jesus. Reprinted by permission of Paulist Press.

p. 220: From *The Cloud of Unknowing*.

p. 226: Ibid.

DE CAUSSADE, JEAN PIERRE (1675–1751)

French Jesuit and ascetic writer. A preacher and spiritual director, he did much to revive mysticism.

p. 85: From *The Sacrament of the Present Moment* by Jean Pierre de Caussade, translated and with an introduction by Kitty Muggeridge, New York: Harper & Row, 1982.

DE DAMPIERRE, PAULINE (contemporary)

French exponent of the Gurdjieff teaching.

p. 59: From "The Human Place: An Interview with Pauline de Dampierre," in *Parabola: Myth and the Quest for Meaning*, Vol. 10, No. 4. Reprinted by permission of *Parabola*.

DE LOMBEZ, AMBROISE (18th century)

The Capuchin theologian's Treatise on Interior Peace was written in Old French and published in Paris in 1756. It was translated into English by the American saint Elizabeth Ann Seton.

pp. 22, 93, 131, and 206: From *A Treatise on Interior Peace* by Ambroise de Lombez, OFM, Capuchin; translated by Saint Elizabeth Ann Seton; edited by Sister Marie Celeste, SC, New York: Alba House, 1996. Permission granted by Alba House.

DENIS (fifth–sixth centuries)

A Syrian monk, also known as Dionysius the Areopagite, and Pseudo-Dionysius, he can be considered the founder of Christian mysticism.

p. 220: From *The Pursuit of Wisdom and Other Works, by the Author of The Cloud of Unknowing*, translated, edited, and annotated by James A. Walsh, SJ, preface by George A. Maloney, SJ, New York: Paulist Press. Copyright © 1998 by the British Province of the Society of Jesus. Reprinted by permission of Paulist Press.

DE PONTE, GUIGO (d. 1297)
Carthusian monk and spiritual writer. Made his monastic profession at the Grande Chartreuse monastery, known chiefly as author of On Contemplation.

pp. 24 and 161: From *Carthusian Spirituality: The Writings of Hugh of Balma and Guigo de Ponte,* translated and introduced by Dennis D. Martin, preface by John van Engen, New York: Paulist Press, 1997. Copyright © 1997 by Paulist Press. Reprinted by permission of Paulist Press.

DESERT FATHERS (fourth–sixth centuries)
Early Christian seekers who withdrew into the deserts of Syria, Egypt, Arabia, and Palestine where they sought a spiritual father or mother and asked for "a word of life."

p. 18: Cited in *Monastery* by M. Basil Pennington, San Francisco: A Scala Book published by Harper San Francisco, 1983.

p. 104: From *The Sayings of the Desert Fathers,* translated by Benedicta Ward, SLG, Cistercian Studies Series 59, Kalamazoo, Mich.: Cistercian Publications, 1975.

p. 168: Cited in *Desert Wisdom: Sayings From the Desert Fathers* by Yushi Nomura, Garden City, N.Y.: Doubleday & Company, Inc. 1982.

p. 170: Ibid.

DONNE, JOHN (1572–1631)
English poet and dean of St. Paul's Cathedral, London. For the 42 years of his life before he entered the ministry, he was a law student, traveler to France and Italy, naval adventurer, and secular poet. A brilliant preacher, his vigorous and vital personality is evident in all his works.

p. 40: From a letter to Sir Henry Goodyere.

p. 43: From a sermon preached at the funeral of Sir William Cokayne, December 12, 1626. Edited and adapted by L. K.

p. 59: From a sermon preached at St. Paul's on Christmas Day, 1624.

p. 75: From *Essays in Divinity* by John Donne. Edited by L. K.

p. 105: From the first sermon preached to King Charles, at St. James, April 3, 1625. Edited and adapted by L. K.

p. 170: [2,8] From a letter to Sir Henry Goodyere.

p. 180: From a sermon preached to the Lords Easter Day, March 28, 1619. Edited by L. K.

p. 205: From a sermon preached at the funeral of Sir William Cokayne, December 12, 1626. Edited by L. K.

p. 214: From a sermon preached at St. Paul's on Christmas Day, 1624. Edited by L. K.

DOROTHEUS, ABBA (sixth century)
Saint, writer, and founder of a Palestinian monastery. His spiritual doctrine places the highest value on humility.

p. 92: From *Early Fathers From the Philokalia*, selected and translated from the Russian by E. Kadloubovsky and G. E. H. Palmer, London: Faber and Faber, 1953.

p. 133: Ibid.

p. 150: From The Divine Office, London: Collins, 1974. Copyright © 1974 by The Hierarchies of England and Wales, Ireland and Australia. Reprinted by permission of A. P. Watt Ltd. on behalf of The Hierarchies of England and Wales, Ireland and Australia.

DOSTOEVSKY, FYODOR (1821–1881)
Russian novelist, author of such titles as The Idiot, Crime and Punishment, *and* The Possessed. *The core of his religious outlook lies in his experience of salvation as a free gift of God.*

pp. 54 and 187: From *The Brothers Karamazov* by Fyodor Dostoevsky, translated from the Russian by Constance Garnett, New York: Macmillan, 1923. Reprinted by permission of Scribner, a division of Simon & Schuster and A. P. Watt Ltd. on behalf of the Executor of the Estate of Constance Garnett.

DU BOIS, W. E. B. (1868–1963)
The richness of Du Bois's scholarly and research legacy can be sampled in his The Suppression of the African Slave Trade *(1896),* The Philadelphia Negro *(1899),* The Souls of Black Folk *(1903),* John Brown *(1909), and* Black Reconstruction *(1935). He was a founder of the World Peace Council and fighter against the Cold War. He fought in the early part of this century for the rights of women, including the vote for Black and white women. The modern civil rights and African liberation movements owe more to Du Bois than any other single person.*

p. 171: From *Prayers for Dark People* by W. E. B. Du Bois, edited by Herbert Aptheker, Amherst: University of Massachusetts Press, 1980.

DUMITRIU, PETRU (1924–)
Romanian novelist and poet, defected to Paris.

p. 80: From *To the Unknown God* by Petru Dumitriu, translated by James Kirkup, New York: Seabury Press, 1982.

ECKHART, MEISTER (1260–1327)

German Dominican mystic and theologian. Entered Dominican abbey and was sent to Paris to study. Famous as a vernacular preacher. Eckhart taught that we should break through to the single ground of all reality where God and the soul are inseparably one.

p. 61: From *Meister Eckhart: A Modern Translation* by Raymond Bernard Blakney, New York: Harper & Row Publishers, Inc., 1941.

p. 84: From *Meister Eckhart: The Essential Sermons, Commentaries, Treatises and Defense*, translation and introduction by Edmund Colledge and Bernard McGinn, preface by Huston Smith, New York: Paulist Press, 1981. Copyright © 1981 by Paulist Press. Reprinted by permission of Paulist Press.

p. 108: From *Meister Eckhart: Teacher and Preacher*, edited by Bernard McGinn with the collaboration of Frank Tobin and Elvira Borgstadt, preface by Kenneth Northcott, New York: Paulist Press, 1986. Copyright © 1986 by Paulist Press. Reprinted by permission of Paulist Press.

p. 109: *Essential Sermons.*

p. 136: Ibid.

p. 137: Ibid.

p. 175: Ibid.

p. 223: From *Meister Eckhart: Selected Writings*, translated by Oliver Davies, London: Penguin Books, 1994. © Oliver Davies, 1994. Reprinted by permission of Penguin Books.

p. 226: *Meister Eckhart: Teacher and Preacher.*

p. 234: Ibid.

ELIOT, T. S. (1888–1965)

Anglo-American poet. One of the most powerful and influential poets of the 20th century.

p. 222: Excerpt from "East Coker" in *Four Quartets*, copyright 1940 by T. S. Eliot and renewed 1968 by Esme Valerie Eliot, reprinted by permission of Harcourt, Inc.

ERASMUS, DESIDERIUS (1466–1536)

Dutch theologian, humanist, and the most renowned scholar of his day. His Greek New Testament with his own Latin translation had a profound influence on theological studies.

p. 115: From *The Paraclesis*, Vol. V, Leyden: 1704. Translated by J. Reginald O'Donnell, CSB. Cited in *The Wisdom of Catholicism*, edited by A. C. Pegis, New York: Random House, 1949.

ERIUGENA, JOHN THE SCOT (810–877)
An Irishman, he was an original thinker and a great theologian and scholar, known as a translator of Greek texts into Latin.

p. 116: Cited in *Treasury of the Kingdom*, compiled by E. A. Blackburn et al., New York: Oxford University Press, 1954.

EVDOKIMOV, PAUL (1901–1970)
One of the most representative figures of the Orthodox Church in the West. He was professor at the Saint-Serge Theological Institute in Paris and director of the Center of Orthodox Studies in the French Language (Paris).

pp. 44, 66, and 110: From *The Struggle With God* by Paul Evdokimov, translated by Sister Gertrude, SP, Glen Rock, N.J.: Paulist Press, 1966. Reprinted by permission of Paulist Press.

FÉNELON, FRANÇOIS (1651–1715)
French Roman Catholic archbishop of Cambrai. He was much sought after as a spiritual director and had considerable influence both in and outside France in the 18th century.

pp. 89, 133, and 138: From *Extracts From the Writings of Francis Fénelon, Archbishop of Cambray*, edited by John Kendall, Philadelphia: Kimber, Conrad, and Co., 1804.

FLAVEL, JOHN (1630–1691)
English minister, spiritual writer, and effective preacher. One of his auditors commented, "That person must have a very soft head, or a very hard heart, or both, that could sit under his ministry unaffected."

p. 181: From *On Keeping the Heart*, circulated in the U.S. by the American Tract Society, cited on www.ccel.wheaton.edu.

p. 184: Ibid. Edited by L. K.

FRANCIS OF ASSISI (1182–1226)
Italian monk, saint, founder of the Franciscan order based on the vows of poverty, chastity, and obedience.

p. 2: From *The Little Flowers of St. Francis*, translated by Thomas Okey, New York: Everyman's Library, 1910. Edited by L. K.

FRANCIS OF SALES (1567–1622)

Saint, bishop of Geneva, and doctor of the church. Exponent of the quietistic trend in mysticism.

p. 127: From *Introduction to the Devout Life* by Francis of Sales, translated by W. W. Hutchins. Cited in *The Wisdom of Catholicism*, edited by A. C. Pegis, New York: Random House, 1949.

GERSON, JEAN (1363–1429)

French churchman and spiritual writer. The Mountain of Contemplation *and* The Perfection of the Heart *are among his major works.*

p. 154: From *Jean Gerson: Early Works*, translated and introduced by Brian Patrick McGuire, preface by Bernard McGinn, New York: Paulist Press, 1998.

GILBERT, HUGH, OSB (contemporary)

Benedictine abbot of Pluscarden Abbey, Scotland.

p. 11: From "The Life of Spiritual Combat," an interview by Philip Zaleski in *Parabola: Myth, Tradition, and the Search for Meaning*, Vol. 24, No. 2, May 1999.

GREGORY OF NYSSA (330–395)

Saint, bishop of Nyssa, Cappadocian father of the church, younger brother of St. Basil. A thinker and theologian of great originality and learning.

p. 147: From *Glory to Glory: Texts From Gregory of Nyssa's Mystical Writings*, edited by Jean Daniélou, translated by Herbert Musurillo, New York: Charles Scribner's Sons, 1961.

GREGORY THE GREAT (d. 604)

Pope Gregory I, doctor of the church, saint. He helped establish the ecclesiastical form of the church that was to last until the Middle Ages.

p. 140: From *Be Friends of God: Spiritual Reading From Gregory the Great*, translated and selected by John Leinenweber, Boston: Cowley Publications, 1990.

p. 182: From *The Homilies of St. Gregory the Great* on *The Book of Ezekiel*, in The Divine Office, London: Collins, 1974. Copyright © 1974, The Hierarchies of England and Wales, Ireland and Australia. Reprinted by permission of A. P. Watt Ltd. on behalf of The Hierarchies of England and Wales, Ireland and Australia.

GREGORY THE SINAITE (1255–1346)

Monk of Sinai and Mount Athos.

p. 92: From *The Philokalia: The Complete Text*, translated from the Greek and edited by G. E. H. Palmer, Philip Sherrard, Kallistos Ware with the assistance of the Holy Transfiguration Monastery (Brookline, Mass.), London and Boston: Faber and Faber, 1981.

GRIFFITHS, BEDE (1906–1993)
English Benedictine monk who spent much of his life in India.
    pp. 197 and 217: From *The Inner Directions Journal,* Summer 1996. Copyright the Inner Directions Foundation. www.innerdirections.org. Reprinted by permission.

GROU, JEAN NICHOLAS (1731–1803)
French Jesuit and spiritual writer. He served as chaplain to a convent of nuns, and from this began the spiritual writing for which he is known.
    p. 202: From *The Hidden Life of the Soul* by Jean Nicholas Grou, translated by W. H. Hutchins, London, 1881.

GUERRIC OF IGNY (12th century)
French Cistercian abbot.
    p. 167: From *Monastery* by M. Basil Pennington, San Francisco: A Scala Book published by Harper San Francisco, 1983.

GUIGO II (12th century)
French Carthusian monk and prior at the Grande Chartreuse monastery.
    p. 122: From *The Ladder of Monks: A Letter on the Contemplative Life, and Twelve Meditations* by Guigo II, translated and with an introduction by Edmund Colledge, OSA, and James Walsh, SJ, Garden City, N.Y.: Image Books, 1978.

HALL, JOSEPH (1574–1656)
English Puritan. His voluminous writings include Heaven Upon Earth.
    p. 202: From *Bishop Joseph Hall and Protestant Meditation in Seventeenth-Century England* by Frank Livingstone Huntley, Binghamton, N.Y.: Center for Medieval and Early Renaissance Studies, 1981.

HAMMARSKJÖLD, DAG (1905–1961)
Son of a former prime minister of Sweden, Hammarskjöld was the second secretary-general of the United Nations. He served from 1953 until his death in an airplane accident on September 18, 1961.

p. 161: From *Markings* by Dag Hammarskjöld, translated from the Swedish by Leif Sjöberg and W. H. Auden, New York: Alfred A. Knopf, 1970.

HANKEY, PATRICK (1886–?)
Dean of Ely Cathedral, and professor of ascetical theology.

p. 131: From *Sign Posts on the Christian Way: A Guide to the Devotional Life* by Patrick Hankey, New York: Charles Scribner's Sons, 1962.

HILTON, WALTER (1343–1396)
English contemplative writer.

p. 205: From *The Scale of Perfection* by Walter Hilton, translated by Dom Gerard Sitwell, OSB, London: Burns, Oates and Washburne, 1953.

HOPKINS, GERARD MANLEY (1844–1889)
English Jesuit priest and poet. His original and profound poetry was unknown during his life.

p. 170: From "The Principle or Foundation," an address based on *The Spiritual Exercises of St. Ignatius Loyola.*

IGNATIUS (30–107)
Saint and bishop of Antioch, known for his Epistles.

pp. 101 and 174: From "Letter to Polycarp," in *The Ante-Nicene Fathers*, the Rev. Alexander Roberts, DD, and James Donaldson, LLD, editors, Grand Rapids, Mich.: Wm. B. Eerdmans Publishing Company, 1887.

JOHN OF THE CROSS (1542–1591)
Spanish saint and mystic.

pp. 219, 221, and 227: From *The Dark Night of the Soul*, translated by E. A. Peers, New York: Image Books, 1959.

JONES, RUFUS M. (1863–1948)
American Quaker. Jones was a professor of philosophy at Haverford College. His many works include A Dynamic Faith *and* The Faith and Practice of the Quakers.

p. 123: From *Practical Christianity* by Rufus M. Jones, Philadelphia: John C. Winston Co., 1899.

JULIAN OF NORWICH (14th century)
English mystic and anchoress. Her revelation of May 1373 consisted of 15 "showings" and another single "showing" the following day. Her book is commonly known as Revelations of Divine Love.

    p. 21: Version by L. K.

    p. 210: From The Divine Office, London: Collins, 1974. Copyright © 1974 by The Hierachies of England and Wales, Ireland and Australia. Reprinted by permission of A. P. Watt Ltd. on behalf of The Hierachies of England and Wales, Ireland and Australia.

JUNG, C. G. (1875–1961)
Jung was one of the great pioneers in the area of depth psychology and the field now known as adult development theory. The collective unconscious, the animus, and anima are only a few of his original and influential concepts.

    p. 177: From *Psychological Reflections* by C. G. Jung, edited and compiled by Jolande Jacobi, Princeton: Princeton University Press, 1953.

KEBLE, JOHN (1792–1866)
Anglican priest. Keble left a brilliant career as a scholar to assist his father in a country church in the Cotswolds. He produced works of scholarship but remained a devoted parish priest. A leader of the Oxford Movement.

    p. 141: From *The Christian Year* by John Keble, Philadelphia: Carey, Lea & Blanchard, 1834.

KELLY, THOMAS RAYMOND (1893–1941)
American Quaker. Born in Ohio of Quaker parents. In 1934 he went to Pendle Hill. He taught at the University of Hawaii in 1935 and went to Germany in 1938.

    pp. 41 and 95: From *A Testament of Devotion* by Thomas R. Kelly, with a biographical memoir by Douglas V. Steere. Copyright 1941 by Harper & Row Publishers, Inc. Renewed 1969 by Lois Lael Kelly Stabler. New introduction copyright © 1992 by HarperCollins Publishers, Inc. Reprinted by permission of HarperCollins Publishers, Inc.

KELPIUS, JOHANNES (1673–1708)
German recluse, mystic, and teacher. Settled in the wilderness near Philadelphia.

    pp. 88 and 210: From *A Method of Prayer* by Johannes Kelpius. Edited and with an introduction by E. Gordon Alderfer, New York: Harper Brothers. In association with Pendle Hill, 1950. Permission granted by Pendle Hill Publications.

KIERKEGAARD, SØREN (1813–1855)
Danish theologian and philosopher who had a great influence on contemporary thought. Christian Discourses *is not as well known as his other works, but it brings to the reader a wealth of understanding of the redemptive work of Christ.*

   p. 26: From *Kierkegaard,* selected and introduced by W. H. Auden, London: Cassell, 1955.

   p. 35: Kierkegaard, Søren, *Works of Love,* edited and translated by Howard V. Hong and Edna H. Hong, Princeton, N.J.: Princeton University Press, 1995. Copyright © 1995 by Princeton University Press. Reprinted by permission of Princeton University Press.

   p. 44: *Kierkegaard.*

   p. 55: Ibid.

   p. 111: *Works of Love.*

   p. 129: From *Christian Discourses,* by Søren Kierkegaard, translated and with an introduction by Walter Lowrie, DD, New York: Oxford University Press, 1939.

   p. 163: From *Purity of Heart Is To Will One Thing* by Søren Kierkegaard. English translation copyright 1938 by Harper & Brothers, renewed © 1966 by Douglas V. Steere. Reprinted by permission of HarperCollins Publishers, Inc.

   p. 214: Ibid.

LAW, WILLIAM (1686–1761)
English contemplative and cleric. Spiritual writer whose famous work, A Serious Call to the Devout and Holy Life, *was inspired by Tauler, Ruusbroec, and Thomas à Kempis.*

   p. 58: From *A Serious Call to a Devout and Holy Life,* by William Law, MA, London: Printed for William Innys, 1929.

   p. 77: From *Selected Mystical Writings of William Law,* edited by Stephen Hobhouse, London: Rockliff, 1948.

   p. 109: *A Serious Call.*

   p. 144: Ibid.

   p. 179: From *The Spirit of Prayer,* or *The Soul Rising Out of the Vanity of Time, into the Riches of Eternity* by William Law, MA, London, 1749.

   p. 184: *A Serious Call.*

   p. 194: *Spirit of Prayer.* Abridged by L. K.

   p. 198: Ibid.

LAWRENCE, BROTHER (1614–1691)

Lay brother among Carmelites in Paris. After being a soldier, and later a hermit, entered the Discalced Carmelites at Paris in 1649, where he was given charge of the kitchen. He led a life of almost constant recollection.

pp. 86, 94, and 208: From *The Kitchen Saint & the Heritage of Islam,* translated by Elmer H. Douglas, Allison Park, Pa.: Pickwick Publications, copyright 1989. Reprinted by permission of Pickwick Publications.

LAWRENCE, D. H. (1885–1930)

An author of novels, short stories, poems, plays, essays, travel books, and letters. His novels Sons and Lovers, The Rainbow, *and* Women in Love *made him one of the most important English writers of the 20th century.*

p. 7: From *The Phoenix: The Posthumous Papers of D. H. Lawrence* by D. H. Lawrence, New York: Viking Press, 1936.

LEWIS, C. S. (1898–1963)

Scholar and Christian apologist. Surprised by Joy *is his spiritual autobiography. Author of the Narnia series for children and the science-fiction novels* Perelandria, That Hideous Strength *and* Out of the Silent Planet.

p. 16: From *A Grief Observed* by C. S. Lewis, HarperSanFrancisco, 1963.

p. 45: From *The Screwtape Letters* by C. S. Lewis, copyright © C. S. Lewis Pte. Ltd. 1942. Extract reprinted by permission.

MACAULAY, ROSE (1881–1958)

English novelist and essayist.

p. 178: From *Letters to a Friend from Rose Macaulay, 1950-1952,* edited by Constance Babington Smith, London: Collins, 1961.

MARSHALL, CHARLES (1637–1698)

English Quaker.

p. 22: From *The Journal, Together With Sundry Epistles and Other Writings of Charles Marshall,* London: Richard Barrett, 1844.

MARY CLARE, MOTHER (1907–)

English nun.

p. 207: From "Listening to God," an address delivered to a conference of Roman Catholic religious. Fairacres Publication 69, SLG Press.

Acknowledgments and Sources

MAXIMOS THE CONFESSOR (580–662)
Greek saint, theologian, and ascetic writer.

p. 230: From *The Philokalia: The Complete Text,* compiled by St. Nikodemus of the Holy Mountain and St. Makarios of Corinth, translated from the Greek and edited by G. E. H. Palmer, Philip Sherrard, Kallistos Ware with the assistance of the Holy Transfiguration Monastery (Brookline, Mass.), Constantine Cavernos, Basil Osborne, Norman Russell, Vol. II, London and Boston: Faber and Faber, 1981. Reprinted by permission of Faber and Faber, Ltd.

MECHTHILD OF MAGDEBURG (1210–1297)
German mystic. Born in Saxony of a noble family, she became a Beguine under the guidance of Dominicans. Her Book of Mystical Revelations *is among the strongest and most poetic of women's writing to have survived from the Middle Ages.*

p. 233: From *Mechthild of Magdeburg, The Flowing Light of the Godhead,* translated and introduced by Frank Tobin, preface by Margot Schmidt, New York: Paulist Press, 1998. Copyright © 1998 by Paulist Press. Reprinted by permission of Paulist Press.

MERTON, THOMAS (1915–1968)
American Cistercian monk. Powerful spiritual writer and influential figure in the Roman Catholic Church and beyond. The autobiographical Seven Storey Mountain *and* Seeds of Contemplation *are among the best known of his many works.*

p. 50: By Thomas Merton, from *New Seeds of Contemplation,* copyright © 1961 by The Abbey of Gethsemani, Inc. Reprinted by permission of New Directions Publishing Corp.

p. 65: From *The Ascent to Truth* by Thomas Merton, New York: Harcourt Brace, 1951.

p. 93: *New Seeds of Contemplation.*

p. 118: Ibid.

p. 174: From *Mystics and Zen Masters* by Thomas Merton, New York: Noonday Press, 1967.

p. 189: From *The Monastic Journey,* edited by Brother Patrick Hart, copyright © 1977 by the Trustees of the Merton Legacy Trust. Reprinted by permission of the Merton Legacy Trust.

p. 197: From *Thomas Merton, Monk: A Monastic Tribute,* edited by Brother Patrick Hart, New York: Sheed and Ward, 1974.

MOLTKE, HELMUTH VON (1907–1945)

German jurist and statesman. The passage quoted is from a letter to his wife written shortly before his execution by the Nazis.

    p. 113: From *Dying We Live* by Helmut Gollwitzer, Kathe Kuhn, and Reinhold Schneider, editors, New York: Pantheon, 1956. Copyright © 1956 by Pantheon Books, a division of Random House, Inc.

MORE, DAME GERTRUDE (1606–1633)

English Benedictine nun and spiritual writer.

    p. 160: Cited in *The English Spirit*, edited by Paul Handley et al., London: Darton, Longman, and Todd, 1987.

MOTOVILOV, N. (c. 1831)

Disciple of St. Seraphim.

    p. 18: Cited in *Russian Mystics* by Sergius Bolshakoff; introduction by Thomas Merton. Kalamazoo, Mich.: Cistercian Publications, 1977. Copyright © 1977 by the Abbey of Gethsemani, Inc. Reprinted by permission of Cistercian Publications.

MUIR, EDWIN (1887–1959)

English novelist and poet.

    p. 193: From *An Autobiography* by Edwin Muir, London: Hogarth Press, 1954.

NEWMAN, JOHN HENRY (1801–1890)

English Roman Catholic cardinal. Convert from the Church of England and a leading spirit of the Oxford Movement, his sermons had a profound influence on the religious life of the whole of England.

    p. 72: From *The Heart of Newman, a Synthesis,* arranged by Erich Przywara, SJ, San Francisco: Ignatius Press, 1997.

NICHOLAS OF CUSA (1401–1464)

German cardinal, theologian, and mathematician.

    p. 191: From *The Vision of God* by Nicholas of Cusa, translated by Emma Gurney Salter, New York: E. P. Dutton, 1928.

Acknowledgments and Sources

OXENHANDLER, NOELLE (contemporary)
Writer and essayist.

p. 24: From "Pascal's Jacket" by Noelle Oxenhandler in *Parabola: The Magazine of Myth and Tradition*, Vol. 19, No. 3. Edited by L. K. Reprinted by permission of Noelle Oxenhandler.

PALAMAS, GREGORY (1296–1359)
Greek theologian and saint. His work stressed Divine Light and the concept of the human being as a single whole—body, mind, and soul together.

p. 20: From *The Triads* by Gregory Palamas, edited and with an introduction by John Meyendorff, translation by Nicholas Gendle, preface by Jaroslav Pelikan, New York: Paulist Press, 1983. Copyright © 1983 by Paulist Press.

PASCAL, BLAISE (1623–1662)
French scientist, polemicist, and Christian apologist. His Pensées *embody a wealth of psychological perception.*

p. 11: From *Selections From the Pensées* by Blaise Pascal. Translated by A. J. Denomy, CSB, New York: Random House, 1949.

PATMORE, COVENTRY (1823–1896)
English poet.

p. 17: From *The Rod, the Root, and the Flower* by Coventry Patmore, London: Grey Walls Press, 1950.

PETER
A contemporary Carthusian novice.

p. 190: From *Interior Prayer: Carthusian Novice Conferences* by a Carthusian, translated by Sister Maureen Scrine, Kalamazoo, Mich.: Cistercian Publications, 1996.

PIOZZI, HESTER LYNCH (1741–1821)
English writer.

p. 37: From *Anecdotes of the Late Samuel Johnson, LL.D.,* by Hester Lynch Piozzi, Cambridge: The University Press, 1925.

POPE, ALEXANDER (1688–1744)
English poet.

p. 61: From *Essay on Man,* edited by Frank Brady, Indianapolis: Bobbs-Merrill Co., Inc., 1965.

RAHNER, KARL (1904–1984)
German Jesuit theologian, and author of a vast number of books and articles. One of the most influential 20th-century Roman Catholic theologians. His difficult technical writing is in contrast to the direct and insightful works quoted here.

p. 41: From *Everyday Faith* by Karl Rahner, translated by W. J. O'Hara, New York: Herder and Herder, 1968.

p. 67: From *On Prayer* by Karl Rahner, SJ, Collegeville, Minn.: The Liturgical Press, copyright © 1993. Permission granted by The Liturgical Press.

p. 79: Ibid.

p. 164: *Everyday Faith.*

p. 211: *On Prayer.*

RICHARD OF ST. VICTOR (?-1173)
Scottish scholastic theologian and mystic.

p. 186: From *Carthusian Spirituality: The Writings of Hugh of Balma and Guigo de Ponte,* translated and introduced by Dennis D. Martin, preface by John van Engen, New York: Paulist Press, 1997. Copyright © 1997 by Paulist Press. Reprinted by permission of Paulist Press.

RODRIGUEZ, ALFONSO (1526–1616)
Spanish Jesuit and spiritual writer.

p. 103: From *The Practice of Christian and Religious Perfection* by Alfonso Rodriguez, written in Spanish, translated from the French, Dublin: James Duffy, 1861.

RUSSIAN PILGRIM (anonymous) (c. 1850)

p. 212: From *The Way of a Pilgrim,* translated from the Russian by R. M. French, with a foreword by George Craig Stewart, Milwaukee, Wis.: Morehouse Publishing, 1931.

Acknowledgments and Sources

RUUSBROEC, JAN VAN (1293–1381)
Flemish mystic and theologian. He studied in Brussels and was prior of a community there. Ruus-broec is the author of authoritative books on the spirtual life such as The Spiritual Espousals, The Kingdom of the Lover of God, *and* The Book of the Spiritual Tabernacle.

p. 97: edited and adapted by L. K. from *The Spiritual Espousals* by Jan van Ruus-broec, edited by J. Alaerts, translated by H. Rolfson, Collegeville, Minn.: Litur-gical Press, 1955, and *John Ruusbroec: The Spiritual Espousals and Other Works*, introduction and translation by James A. Wiseman, New York: Paulist Press, 1985. Copyright © 1985 by Paulist Press.

p. 105: *John Ruusbroec.* Reprinted by permission of Paulist Press.

p. 152: Ibid.

p. 232: From *Ruysbroek and the Mystics,* with selections from Ruysbroek by Mau-rice Maeterlink, translated by James T. Stoddart, London: Hodder and Stoughton, 1894.

SAYERS, DOROTHY L. (1893–1957)
English novelist, playwright, and apologist.

p. 15: From *Further Papers on Dante* by Dorothy L. Sayers, London: Methuen & Co. Ltd., 1957.

SCUPOLI, LORENZO (1530–1610)
Italian Roman Catholic priest. Unseen Warfare *by Nicodemus of the Holy Mountain is a variant of Scupoli's work.*

p. 147: From *The Spiritual Combat of Dom Lorenzo Scupoli,* translated from the Ital-ian by Rev. Thomas Barns, MA Oxon., London: Methuen & Co. Ltd., 1909.

SERGIEFF, FATHER JOHN (St. John of Kronstadt) (1829–1909)
Russian monk.

p. 199: From *My Life in Christ, Extracts from the Diary of John Iliyitch Sergieff,* trans-lated by E. E Goullaeff. London: Cassell and Co., Ltd., 1897.

SHAKESPEARE, WILLIAM (1564–1616)
England's bard.

p. 182: From *The Merchant of Venice,* I.2.13.

SIMEON THE NEW THEOLOGIAN (949–1022)
Byzantine saint, mystic, and spiritual writer. Assigned a central place to the vision of Divine Light.

    p. 18: From *Writings From the Philokalia on Prayer of the Heart*, London: Faber and Faber, 1951.

    p. 33: Cited in *The Lenten Spring: Readings for Great Lent* by Thomas Hopko, Crestwood, N.Y.: St. Vladimir's Seminary Press, 1983.

SMART, CHRISTOPHER (1722–1771)
English poet.
p. 2: Cited in *The Norton Anthology of Poetry.* New York: W. W. Norton & Co., Inc., 1970.

SMITH, HENRY [The Silver-Tongued] (1550–1600)
English clergyman. Held the office of lecturer at the Church of St. Clement Danes, London.

    p. 72: Cited in *A Treasury of the Kingdom* compiled by E. A. Blackburn et al., New York: Oxford University Press, 1954.

SMITH, JOHN (1618–1652)
English Platonist.
    p. 219: From *Selected Discourses* by John Smith, London, 1821.

SUSO, HENRY (1300–1366)
One of the foremost German contemplatives, follower of Eckhart.
    p. 186: *A Little Book of Eternal Wisdom* by Blessed Henry Suso, London: Burns, Oates & Washbourne, Ltd. Publishers to the Holy See, 1910.

SWEDENBORG, EMANUEL (1688–1772)
Swedish scientist, mystical thinker, and visionary. The basis of his thought was a "doctrine of correspondence" between physical and spiritual worlds. His prolific writings include the eight-volume Arcana Coelestia. *He influenced Blake.*

    pp. 128, 169, and 228: From *A Compendium of Theological Writings of Emanuel Swedenborg,* edited by Samuel Warren, New York: Swedenborg Foundation, 1974.

TAULER, JOHANNES (1300–1361)
German Dominican contemplative. Along with Meister Eckhart and Henry Suso, one of the most influential German mystical writers of the 14th century.

p. 48: From *Johannes Tauler: Sermons*, translated by Maria Shrady with an introduction by Josef Schmidt, preface by Alois Haas, New York: Paulist Press, 1985. Copyright © 1985 by Paulist Press. Reprinted by permission of Paulist Press.
p. 106: Ibid.
p. 167: From *The Life and Sermons of Dr. John Tauler*, translated by Susanna Winkworth, New York, 1858.
p. 192: From *Johannes Tauler*.
p. 225: Ibid.

TAYLOR, JEREMY (1613–1667)

English bishop and writer. Native of Cambridge and educated there. His Holy Living and Holy Dying *is a classic, embodying the temperance and moderation of Anglican spirituality. One of the most celebrated preachers of his day.*

pp. 57, 125, and 176: From *Selected Works: Jeremy Taylor*, edited with an introduction by Thomas K. Carroll, preface by John Booty, New York: Paulist Press, 1990. Copyright © 1990 by Paulist Press. Reprinted by permission of Paulist Press.

TEILHARD DE CHARDIN, PIERRE (1881–1955)

French paleontologist and Jesuit priest.

p. 7: From *The Divine Milieu: An Essay on The Interior Life* by Pierre Teilhard de Chardin. Copyright © 1957 by Editions du Seuil, Paris. English translation copyright © 1960 by Wm. Collins Sons & Co., London, and Harper & Row Publishers, Inc. New York. Renewed © 1988 by Harper & Row Publishers, Inc. Reprinted by permission of HarperCollins Publishers, Inc..
p. 14: Ibid.
p. 141: Ibid.
p. 172: From *Letters From a Traveller*, edited by Claude Aragonnès, London: Collins, 1962.

TEMPLE, WILLIAM (1881–1944)

English archbishop of Canterbury. He had a lifelong concern with educational and social issues and was a trained philosopher and independent thinker.

p. 42: Readings in St. John's Gospel. Cited in *From The Fathers to the Churches*, edited by Brother Kenneth, CGA, London: Wm. Collins, 1983.

TERESA OF ÁVILA (1515–1582)

Spanish Carmelite saint, nun, and mystic. The Way of Perfection *and* The Interior Castle *are the best-known among her many works. She described the life of prayer from meditation on sacred texts to the mystic marriage. An active reformer and organizer, her life is the classic example of the union of the active and contemplative life.*

p. 38: From *The Interior Castle* by St. Teresa of Ávila, translated by E. A. Peers, New York: Sheed and Ward, 1946.

p. 193: From *The Way of Perfection* by St. Teresa of Ávila, translated by E. A. Peers, New York: Sheed and Ward, 1946.

p. 199: *Interior Castle.*

p. 212: From the *Life of St. Teresa of Ávila* by E. A. Peers, New York: Sheed and Ward, 1943.

TERTULLIAN (160–230)

Latin ecclesiastical writer of Carthage. A leading authority and father in the early church.

p. 1: From *Tertullian: Treatise on Prayer*, chapter 29 in The Divine Office, London: Collins, 1974. Copyright © 1974 by The Hierarchies of England and Wales, Ireland and Australia. Reprinted by permission of A. P. Watt Ltd. on behalf of The Hierarchies of England and Wales, Ireland and Australia.

THEOLOGICA GERMANICA (14th century)

This work of unknown German authorship was discovered and published in 1516 by Martin Luther, who said of it that "Next to the Bible and St. Augustine, no book has ever come into my hands from which I have learnt more of God and Christ, and man and all things that are."

p. 145: From *Theologica Germanica*, edited by Dr. Pfeiffer, translated from the German by Susanna Winkworth, London: Golden Treasury Series, 1893.

THEOPHAN THE RECLUSE (1815–1894)

Russian Orthodox monk and saint.

p. 81: From *The Spiritual Life and How to Be Attuned to It* by St. Theophan the Recluse, translated by Alexandra Dockham, Platina, Calif.: St. Herman of Alaska Brotherhood, 1995. Reprinted by permission of St. Herman of Alaska Brotherhood.

p. 139: Ibid.

p. 201: From *Russian Mystics* by Sergius Bolshakoff; introduction by Thomas Merton, Kalamazoo, Mich.: Cistercian Publications, copyright © 1977 by the Abbey of Gethsemani, Inc. Reprinted by permission of Cistercian Publications.

THE GOSPEL OF THOMAS (first century)

A collection of traditional wisdom sayings, parables, and proverbs attributed to Jesus.

p. 117: From *The Other Gospels: Non-Canonical Gospel Texts*, edited by Ron Cameron. Philadelphia: The Westminster Press, 1982.

THOMAS À KEMPIS (1380–1471)

Dutch ecclesiastic and ascetical writer. Educated at the school of the Brethren of the Common Life, he took the habit in 1406. A spiritual advisor and writer, he is most celebrated for his Imitation of Christ.

p. 104: From *The Imitation of Christ: A Timeless Classic for Contemporary Readers* by Thomas à Kempis, translated by William Creasy, Notre Dame, Ind.: Ave Maria Press, 1989.

THOREAU, HENRY DAVID (1817–1862)

American poet, essayist, and naturalist. His journal of 14 volumes was published posthumously.

p. 8: From *The Journals of Henry D. Thoreau*, edited by Bradford Torrey and Francis H. Allen, Boston: Houghton Mifflin, 1906.

TIKHON OF ZADONSK (1792–1866)

Russian bishop and spiritual writer.

p. 132: From *Russian Mystics* by Sergius Bolshakoff, introduction by Thomas Merton, Kalamazoo, Mich.: Cistercian Publications, copyright © 1977 by the Abbey of Gethsemani, Inc. Reprinted by permission of Cistercian Publications.

TRACOL, HENRI (1909–1997)

French journalist and sculptor.

p. 120: From "The Mystery of Rebirth" by Henri Tracol, translated and adapted by Dorothea Dooling from *"Homme, ciel, terre,"* which first appeared in *L'Age Nouveau*, No. 112. Cited in *Parabola: Myth and the Quest for Meaning*, Vol. 10, No. 3. Reprinted by permission of Ellen Dooling Draper.

TRAHERNE, THOMAS (1637–1674)

Obscure cleric of Herefordshire. An anonymous manuscript bought in London in 1896 contained his poems, which were first published in 1908.

pp. 6, 16, 56, and 163: From *Centuries of Meditations* by Thomas Traherne, edited by Bertram Dobell, London: P. J. & A. E. Dobell, 1908.

TUTU, DESMOND (1931–)

Archbishop Tutu was born in South Africa and studied theology in England. In 1978 he became the first Black general secretary of the Anglican South African Council of Churches. Tutu is an honorary doctor of a number of leading universities in the United States, Britain, and Germany. A fierce antiapartheid leader, he was the 1984 Nobel Peace Prize Laureate.

p. 192: From *An African Prayer Book*, Selected and with an Introduction by Desmond Tutu, New York: Doubleday, 1995.

UNDERHILL, EVELYN (1875–1941)

English exponent of mystical life. Educated at King's College, London. Mysticism is her most well-known book and has become a standard work. A prolific writer and later a much sought-after retreat leader.

pp. 37, 69, and 143: From *The Spiritual Life* by Evelyn Underhill, New York: Harper & Brothers, Inc., 1937.

UNSEEN WARFARE

In its original form Unseen Warfare *was Lorenzo Scupoli's sixteenth-century work,* Combattimento spirituale. *In the eighteenth century, a monk of Mount Athos, Nicodemus, translated, edited, and adapted it to the needs of Orthodox readers. Later, in the nineteenth century, Theophan the Recluse translated* Unseen Warfare *into Russian, and also substantially adapted and added to it. The English version is translated from Theophan's Russian version.*

pp. 101, 124, and 134: From *Unseen Warfare*, translated by E. Kadloubovsky and G. E. H. Palmer, introduction by H. A. Hodges, London: Faber and Faber, 1952. Reprinted by permission of Faber and Faber.

VAN GOGH, VINCENT (1853–1890)

Dutch painter.

pp. 40 and 172: From *The Complete Letters of Vincent van Gogh* (Vincent van Gogh Foundation). Reprinted by permission of the Van Gogh Museum, Amsterdam.

WARE, KALLISTOS (1934–)

Greek Orthodox archbishop.

pp. 28 and 63: From "Image and Likeness: An Interview with Bishop Kallistos

Ware" by James Moran in *Parabola: Myth and the Quest for Meaning*, Vol. 10, No. 1. Reprinted by permission of *Parabola*.

WEIL, SIMONE (1909–1943)
French scholar, mystic, and philosopher.

p. 13: From *Waiting for God* by Simone Weil, New York: HarperPerennial Library, 1992.

WESLEY, JOHN (1703–1791)
Founder of the Methodist Movement and central figure in the rise of Methodism.

pp. 142 and 183: From *Christian Perfection* by John Wesley, edited by Thomas Jackson, 1872.

WILDE, OSCAR (1854–1900)
English playwright who outraged the conventions of his day. Behind the facade that shocked people, however, there was a man sympathetic to Christian teachings.

p. 162: From his essay "The Ballad of Reading Gaol."

WILLIAM OF ST. THIERRY (1075–1148)
Belgian Benedictine monk and theologian.

p. 224: From *The Pursuit of Wisdom and Other Works*, by the Author of *The Cloud of Unknowing*, translated, edited, and annotated by James A. Walsh, SJ, preface by George A. Maloney, SJ, New York: Paulist Press. Copyright © 1998 by the British Province of the Society of Jesus. Reprinted by permission of Paulist Press.

WILLIAMS, CHARLES (1886–1945)
English novelist, essayist, poet, and theological writer. Theological writings such as Descent of the Dove *explored the activity of the Holy Spirit in history. Part of a literary circle that included C. S. Lewis and Dorothy L. Sayers.*

p. 30: From *Charles Williams: Essential Writings in Spirituality and Theology.* Copyright 1993 by Charles Hefling. All rights reserved. Available from Cowley Publications, 28 Temple Place, Boston, MA 02111 (www.cowley.org 1-800-225-1534).

ABOUT THE EDITOR

For more than twenty years, Lorraine Kisly has studied and worked with the texts of the great religious traditions. She was the editor of *Parabola: Myth, Tradition, and the Search for Meaning;* the founding publisher of *Tricycle: The Buddhist Review* and editor of Tricycle Books; and publisher of Pilgrim Press. She lives in rural Pennsylvania.

OTHER
BELL TOWER BOOKS

Books that nourish the soul, illuminate the mind,
and speak directly to the heart

Rob Baker
PLANNING MEMORIAL CELEBRATIONS
A Sourcebook
A one-stop handbook for a situation
more and more of us are facing as we grow older.
0-609-80404-9 Softcover

Thomas Berry
THE GREAT WORK
Our Way Into the Future
The grandfather of Deep Ecology teaches us how to move from a
human-centered view of the world to one
focused on the earth and all its inhabitants.
0-609-60525-9 Hardcover
0-609-80499-5 Softcover

Cynthia Bourgeault
LOVE IS STRONGER THAN DEATH
The Mystical Union of Two Souls
Both the story of the incandescent love between two hermits
and a guidebook for those called to this path of soulwork.
0-609-60473-2 Hardcover

Madeline Bruser
THE ART OF PRACTICING
Making Music from the Heart
A classic work on how to practice music that combines
meditative principles with information on body mechanics and medicine.
0-517-70822-1 Hardcover
0-609-80177-5 Softcover

Marc David
NOURISHING WISDOM
A Mind/Body Approach to Nutrition and Well-Being
A book that advocates awareness in eating.
0-517-88129-2 Softcover

Joan Furman, MSN, RN, and David McNabb
THE DYING TIME
Practical Wisdom for the Dying and Their Caregivers
A comprehensive guide filled with physical, emotional, and spiritual advice.
0-609-80003-5 Softcover

Bernie Glassman
BEARING WITNESS
A Zen Master's Lessons in Making Peace
How Glassman started the Zen Peacemaker Order and
what each of us can do to make peace in our hearts and in the world.
0-609-60061-3 Hardcover
0-609-80391-3 Softcover

Bernard Glassman and Rick Fields
INSTRUCTIONS TO THE COOK
A Zen Master's Lessons in Living a Life That Matters
A distillation of Zen wisdom that can be used equally well as
a manual on business or spiritual practice, cooking or life.
0-517-88829-7 Softcover

Niles Elliot Goldstein
GOD AT THE EDGE
Searching for the Divine in Uncomfortable and Unexpected Places
A book about adventure, raw experience, and facing inner demons.
Hardcover 0-609-60499-6

Greg Johanson and Ron Kurtz
GRACE UNFOLDING
Psychotherapy in the Spirit of the Tao-te ching
The interaction of client and therapist illuminated
through the gentle power and wisdom of Lao Tsu's ancient classic.
0-517-88130-6 Softcover

Jack and Marcia Kelly
SANCTUARIES
A Guide to Lodgings in Monasteries, Abbeys, and Retreats of the United States
For those in search of renewal and a little peace;
described by the *New York Times* as "the *Michelin Guide* of the retreat set."
0-517-88517-4 Softcover

Selected by Marcia and Jack Kelly
ONE HUNDRED GRACES
Mealtime Blessings
A collection of graces from many traditions,
inscribed in calligraphy reminiscent of the manuscripts of medieval Europe.
0-609-80093-0 Softcover

Barbara Lachman
THE JOURNAL OF HILDEGARD OF BINGEN
A year in the life of the twelfth-century German saint—
the diary she never had the time to write herself.
0-517-88390-2 Softcover

Stephen Levine
A YEAR TO LIVE
How to Live This Year as if It Were Your Last
Using the consciousness of our mortality
to enter into a new and vibrant relationship with life.
0-609-80194-5 Softcover

Gunilla Norris
BEING HOME
A Book of Meditations
An exquisite modern book of hours,
a celebration of mindfulness in everyday activities.
0-517-58159-0 Hardcover

Marcia Prager
THE PATH OF BLESSING
Experiencing the Energy and Abundance of the Divine
How to use the traditional Jewish practice of calling down a blessing
on each action as a profound path of spiritual growth.
0-517-70363-7 Hardcover
0-609-80393-X Softcover

Saki Santorelli
HEAL THY SELF
Lessons on Mindfulness in Medicine
An invitation to patients and health-care professionals to bring mindfulness
into the crucible of the healing relationship.
0-609-60385-X Hardcover
0-609-80504-5 Softcover

Rabbi Rami M. Shapiro
MINYAN
Ten Principles for Living a Life of Integrity
A primer for those interested to know
what Judaism has to offer the spiritually hungry.
0-609-80055-8 Softcover

Rabbi Rami M. Shapiro
WISDOM OF THE JEWISH SAGES
A Modern Reading of Pirke Avot
A third-century treasury of maxims on justice, integrity, and virtue—
Judaism's principal ethical scripture.
0-517-79966-9 Hardcover

Jean Smith
THE BEGINNER'S GUIDE TO ZEN BUDDHISM
A comprehensive and easily accessible introduction
that assumes no prior knowledge of Zen Buddhism.
0-609-80466-9 Softcover

Rabbi Joseph Telushkin
THE BOOK OF JEWISH VALUES
A Day-by-Day Guide to Ethical Living
Ancient and modern advice on how to remain honest
in a morally complicated world.
0-609-60330-2 Hardcover

James Thornton
A FIELD GUIDE TO THE SOUL
A Down-to-Earth Handbook of Spiritual Practice
In the tradition of *The Seat of the Soul, The Soul's Code,* and *Care of the Soul,*
a primer readers are calling "the Bible for the new millennium."
0-609-60368-X Hardcover
0-609-80392-1 Softcover

Joan Tollifson
BARE-BONES MEDITATION
Waking Up from the Story of My Life
An unvarnished, exhilarating account of one woman's struggle
to make sense of her life.
0-517-88792-4 Softcover

Michael Toms and Justine Willis Toms
TRUE WORK
Doing What You Love and Loving What You Do
Wisdom for the workplace from the husband-and-wife team
of NPR's weekly radio program *New Dimensions.*
0-609-80212-7 Softcover

BUDDHA LAUGHING
A Tricycle *Book of Cartoons*
A marvelous opportunity for self-reflection
for those who tend to take themselves too seriously.
0-609-80409-X Softcover

Ed. Richard Whelan
SELF-RELIANCE
The Wisdom of Ralph Waldo Emerson as Inspiration for Daily Living
A distillation of Emerson's spiritual writings for contemporary readers.
0-517-58512-X Softcover

*Bell Tower books are for sale at your local bookstore, or you may
call Random House at 1-800-793-BOOK to order with a credit card.*